Advertising, Competition and Consumer Behaviour

Public Policy and the Market

Advertising, Competition and Consumer Behaviour

Public Policy and the Market

Christina Fulop, BSc(Econ), PhD
Principal Lecturer in Marketing,
School of Business Studies,
City of London Polytechnic

HOLT, RINEHART AND WINSTON
London · New York · Sydney · Toronto

with

THE ADVERTISING ASSOCIATION

Holt, Rinehart and Winston Ltd: 1 St Anne's Road,
                    Eastbourne, East Sussex BN21 3UN

British Library Cataloguing in Publication Data

Fulop, Christina
  Advertising, competition and consumer
  behaviour.
  1. Advertising
  I. Title
  659.1   HF5821

ISBN 0–03–910295–5

Printed and bound in Great Britain by The Pitman Press, Bath

Last digit is print no: 9 8 7 6 5 4 3 2 1

Contents

Introduction

This study analyses and compares the theories and empirical research relating to advertising and competition in economics literature with their operation in the market-place. The divergences which are found to occur between theory and practice are then compared with the attitudes and pronouncements of public policy towards advertising and competition. The subject matter is dealt with in three sections.

Part 1 is a review of the main literature in economic theory concerned with advertising and competition; that is, the theory of value, the concept of consumer sovereignty, the theory of the firm, perfect and imperfect competition, and theories and empirical studies on the effects of advertising and imperfect competition (in particular, oligopoly) on prices, profits, barriers to entry and product differentiation. It also includes a brief outline of the theory of the economics of information which analyses the benefits which buyers of advertised products gain from advertising as opposed to the traditional approach of considering advertising almost entirely from the viewpoint of the sellers of advertised products. Since there is by no means general agreement on these theories and studies, the review is interspersed with criticisms which have been made about specific features of them.

This survey is followed by an outline of three theories which are considered to give a more accurate account of the behaviour of firms in the real world: managerial economics; management of demand; and competition as a process and not as a situation. However, many of the criticisms of the theory of the firm have been rejected as being misconceived for a variety of reasons, viz. (1) since the theory was only ever intended as an abstract model conceived for theoretical reasoning, it is not surprising that it should diverge from reality, and should not therefore be taken at its face value; (2) that it provides a limiting case against which real situations can be compared and evaluated; and (3) that the major decisions of firms in the real world are dealt with in the literature of the economics of industrial structure and organization. Finally, Part 1 outlines the concept of 'workable' competition which has developed parallel with the traditional theory of the firm to explain how, under conditions of oligopoly and imperfect competition, it is nevertheless possible for competition to flourish.

Part 2 studies the consumer in the market from three points of view: a brief survey of the major academic theories of consumer behaviour is followed by examples of empirical research into consumer behaviour, including brand loyalty and brand share prediction, and, finally, 9 case histories illustrate how products are developed and introduced on the market, how firms compete, and the different forms that competition can take.

Part 3 compares the economic theories on advertising and competition as outlined in the mainstream of economics literature in Part 1 with examples taken from the case histories and the empirical research in Part 2. In turn, the theory and practice of advertising and competition are compared with examples taken from the Reports of such bodies as the Monopolies and Mergers Commission, the Price Commission and the Office of Fair Trading which illustrate the attitude of public policy towards advertising and competition.

The conclusions draw attention to the major discrepancies which appear to exist between theory and practice, and the implications that follow for public policy which seems to be based predominantly on the traditional theory of the firm and the need to eliminate imperfections in the market such as product differentiation, advertising and non-price competition.

The issues raised in the book will interest businessmen, practitioners in advertising and legislators in the continuing debate on the appropriate framework for competition policy. It is hoped that it will also help students experiencing difficulty in reconciling the contradictory information presented to them on advertising and competition.

Christina Fulop

Acknowledgements

This book is based on a PhD thesis undertaken at Brunel University under the supervision of Professor the Lord Vaizey. In its present form, it differs in some respects from the thesis, notably by the inclusion of additional case history material.

I wish to thank Lord Vaizey for his guidance, advice and constant encouragement. In particular, the study benefited from his willingness to discuss the difficulties and frustrations which seemed to beset the thesis at various stages, and from his pertinent criticisms on the several drafts of it which he read. Professor Patrick Lynch, University College, Dublin, the external examiner of the thesis, also made helpful comments which led to revision of some of the original material. On a more general note, I would like to acknowledge the benefit I have derived from discussions over several years with Dr Harold Lind, AGB Ltd, and my colleague, Tony Lee, City of London Polytechnic, which helped to clarify some of my initial views on the subject.

The case histories of the methods used by firms to market their products and services are an important constituent of the study. Unfortunately, many firms in this country are still reluctant to reveal such information either because they fear that it may prove commercially sensitive, and/or because they are unwilling to divert their executives from their day-to-day activities. I am therefore extremely grateful to those firms (and their advertising agencies) who were prepared to cooperate, and to members of their staffs who willingly participated in lengthy discussions and dealt courteously and patiently with the many queries which I sent to them. I would like especially to acknowledge the generous assistance I received from: Geoffrey Dodds and Nick Phillips, Beecham Proprietaries; David Rayner, British Railways Board; Ron Hammond, Van den Berghs; Geoffrey Batchelor, Unilever Ltd; Fred Lewis and Peter Dart, Lever Bros Ltd; Ken Clarke, Batchelors Foods Ltd; Stephen King and Patricia Mann, J. Walter Thompson Ltd; David Berliner, BAT Stores Holdings Ltd; Peter Fishbourne, Argos Distributors Ltd; Sidney Bushell,

Davidson, Pearce Ltd; Charles Barr, Lansing Ltd; and Stephen White, Holt-Saunders Ltd.

I am indebted to the City of London Polytechnic for a year's sabbatical leave. This provided me with that very precious commodity, time, which enabled me to concentrate wholeheartedly on my researches.

Finally, I am very appreciative of the support and encouragement I have always received throughout my academic career from my husband Walter, and, not least, of the patience which he and my children, Ruth, Naomi and Mark, displayed during the final stages of the thesis and its translation into book form.

Part 1

A review of economic theories of advertising and competition

1   Traditional neoclassical economic theory

THEORY OF VALUE

The factors which determine demand, supply and price comprise the theory of value and distribution. This forms the core of orthodox economic theory and is based on the 'principle of equal net advantage'; that is, that under the stimulus of prices and profits resources move from one occupation to another, and from the production of one type of product or service to another.

Adam Smith's concept of 'effective demand' contains the germ of the modern theory of demand and supply (Book 1, chapters 7 and 9). Briefly, Smith put forward the idea that producers sought to earn the largest possible profit, but in order to do so they had to produce goods desired by the community. Furthermore, they must produce them in the right quantities, otherwise too much would cause a low price and a low profit, while too small a supply would cause an increase in price. The delicate mechanism of the 'invisible hand' was also at work in the markets for the factors of production—capital, land and labour—providing harmony as long as factors sought the largest possible earnings. This was one part of the system of social harmony in an economic society which was dependent on the delicate balance of man's conflicting motives.

Ricardo's main achievements in the theory of value and distribution are set out in *The Principles of Political Economy and Taxation* (1817). His theory of value was a quantity-of-labour theory. He dismissed 'scarce' (i.e. irreproducible) commodities; he concentrated on the mass of goods that may be 'increased by human industry' and tried to demonstrate that the exchange values of commodities will be proportional to the quantities of labour embodied in them (included 'stored-up' labour in the form of machines, etc.). The simplicity of this proposition was amended in later sections of the book, to production requiring the use of proportions of capital and labour of varying qualities, but Ricardo retained it as a fundamental element in his theory.

3

After Ricardo, most of the energies of the classical school were devoted to the labour theory of value, vaguely formulated by Adam Smith and developed by Ricardo. It was widely criticized but not replaced until the 'full cost' theory of John Stuart Mill, which stated that the value of a commodity depended on the amount of all the factors used to produce it.

The modern theory of value and distribution dates from the latter part of the nineteenth century. The beginnings of the 'marginal utility school' developed simultaneously around Jevons in England, Carl Menger in Austria and Walras in Switzerland who approached the problem of value from the side of demand and produced the theory that the value of a commodity depended on the 'utility' or satisfaction of a final marginal unit. This led to the exposition of the utility analysis as the foundation of both demand and supply, and as a general theory of choice. Much of what the marginal utility school proclaimed is implicit in the classical economists, but now, for the first time, the dependence of value on scarcity, in relation to demand, and the dependence of scarcity on cost of production were made explicit. The shift in emphasis away from cost of production towards demand and final consumption caused the change to be described in terms of a shift to a subjective theory of value.

Although this theory was refined and developed by Wieser and Bohm-Bawerk in Austria, it met with opposition in Great Britain and was not finally accepted until the publication of Alfred Marshall's *Principles of Economics* in 1890 (see Marshall, 1920). Marshall's contribution was to bring together what had formerly been two competing theories into a single theory of value and distribution. His basic proposition is that any price tends to be that at which the quantity of the commodity demanded is equal to the quantity supplied. Marshall showed how the demand curve depended on the underlying utility relationships, and how the supply curve was related to costs. Man's economic behaviour was based upon a balance between the search for satisfaction (utility) and the avoidance of sacrifice; this approach enabled Marshall to treat utility and costs as the joint determinants of value. They were like the blades of a pair of scissors, neither cutting solely by its own action.

He applied this general scheme to the whole field of economic activity. The individual consumer obtained income by balancing the disutility of effort with the utility derived from spending the income derived from it. Likewise, the pattern of his expenditure was determined by the utility to be obtained from a commodity at the expense of the utility forgone in not buying others.

The two principles underlying this theory are (1) that price tends to reflect opportunity costs, that is, the sacrifice of the alternatives forgone in producing a commodity or service, and (2) that consumers spend their incomes in the ways they prefer, that is, there is consumer sovereignty. (Consumer sovereignty, in its simplest form, signifies that it is the preferences of consumers, as shown by the ways in which they spend their money, that determine what merchandise is produced and which services supplied.)

This proposition would naturally be easier to accept if all goods were produced to order. The direction of economic activity would then be determined by consumers' orders. Retailers would pass them on to wholesalers, wholesalers to manufacturers, manufacturers to producers of intermediate products, and so on. In practice, of course, the vast majority of merchandise is manufactured in anticipation of consumers' demands. Nevertheless, even under round-about methods of production, which are continually lengthening as technical processes become more complex, consumer sovereignty implies that businessmen whose anticipations are correct earn a larger money return than if they are wrong. If they are shown by events to be wrong, businessmen are compelled sooner or later to change their plans, and to bring them more closely in line with the wishes of consumers. In this way, it is still possible to maintain that production is controlled by demand, or rather for the most part by expected demand. Broadly, consumer sovereignty is more effective the more competitive the market, and less effective where there is an element of monopoly.

The theory of consumer sovereignty is subject to three limitations. First, the amount of available resources and the state of technical knowledge impose an inherent limitation on the power of consumers to determine what shall be produced. Second, the distortion implicit in inequality of income permits the pull on the market exerted by the rich man to be disproportionately stronger than that exerted by the less wealthy. Third, there are the limitations imposed by the state: the sale of some goods, such as certain drugs, may be prohibited; the consumption of others, such as alcoholic drink before driving, is effectively restricted. The first limitation is inherent; the second can be alleviated by the state through progressive taxation; the third is generally believed to be beneficial.

In several important respects Marshall's concept of the theory of value differed from that of the marginal utility school:

1. In contrast to the concept of 'timeless equilibrium' Marshall stressed continually the importance of the time element in determining price and value:

   '. . . the margin, which must be studied in reference to long periods and enduring results, differs in character as well as in extent from that which must be studied in reference to short periods and to passing fluctuations.'
   [1920, Preface, p. xvi]

   As a consequence, he considered the factors influencing the determination of value under three time periods relevant to supply: the *momentary* period in which equilibrium conditions relate to the disposal of a given stock of a commodity; the *short run* in which the equilibrium output is related to a given number of producers operating with given stocks of equipment; and the *long run* in which the number of producers and the scale of equipment at their disposal are assumed to be variable. Finally, it was necessary for value to be considered in the 'non-static' period when all economic data such as tastes, technology, populations, etc., are likely to change. The importance of making these time distinctions was to clarify that the influence of utility on value predominates during short periods, but that of cost of production predominates in the long run.

2. The marginal utility school considered the supply of factors of production as given because it was taking just the immediate (i.e., timeless) period. On the other hand, Marshall did not take the factors of production as given but as having a supply price; there is a certain rate of return which it is necessary for a

factor to receive to call forth a certain quantity of it. The price is not a cost, but it measures cost.

3. The implicit assumption of the marginal utility school that wants are fixed was not accepted by Marshall:

    '. . . although it is man's wants in the earliest stages of his development that give rise to his activities, yet afterwards each new step upwards is to be regarded as the development of new activities giving rise to new wants, rather than of new wants giving rise to new activities.' [1890, p. 89]

Furthermore, Marshall pointed out the 'high theme of economic progress' and was anxious to distance himself from the idea of treating economic problems in terms of 'statical equilibrium', which he maintained was not only an imperfect introduction but 'barely even an introduction to the study of the progress and development of industries which show a tendency to increasing returns'. Since Marshall was well aware of the intricate nature of economic rivalries in the real world, his comment was presumably intended as a rebuke to those who had taken the analogy of Jevons seriously (statical mechanics) so that economic analysis became preoccupied with equilibrium positions under conditions of competition. A second consequence followed from this preoccupation, as Dobb pointed out,

    '. . . following from this, dynamic considerations tend to be ignored . . . could not deal with the stability or instability of paths of movement, and hence with fluctuations or with change as a process.' [1973, p. 173]

The differences between the two views of the neoclassical doctrine were synthesized by Pigou by placing it in a setting of stationary equilibrium which turned it into a neat logical system, but which also neglected some of the Marshallian concepts relating to time, wants, and competition.

THE TRADITIONAL THEORY OF THE FIRM: PERFECT AND IMPERFECT COMPETITION

Perfect competition is the basis of the traditional theory of the firm as it has become familiar in economic textbooks. For an industry to be perfectly competitive two conditions must be met:

1. The product must be homogeneous so that the products of one firm will be perfectly substitutable in the minds of the buyers for the product of any other firm in the industry.
2. The most profitable output of the individual firm must be small relative to the total output coming on to the market. The latter condition will be fulfilled only if the average cost of production in each individual firm reaches its minimum at a relatively small output. It will also be fulfilled only if the commodity is readily transportable and if the buyers and sellers are in close physical proximity.

Perfect competition is then an analytical 'model' of the pure form that a market would take if:

(a) there were many sellers of absolutely identical products in relation to their total sales so that none could influence market price by varying the quantity he was prepared to market (i.e., every seller is faced by a horizontal demand curve). It follows that a firm with perfect markets will not have any selling costs; there is no point in trying to increase the amount that can be sold at the market price when any amount within the limits of the firm's capacity is saleable.

(b) buyers and sellers were aware with complete certainty of prices and opportunities available everywhere in this and other markets (i.e., there is perfect knowledge and therefore the absence of advertising and other marketing costs);

(c) significant economies of scale were absent so that no one seller could grow to dominate the market (i.e., producers would remain relatively small scale); and

(d) there were no barriers of any kind to the movement of land, labour, and capital or of entrepreneurs from or to the rest of the economy.

The assumption is also made in this static theory that in the short run incomes and tastes remain the same, and the state of technology is given.

Under these circumstances competition among producers would in the long run ensure that every producer was operating with the most efficient size of plant and equipment, producing the most efficient (low cost) output, and was earning only the minimum amount of profit necessary to maintain the minimum necessary number of producers in the industry.

Equilibrium is reached when prices are such that supply of every commodity equals the demand for it, and no factors of production have any incentive to move into another industry or occupation. It is true that the prices of products are related to the prices of the factors of production employed in producing them. But it is also true that the prices of those factors depend on the value of their products both in the industry under consideration and in other industries.

The prices of products in one industry are affected by the prices of the possible substitutes produced by other industries. Everything depends on everything else. The price system is a system; all prices are mutually dependent on one another.

The model of perfect competition yields an 'ideal' output in the sense that the price consumers would have to pay to obtain additional supplies of a commodity produced under these conditions would, in both the short run and the long run, be just sufficient to bid the necessary productive resources away from alternative uses. If production were everywhere organized in this ideal manner the price system would thus secure an optimum distribution of economic resources to reflect consumers' preferences in the most efficient way. The model thus provides a yardstick of economic efficiency in the allocation of resources.

In the exposition of perfect competition, pure monopoly is treated as a special case, and consists of the opposite of the three essential elements of perfect competition; that is, (1) one firm in the industry; (2) producing a product wholly unlike the product of any other firm; and (3) no possibility for new firms to enter the industry. Then it is traditionally assumed that a single producer will be able to raise his price and thereby earn a monopoly profit, depending upon the shape of his demand curve.

Although both perfect competition and monopoly were seen to be operating in the economy (many agricultural products and commodities operate under conditions close to perfect competition; 'public utilities' operate under conditions close to pure monopoly) the bulk of economic activity clearly operated between the extremes of perfect competition and pure monopoly. Consequently, there were several attempts made to replace or supplement the model of perfect competition. Most notable were the concepts of monopolistic and imperfect competition developed during the 1930s by, respectively, E. H. Chamberlin and Joan Robinson. As Robinson pointed out in 1969,

> '. . . by showing that perfect competition cannot obtain in manufacturing industry (imperfect competition) undermines the complex of ideas erected on the slogan of "price equals marginal cost".' [Preface, p. xi]

Imperfect competition covers the economic models of market forms used in economic analysis other than perfect competition (i.e., monopolistic competition, oligipoly, duopoly through to monopoly). In both perfect and imperfect competition, freedom of entry of firms or of other resources into the industry is assumed. The different types of competition are then defined by varying two basic conditions: the homogeneity of the product and the number of firms. Perfect competition assumes many firms and a homogeneous product, but many firms producing products which are similar but not identical is monopolistic competition. When a few firms are selling a homogeneous product there is perfect oligopoly, whereas when a few firms are selling heterogeneous products imperfect oligopoly exists.

Thus imperfect competition depicts a market situation which does not fulfil all the conditions necessary for perfect competition and is characterized by one or more of the following features: the ability of sellers to influence demand by persuading consumers that their product is different from others of the same kind and thus to generate some degree of monopoly by such practices as product differentiation, branding, advertising; restraints on the entry of competitors into any line of production either because of the large scale of initial investment required or because of restrictive and collusive practices; the existence of uncertainty and imperfect knowledge about prices and profits elsewhere; the decrease of price competition. There is a clear distinction drawn between restrictive practices employed by a group to convert an otherwise competitive situation into a monopoly and an individual monopoly or near-monopoly which arises from the economies of large-scale production.

The distinctive contribution of Chamberlin and Robinson was to show that in contrast to neoclassical economics it is more appropriate to set out the analysis of monopoly, and treat perfect competition as a special case. Then the condition noticed under perfect competition that the most profitable output occurs where price equals marginal cost is only a special case of the general proposition that all firms are most profitable at the output where the marginal revenue equals marginal cost.

If the simplifying assumption is then adopted, as it is, that the monopolist or the producer in an imperfectly competitive market will produce such an output as will maximize his profits, output will tend to be smaller, other things being equal (e.g., costs), than it would be in a more competitive market. Whereas under perfect competition sellers are price takers because the price is constant for all outputs, under all degrees of imperfect competition the supplier is a price searcher because he is faced by a declining demand curve so that an additional quantity can be sold only if the price of all output is lowered. However, just as with perfect competition, imperfect competition is also a static theory which takes demand as given, and does not inquire how consumer preferences are formed. As Robinson (1969) put it,

> 'The whole analysis, which in reality consists of comparisons of static equilibrium positions, is dressed up to appear to represent a process going on through time. To put the argument into a dynamic setting it is necessary to distinguish between the short-period aspect of competition . . . and the long period aspect.' [Preface, pp. vi–vii]

Under the imperfect competition analysis, the more markets are imperfect the smaller the output because the higher the price has to be in order to maximize profits; since the high price may attract new competitors, output may remain below the optimum level.

It is therefore only under perfect competition, with perfect mobility of resources, that private interest and social interest coincide. Imperfect competition does not yield the best results in terms of economic welfare because it does not conform to the premise that consumers should get the goods that they value more highly, and should go on getting them.

Thus in traditional theory the firm has been regarded mainly as a vehicle for maximizing profits and allocating resources or, where it was admitted that in the presence of imperfect competition this might no longer be possible, the alternative behaviour of the firm has been considered almost entirely in terms of price theory. Traditional theory, too, has been concerned predominantly with whether profits are normal or contain an element of monopoly profit.

Finally, the simplifying assumptions made in the theory of the firm for purposes of analysis have the effect of confining the entrepreneur to a straitjacket, and thereby reducing his role, in the words of Benson, to a

> '. . . creature that moves
> In predestinate grooves
> He is not even a bus; he's a tram.'

ADVERTISING AND ECONOMIC THEORY

The adjective 'perfect' is a technical term used in economic analysis; it has no necessary moral implication. An equivalent in the physical sciences is 'perfect' vacuum which means *complete* not necessarily *best*. Nevertheless, imperfect competition is often regarded as less desirable competition, in particular the 'imperfection' of the market brought about first by advertising and other selling techniques, and second by a market structure characterized by seller concentration—oligopoly. Since discussions on advertising and oligopoly are inextricably linked, before proceeding to the relationship between advertising and competition, the concept of oligopoly—the domination of an industry by a few firms—requires elucidation.

The theory of the firm predicts that industries in which output is produced by a few dominant firms may in the long run earn higher rates of return. For this to occur, the assumptions are made (1) that collusion rather than competition increases with concentration; and (2) that there are barriers to entry. Without these conditions monopoly profits will not arise.

The other major feature of oligopoly under this theory is a diminution of price competition among firms as a direct result of their mutual interdependence. It is argued that there will be a general unwillingness to lower prices because this action will cause competitors to follow suit, and since market shares will remain unchanged all the firms will suffer a fall in profits. Conversely, no firm will readily raise its prices, because if others refuse to do likewise the company which raises its prices will lose a share of the market. This will lead to a stagnant situation in which prices will change only very slowly even when costs are changing, and the market shares of the few large companies will remain fairly stable. The appreciation among oligopolists of the interdependence of their market behaviour leads them to forgo independent price initiatives in favour of coordinating pricing (tacit or overt). More commonly, oligopolistic markets are characterized by non-price competition in the form of advertising and sales promotion activities aimed at product differentiation and the development of brand loyalty, and these factors rather than price competition will determine market shares.

The lack of independent pricing under an oligopolistic market structure therefore leads to the prevalence of parallel prices and price leadership. A distinction is, however, made between disciplined and barometric price leadership. The major conditions contributing towards disciplined price leadership include not only high seller concentration but also security against the entry into the market of new competitors, similarity of products, the degree of elasticity of demand, and similarity of cost levels and cost structures. The greater the discipline and the more unresponsive the demand, the higher, other things being equal, are prices and profits likely to be.

Barometric price leadership comprises a much looser form of price leadership where, in the presence of frequent changes and differences in cost and demand, products and production methods, and competitive conditions, it is much more difficult for firms to sustain highly coordinated pricing. In this more volatile situation the price leader will be followed immediately only if his decisions are felt to be an accurate reflection of changes in cost and market conditions. According to Stigler, in barometric pricing the price leader

'Commands adherence of rivals to his price only because and to the extent that his price reflects market conditions with tolerable promptness.' [1947, p. 446]

It has been further argued (Markham, 1951) that the factors responsible for barometric price leadership result in a less orderly form of price parallelism and a type of behaviour closer to that expected in an industry composed of a larger number of sellers. As a result, the levels of prices and profits are likely to diverge less from the competitive norm than with the disciplined forms of parallel pricing.

The position of economic theory on the place of advertising in the traditional theory of the firm has been the subject of controversial debate among economists for many years. The first major economist to acknowledge advertising as a subject for economic analysis was Marshall (1919), who made a distinction between 'constructive' advertising which was considered beneficial because it was informative, and 'combative' advertising which was considered as wasteful because it was repetitive and persuasive. A major critic of advertising at a later date has been Kaldor (1950) who postulates inter alia in his seminal article, 'The economic aspects of advertising', that although the primary 'direct' function of advertising is to provide information it does not do this efficiently, namely the volume of advertising expenditures is excessive because it is jointly supplied with products, advertising fails to provide enough unbiased information, and it is costly. Kaldor also claimed that one 'indirect' effect of advertising is to promote concentration. This article has stimulated many of the empirical studies of the past 30 years.

Broadly, the debate has focused on the kind and amount of advertising required in the provision of information, and the effects of advertising on competition. In addition, there has been a separate and comparatively recent sector of economics—the theory of the economics of information—which has considered advertising from the point of view of buyers of advertised products in contrast to the sellers of these products which has been the traditional approach.

These various issues of advertising and economic theory are closely related and tend to overlap, but will be dealt with separately as far as possible for ease of exposition.

Advertising and information

If, as is assumed under perfect competition, buyers and sellers have perfect knowledge, advertising would be superfluous and represent a waste of resources. If, on the other hand, there was not always perfect knowledge, advertising could perform a useful function. It has been generally accepted that in the real world some selling techniques are necessary because information is not perfect, or because indivisibilities in production techniques require markets to be expanded.

However, in the provision of information, advertising expenditure has been deemed to be wasteful and excessive, and therefore to have undesirable effects on welfare on two major accounts. First, many advertisements are persuasive rather than informative; persuasive advertisements help to stimulate product differentiation and brand loyalty, and hence encourage imperfect competition. A related criticism is the Kaldor contention that advertising fails to provide enough unbiased information, and that the information supplied by advertising (at a cost in 1938 of M£68) could be provided more cheaply by an independent information service (around M£14 in 1938). Kaldor also suggested that retailer advertising is more informative than manufacturer advertising, so that retailers 'disseminate market information in a strict sense, and tend to reduce market imperfection' (p. 7) while the opposite result is more likely for advertising by manufacturers of consumer goods. Second, since advertising is jointly supplied (Kaldor) with the product in the sense that the buyer must pay for both even though he may only wish to purchase the latter, he would buy less than he does under this arrangement if advertising were separated from the product.

Advertising: informative or persuasive?

It was Marshall who made the distinction between 'constructive' advertising, designed to inform people about products offered for sale, which he thought was beneficial, and 'combative' advertising which was primarily not informative but repetitive and persuasive, and which was wasteful, even if it raised output and lowered costs, because such economies could have been reaped without it (1919, p. 305).

Marshall's separation of advertising content into two kinds was adopted by Pigou during the 1920s, and he drew a similar but more extreme distinction between 'informative' and 'competitive' advertising. The latter advertising had

'. . . the sole purpose of transferring the demand for a given commodity from one source of supply to another.' [1932, pp. 196–200]

He considered that most advertising was 'competitive' and therefore undesirable. Advertising could lead to arrangements between formerly independent firms and therefore to monopoly; it could be self-defeating because the advertising efforts of competing firms cancelled one another out; and it could merely substitute the products of one firm for those of another and more efficient firm. Pigou suggested that the wasteful element in advertising might be prevented by taxing or even prohibiting 'competitive' advertising.

The distinction of advertising into two kinds was made with apparently little empirical investigation. According to Stuart Chase,

'Nine-tenths and more of advertising is largely competitive wrangling as to the relative merits of two indistinguishable compounds.' [1925, p. 113]

The distinction between informative and other advertising was considered illogical and impracticable by Braithwaite (1928). She judged, however, that most advertising was not informative. If advertising increased output by facilitating standardization and mass production, and reduced costs per unit and therefore prices, then it could be considered beneficial. On the other hand, if it merely redistributed demand for different commodities, resources were used in a less desirable pattern from the community's point of view.

Implicit in the distinction made between 'informative' and 'competitive' advertising seemed to be the belief that it was the latter type of advertising which was responsible for product differentiation. Braithwaite, for instance, propounded that advertising could restrict competition because price and quality lost their powers as instruments of competition and were replaced by the power of producers to win markets by creating 'reputation'. This process of creating 'reputation' monopolies then became cumulative and a vicious advertising circle was set in motion.

In the 1930s Chamberlin and Robinson developed Braithwaite's notion of reputation monopolies by claiming that advertising could be used to 'differentiate' products from one another by emphasizing the less important advantages and so create 'loyalty' for each brand; this gave each advertiser a pocket of monopoly and he could then charge a higher price for his product, but his output was lower than it would be in perfect competition.

Later, Robinson (1969) put this view more forthrightly:

'. . . non-price competition, such as artificial product differentiation, advertising and sales promotion . . . accounts for the greatest part of the wastefulness of imperfect markets.' [Preface, p. ix]

Comanor and Wilson (1974) also seemed to imply that advertising was the essential requirement for the introduction of product differentiation:

'. . . advertising in this analysis acts as a proxy for product differentiation, or, more specifically, for the product and market characteristics that permit heavy advertising expenditures to differentiate effectively the products of a firm from those of its rivals. Although these product and market characteristics are not easily measured, they are typically characterized by heavy advertising expenditures.' [pp. 130–131]

The distinction between 'informative' and 'combative' advertising was applied by Lewis (1945, 1949), as by Kaldor, to retailers' and manufacturers' advertising respectively. Lewis argued further that consumers are better guided by retailers into buying (standardized or mass-produced) goods they have chosen on the basis of their expert knowledge and experience than by manufacturers, each of whom is intent on pushing his own brand or variety on ill-informed purchasers:

'It should not be on the manufacturer's strident claims that the public has to rely for information . . . much advertising by manufacturers is wasteful (because buyers and sellers already know the facts, or when it is false or misleading).' [1945, pp. 218–220]

In this view, therefore, retail advertising is distinguished as 'desirable' because it is informative; manufacturer advertising is considered 'undesirable' because it is mainly combative or persuasive.

The thesis that advertising was one way of conveying information to consumers about a product they knew existed, but to mix information with persuasion seemed undesirable, and the amount of resources devoted to advertising seemed excessive persisted through the 1920s and 1930s to the 1950s and 1960s. Harbury (1958), for instance, explains that most advertising is 'largely persuasive in character and the information supplied is selective'. And Boulding suggested that while there was a case for a certain amount of purely informative advertising which describes the qualities and prices of commodities,

'This virtuous advertising . . . does not bulk very large in total. Most advertising, unfortunately, is devoted to an attempt to build up in the minds of the consumers irrational preferences for certain brands of goods.' [1955, p. 672]

There were, however, economists who questioned the belief that it was possible to isolate 'informative' from 'competitive' advertising, and that one component of the content of advertisements could manipulate demand against consumers' interests:

1. It has been pointed out, for instance (Harris and Seldon, 1962, p. 74; Economists Advisory Group, 1967, p. 79), that the ability of 'persuasive' advertising to manipulate demand contrary to the consumer's interest is at variance with economic theory in which consumers' preferences are given and changes in them are largely ignored. Moreover, conventional demand theory does not inquire into how consumers' preferences are formed in the first place.
2. It has been argued that the distinction drawn between 'informative' and 'competitive' advertising is a matter of semantics, and one which in practice it is impossible to draw. Consequently, advertising per se should be considered as providing some kind of information; for example, Hicks:

    'The attention of the consumer has to be attracted and his attention aroused. In order to perform its social function, advertising has to be attractive and (let us not be afraid to say) persuasive.' [1962, p. 257]

    and Alderson:

    'All effective communication is persuasive . . . both information and recommendation must be presented persuasively if they are to have any effect on purchasing decisions.' [1968, p. 582]

3. The artificial distinction drawn between 'informative' and 'persuasive' advertising is based on a misunderstanding of the nature, purpose and rationale of advertising which is wider than conveying information to the consumer about products which are already in existence (new products; continually changing consumers—baby products; new uses of an established product; changes in the product itself—Telser, Ozga, Marris); for example, as Kirzner stated:

    'The entrepreneur's task is not completed when he makes information available to the consumer. He must also get the consumer to notice and absorb the information . . . It is not so much perhaps that effective communication needs to be persuasive as that it needs to be eye-catching, mind-catching, and re-inforced by constant repetition'. [1973, p. 162]

Despite these counter-arguments to the conventional distinction made between 'informative' and 'persuasive' advertising, the traditional view persisted. Together with Kaldor's contrast of the higher cost of advertising compared with that of an independent information service plus his contention that advertising is biased, these views led to the proposal that a more efficient and unbiased method of spreading necessary information might be reports by independent consumer advisory units. Thus Meade:

'Consumers are ignorant and gullible. It is, therefore, desirable for the State to discourage private commercial advertisement and to foster disinterested consumer research and information services.' [1964, p. 12]

More recently, Meade expanded this proposal:

'Of course much advertisement of an informative nature is necessary and desirable. But much advertisement is not of this kind. A tax on advertisement would increase the incentive for firms to seek markets by cutting prices rather than by persuasive bamboozlement . . . Measures might be taken to replace much interested persuasive advertisement with impartial information through the promotion by the State of bodies for consumers' research and education. The provision and widespread dissemination by a number of independent semi-public bodies of information about the real qualities of different products would increase the forces of the market mechanism to which the producers would have to submit.' [1975, pp. 49–50]

A more extreme view that even an independent consumer advice system might not be adequate to counterbalance the power of advertising was put forward by Robinson:

'. . . consumer sovereignty can never be established as long as the initiative lies with the producer. For the general run of consumer goods, the buyer is necessarily an amateur while the seller is a professional . . . The great chain stores exercise some monopsonistic influence in imposing a kind of synthetic perfect market on small-scale producers, but they cannot offer a counter-weight to the great oligopolists.' [1969, p. xii]

That independent information services for consumers are necessary because the information provided by advertisements is designed by the sellers of goods and is consequently biased was also propounded by the Economists Advisory Group (1967, p. 78); while Reekie agrees with their view that there is 'too little information in particular' and suggests 'establishing some sort of rival to the Consumers' Association' (1977, pp. 86–88).

As a means of reducing advertising expenditure and other selling costs both Kaldor and Lewis maintained that the distributive system should be dominated by the retailer, and by retailer brands rather than those of manufacturers. The manufacturers would supply large retailers (chain stores, cooperative societies) who would tell them what consumers wanted. It was also envisaged by both Lewis and Kaldor that the pressure of retailer domination would lead to a reduction in the variety of products.

Advertising: joint supply

Kaldor claimed that advertising is wasteful of resources because advertisers buy more advertising than the public require, with the result that there are socially undesirable effects on welfare. This contention is expounded from the classical economist's viewpoint of consumer sovereignty. For example, Kaldor defines advertising as a subsidized commodity which is offered by the manufacturer to the consumer at nil cost in the expectation that there will be a consequential increase in the demand for his products. In other words, the manufacturer is the seller of the advertising and the consumer is the buyer. Since advertising is not bought separately but is purchased as an integral part of the product, consumers cannot easily evaluate whether or not they want it and, as a consequence, its true cost is not known, nor whether resources are economically used for supplying it.

The joint supply argument has been criticized for the most part by questioning the various economic assumptions behind Kaldor's hypothesis.

Telser (1966), for instance, dissents from Kaldor's reasoning because (1) existing economies of joint production would be lost with a separate market for advertising messages, and (2) as long as there are unadvertised or lightly advertised goods available in the market, the price differential between these and advertised goods cannot exceed the amount consumers are willing to pay for the extra advertising involved. This last point has also been made by Stigler, who further commented:

'The assimilation of information is not an easy or pleasant task for most people, and they may well be willing to pay more for the information when supplied in an enjoyable form. In principle this complementary demand for information and entertainment is exactly analogous to the complementary demand of consumers for commodities and delivery service or air-conditioned stores'. [1961, pp. 213–225]

It has been argued by Ozga (1960) that real consumer demand for advertising is a great deal higher than Kaldor suggests because it forms part of consumers' continual learning and remembering process. All these criticisms assume that the argument is essentially whether the consumer demand curve and the media supply curve are as far apart as Kaldor suggests.

Lind (1975), on the other hand, has pointed out that it is the manufacturer rather than the consumer who demands and buys the advertising, and it is the media rather than the manufacturer who supply it. He argues that it is illogical, therefore, to consider advertising as a separate entity from the product, as much as it would be illogical to consider delivery vans, for example, as separate from the product. On Lind's analysis advertising is an input to business, the amount of which is determined on exactly similar lines and with a roughly similar possibility of error, to those of any other capital, labour or marketing input.

Advertising and competition

The view of many economists regarding the relationship between advertising and competition is summed up by H. C. Simons:

'A major barrier to really competitive enterprise and efficient service to consumers'. [1948, p. 95]

Most recent discussion of advertising in relation to the theory of the firm, and in the branch of economics dealing with industrial structure/organization, has tended to concentrate on the welfare implications of the effect of advertising on competition, and particularly on market structure, for instance the association of advertising with product differentiation in building up brand loyalty, and thus causing imperfections in the market, excess capacity and higher prices; the significance of advertising as an important cause of industrial concentration; and the role of advertising as a barrier to entry which reinforces concentration and enables firms to earn monopoly profits.

Kaldor (1950) suggested that the anti-competitive effect of advertising is to switch demand from some products to others, which is undesirable; that is, advertising shifts demand from smaller to larger firms, so reducing the number of firms until the whole output of a product is manufactured by a small number— oligopoly. As a consequence, competition no longer takes place by means of prices, but by means of packaging, samples, coupons, gifts and other attractions that might be considered secondary. He maintained that this method of competition has advantages and disadvantages when compared with more perfect competition. Among its advantages are the encouragement of economies of large-scale production, finance, long-term research and more risk taking. On the other hand, its disadvantages include higher costs of management, high selling costs (including advertising), higher prices, barrier to entry to new firms with new ideas and methods because of the high cost of breaking into the market, and a possibly dangerous concentration of economic power. Kaldor concluded from this analysis that there are monopolistic and oligopolistic tendencies inherent in advertising, which lead to a progressive concentration of market power in the hands of large firms, so that this concentration leads in turn to a reduction in the degree of freedom of entry into the market for newcomers, and that consequently it is possible for existing firms to enjoy a higher level of profit without attracting new competitors than would be possible if there were no advertising, viz:

> 'The economic effects of advertising must be judged therefore in terms of the advantages of the manufacturers' oligopoly (as against the polypoly under wholesalers' domination) which it helped to create and maintain . . . after advertising has been generally adopted . . . sales will have been concentrated among a smaller number of firms and the size of the representative firm will have increased.' [1950, p. 13]

Advertising, concentration and profits. The view that seller concentration is higher than it would be if firms advertised less has stimulated a series of empirical investigations which have tried to ascertain, first, whether there is a systematic association between advertising intensity and industry concentration and, second, the relationship between advertising intensity and profitability. The assumptions underlying the argument that advertising increases monopoly power is that it leads to an increase in the minimum efficient size of firm, and that there are increasing returns to advertising.

Concentration: increasing or decreasing?

Before discussing the specific relationship that is claimed to exist between advertising and concentration, it is necessary to point out that there is by no means general agreement on whether the degree of concentration in industry has been increasing or decreasing in the economy as a whole, nor into the factors which increase, decrease and maintain concentration in particular industries.

In the United States of America in the 1930s and 1940s there was a general consensus (Berle and Means, 1932; Burns, 1936; Galbraith, 1948) that increasing concentration had been evident since the beginning of the century and that its continuing increase was inevitable. In the 1950s, as a result of empirical and theoretical research, these views were contested (Adelman, 1951; Penrose, 1959), and their conclusions were confirmed by official statistics which showed a very stable structure of industry between 1954 and 1972, and investigations into concentration ratio (the proportion of total industry output accounted for by the largest three or four firms in industry) which did not show a diminution in competition because the firms do not remain the same.

In the 1970s the view that industrial concentration had been growing in the United Kingdom was put forward (Aaronvitch and Sawyer, 1974; Bannock, 1971; Marris, 1964; and in particular by Prais, 1976). The dangers of this development were emphasized as well as its implications for industrial policy.

Jewkes (1977) has, however, pointed out that Prais has frequently revised downwards the percentage of output he attributes to the 100 largest companies for the year 1970 from 52 per cent to 40 to 41 per cent, while the Department of Industry in an official study gave the figure for 1970 at 37.7 per cent. He concludes:

> 'The stability (around 33 per cent) of the corresponding percentage in American industry is now accepted by all informed observers. It may be that in the UK we too are reaching a stability around 38 per cent, the higher figure for the UK perhaps being accounted for by our smaller economy than the American . . .' [1977, p. 24]

Other economists (Parkin, 1972; Hart, 1965) have pointed out some of the limitations in Gibrat's Law which Prais has used to support his statistical findings. The Gibrat hypothesis maintains that if there is a random element in firms' growth, but all firms (regardless of size) have the same probability of growth, the distribution of firms' sizes will approach the log-normal distribution. Jewkes further maintains that other mathematical economists have sought to understand the process of industrial concentration by taking into account the entry and exit of firms into and out of the market and that the conclusion of Adelman (1958) was the opposite of Prais, namely, that a tendency towards deconcentration could be expected and a growth in the size of the median firm.

Extensive analysis by Telser failed to find a correlation between advertising expenditures and market structure when he compared market concentration data with advertising intensity for 42 industries:

> 'There is little empirical support for an adverse association between advertising and competition, despite some plausible theorizing to the contrary.' [1964, p. 558]

His general findings were that initial injections of advertising in an industry are not decisive, and that it is not the case that a given firm can take a major advertising initiative, which then gives it a monopoly which persists. On the contrary, Telser suggests that industries tend towards equilibria without being determined by historical advertising events.

A study by Mann et al of 14 industries, however, found a positive correlation between four-firm concentration ratios and average advertising–sales ratios (the simple correlation coefficients range from 0.41 to 0.72 among their several regressions) and concluded that

'enough of the variance in concentration is explained by advertising intensity to raise an issue for public policy.' [1967, p. 38]

These findings sparked off considerable controversy. Ekelund and Maurice (1969), Telser (1969) and Ekelund and Gramm (1970, 1971) have argued that no correlation between advertising intensity and concentration exists in the United States. Doyle (1968), Reekie (1977) and Schnabel (1970) report similar negative findings with United Kingdom data. Conversely, Marcus (1969), Mann et al (1969) and Mann and Meehan (1971) have contended that there is a significant correlation.

In a critical review of the literature J. L. Simon was less convinced of the causal relationship between advertising and concentration:

'. . . it is the structural features of an industry rather than decisions by single firms which determine the intensity of advertising on the industry . . . in any case the existing data are not well suited to a test of causality from advertising to concentration because it is not very reasonable to think of advertising as exogenous.' [1975, p. 169]

Thus the empirical data and the interpretation of them conflict about whether or not there is a correlation between advertising and concentration. It has been argued, however, that higher concentration alone does not lead to higher profits, but that conditions of entry are an equally important determinant.

The association between profitability and advertising intensity was first noted by Comanor and Wilson. Their paper, which used similar data to those of Telser, supplied empirical support for implications precisely the opposite to his conclusions (this contradiction is primarily a reflection of differences in the conceptual and statistical approaches adopted rather than differences in data or sample):

'. . . advertising has a statistically significant and quantitatively important impact upon profit rates which provide a measure of market performance as well as indicate the existence of market power.' [1967, p. 423]

Their findings showed that industries with high advertising outlays had a profit rate that exceeded that of other industries by nearly four percentage points, that is, nearly half as high again as the other industries in the sample. Their findings were confirmed by Guth (1971), whose investigations showed that advertising affects the distribution of firm sizes in an industry, and that advertising increases the industry average profit level. Furthermore, while a study by Lambin (1975) covering eight different Western European countries found no significant association between measures of market concentration and advertising intensity, it did find some support for the contention that advertising intensity increases the capacity of the firm to charge higher prices and did find that advertising could be an entry barrier for new firms, though this was neither general nor systematic of the countries and markets studied.

However, Telser has commented on investigations which show this causal link between advertising and profits:

> '. . . were matters so simple it would be hard to explain why all companies do not travel the same road to riches.' [1968, p. 169]

The effect of advertising on profitability in different product groups has also been studied. Strickland and Weiss (1976), for instance, showed by means of a three equation model in which advertising–sales ratios, concentration ratios, and price–cost margins are the dependent variables that when their sample was divided into consumer and producer goods, advertising was unexpectedly more effective in the latter than in the former. This finding was not confirmed by Martin (1978), however, when he adopted a slightly different model. In this investigation the advertising coefficients remained statistically significant in the margin equations for consumer goods as well as for producer goods. In another investigation Porter (1974) divided consumer goods industries into their traditional sectors of convenience and shopping goods. He points out that since unit prices for convenience goods are low and purchases are generally made from easily accessible outlets the 'probable gains from making price and quality comparisons [are] small relative to [the] consumer's appraisal of search costs' (p. 422) whereas shopping goods warrant price and quality comparisons before a purchasing decision is made because the potential gain is large compared with the cost of search. Consequently Porter suggests that the impact of advertising is likely to be much greater for convenience goods than for shopping goods, and concludes that 'previous empirical work in consumer goods industries . . . has mixed two very different samples. The results obtained . . . represent a curious averaging of these two diverse groups' (p. 432).

The results of these investigations have led Comanor and Wilson (1979) to comment that the 'competitive effects of advertising are likely to be found in a small group of industries with particular characteristics' (p. 462), and that unfortunately there has been no test of possible simultaneous equation bias in regression estimates limited to convenience goods industries.

In a critical assessment of the available evidence Schmalensee (1972) analysed the impact of advertising on a firm's ability to earn monopoly profits. He concluded that a correlation between advertising intensity and profitability is to be expected even in the absence of a causal flow from advertising to profits. He can find no evidence that advertising increases the minimum efficient firm size, or that there are increasing returns to advertising, or that advertising creates durable preference changes that serve as entry barriers to new firms. He therefore concludes that nothing is really known about the impact of advertising on monopoly profits.

Ferguson (1974), when he examined the limited evidence, could also find no support for the contention that there are increasing returns to advertising. He also pointed out the formidable econometric and measurement problems present in the single-equation multiple-regression tests of the hypothesis that advertising decreases competition which are used in most studies.

Advertising as a barrier to entry. Stigler defines a barrier to entry as

'. . . a cost of producing (at some or every rate of output) which must be borne by a firm which seeks to enter a business but is not borne by firms already in the industry'. [1968, p. 67]

A high level of expenditure on advertising in association with product differentiation has been seen as an effective method of discouraging new entrants. This is contended to result from higher penetration costs of new firms, consumer inertia, and the economies of scale in advertising available to larger extant firms. Advertising has been criticized, therefore, as a source of monopoly power through its impact on conditions of entry; for example, as R. E. Cave states:

'. . . research in the USA has revealed that "heavy advertising" worsens industry performance by raising barriers to entry and increases market power.' [1968, p. 312]

However, there has by no means been a unanimity of view resulting from the continuous theoretical debate and empirical investigations which have taken place.

The pioneering work in this field is that of Bain (1956), who measured the influence of barriers to entry—classified as very high, substantial and moderate to low—on the profit rates of the leading firms in a sample of oligopolistic industries for the periods 1936 to 1940 and 1947 to 1951. He found that

'product differentiation is of at least the same general order of importance as an impediment to entry as are economies of large-scale production and distribution'. [chapter 4]

This investigation was followed up by Mann (1966) who undertook research into the relationship between seller concentration, barriers to entry, and profit rates for 1950 to 1960 to determine whether the pattern Bain had discovered was compatible with a period of time that was not part of the Great Depression or of rapid postwar inflation. His findings supported Bain's results. Furthermore, Bain (1968) has asserted that advertising does inhibit entry:

'The product differentiation advantages of established firms loom larger than any other sources of barriers to entry, and especially large as a source of high and very high barriers . . . This superiority of established firms in turn typically hinges in important or major degree upon the susceptibility of buyers to persuasion through heavy advertising or other sales promotion effort.' [1968, pp. 281–282]

Schmalensee (1972, p. 243), however, could find no evidence in support of Bain's conclusion. He further criticized the original Bain (1956) investigation on the grounds that it performed no tests of hypotheses; advertising was held to be a major source of entry barrier mainly when it was intensive or when industry sources voiced the opinion that it limited entry possibilities. Stigler (1968) has also passed critical judgement on the Bain concept of limit pricing which is deployed to determine the heights of his barriers.

In Bain's 1936 to 1940 study based on 42 United States industries, in the group of highly concentrated industries where the eight largest firms accounted for 70 per cent or more of value added, the average profit rate was significantly higher than in the less concentrated industries. A re-examination of these industries by Brozen (1970) showed that even if concentration had facilitated collusion initially this had been a short-term phenomenon because 15 years later the high and low profit rates in these industries had moved back towards the average. Brozen's later work (1971) also showed that Bain's results were biased by a statistical error resulting from the incorrect assumption that industries were in long-run equilibrium.

There is an alternative view to that of Bain regarding concentration which does not rest on economies of scale and which, therefore, does not state that barriers to entry increase with concentration. Both Demsetz (1973) and Brozen (1971) have concluded that concentration can arise as the result of the relative efficiency of large firms compared with that of smaller firms in a particular industry. In Demsetz's analysis profits do not arise due to output restriction or collusion, but to superior performance resulting from uncertainty plus luck or extraordinary insight by management:

> 'Since information is costly to obtain and techniques difficult to duplicate, the firm may enjoy growth and a superior rate of return for some time.' [1973, p. 3]

Ferguson concludes that if this view of concentration as a measure of the relative efficiency of large firms is correct,

> '. . . finding advertising expenditure positively related to concentration (and rates of return) does not indicate that advertising is a barrier to entry or a source of monopoly power.' [1974, p. 61]

Ferguson has also made some fundamental criticisms of the studies linking advertising with monopoly power: that these investigations have been conducted within an incomplete theoretical framework of the model of structure–conduct–performance—for example, it has been questioned whether market structure is a good indicator or determinant of monopoly power; it is possible to question the economic significance of concentration ratios because of shortcomings and inaccuracies in the data; there are serious doubts concerning the assumption of one-way causality of market structure and conduct; there is no generally agreed theory of collusion; there is no measure of the conditions of entry—the extent to which established firms can raise prices above marginal cost without attracting entry.

Since a theoretical basis on which to draw practical conclusions on the relationship between advertising and monopoly power does not appear to exist, and the variety of studies undertaken to assess the effects of advertising on monopoly and industrial concentration have either been inconclusive, or have been shown by later studies to have reached unjustified conclusions, some economists have suggested that there is no theoretical or empirical basis for any public policy based on the presumption that advertising decreases competition (Ferguson, 1974; Needham, 1971).

In a recent survey of the literature on the effects of advertising on competition which concentrated on those papers which examine the impact of advertising on barriers to entry and on the extent of price competition, Comanor and Wilson admit that no consensus view has developed on the theoretical models, and that there are differences of opinion on the interpretation of the many econometric studies of advertising and profitability:

'At the end of this discussion as at the beginning much depends on the effect of advertising on demand elasticities, and there appears to be no general rule. There are plausible models on both sides of the issue, so that any resolution of this controversy depends on the empirical evidence. Unfortunately, there are also substantial differences as to how the various statistical results should be interpreted.' [1979, p. 457]

Nevertheless, Comanor and Wilson draw the primary conclusion from empirical research that 'heavy advertising does contribute to high levels of market power in some industries' (p. 473), and if this power could be reduced without limiting the information provided by the current volume of advertising social welfare would be improved. Since, however, no accepted theoretical basis yet exists for assessing the gains to consumers from the information contained in advertising, Comanor and Wilson suggest that this should be the next issue for examination, and on which public policy judgements should also depend.

Advertising and the theory of the economics of information

As has been seen (Marshall et al) it has been acknowledged that advertising may fulfil a useful role in providing information where buyers and sellers do not have perfect knowledge—even if the concept of what constitutes information is some-what ambiguous. On the other hand, the assumption of perfect knowledge which is made in the conventional theory of the firm means that the acquisition of knowledge of prices or exchange opportunities in a perfect market is costless, so that knowledge is, as it were, a free good.

Since in the real world information about available products is not a free good automatically available to anyone and everyone, a different way of considering advertising has emerged comparatively recently in the economics of information by concentrating on analysing the benefits which buyers of advertised products gain from advertisements as opposed to the traditional approach of considering advertising almost entirely from the viewpoint of the sellers of advertised products.

The seminal article by Stigler criticized the neglect in economic theory of the cost of search for information:

'. . . information . . . occupies a slum dwelling in the town of economics . . . Mostly it is ignored . . . And one of the information-producing industries, advertising, is treated with a hostility that economists normally reserve for tariffs or monopolists.' [1961, p. 213]

He illustrated his criticism by analysing one important role of advertising for buyers: the identification of sellers and the ascertainment of market price. The expansion of recruitment advertising over the past two decades has been an important factor, for example, in bringing job opportunities and current wages and salaries to the attention of job seekers, thus reducing the cost and time of search for employees (Fulop, 1971, p. 65). In the absence of advertising, buyers must acquire information in other ways, or make decisions without it. In certain circumstances this may be more costly for buyers than the cost of resources devoted to advertising.

Furthermore, once there is an awareness of the cost of the search for information, it becomes possible to explain why buyers attach importance to 'reputation'; it economizes on search because it denotes the persistence of quality. As Stigler points out:

> 'When economists deplore the reliance of the consumer on reputation . . . they implicitly assume that the consumer has a large laboratory, ready to deliver current information quickly and gratuitously.' [1961, p. 224]

Johnson has also emphasized that information is not a free good, and maintains that this misconception arises as a result of the basic assumption of perfect knowledge in the theory of the firm:

> 'The approach of politicians and the general public to advertising, like that of economic theory, is still dominated by the idea that everyone knows what he wants.' [1967, p. 14]

Consequently, Johnson maintains that

> 'Information is important, worth spending resources on acquiring, and advertising is only one of the many ways of providing information.' [1967, p. 14]

2 Alternative theories to the theory of the firm

In the neoclassical theory of the firm it has been seen that competition is used in a technical sense to classify market conditions according to the degree of control over prices exercised by producers or consumers. In this technical meaning of market situations, competition embraces only impersonal adaptations to given conditions, and it is assumed that the most wanted products and the least cost methods and scales of production are known. Despite adaptations and modifications which have been incorporated in the theory to explain a variety of market conditions such as oligopoly, etc., the raison d'être of the theory has remained unchanged—a method of specifying the mechanisms by which resources are allocated in the market-place.

There are three major criticisms of the theory:

1. That its basic assumptions that the objective of the firm is to maximize net revenue, and that decision behaviour is guided by the precepts of utility maximizations, do not accord with the behaviour of firms in the real world where the motives underlying behaviour are more complex and multi-dimensional, and where perfect maximization would be too expensive and time-consuming to achieve in a world of imperfect knowledge for firms and consumers.

2. That the theory is inadequate because insufficient attention has been paid to the behaviour of the large corporation or firm which has become the norm over wide areas of industry as a consequence of technological developments, economies of scale, and the separation of ownership and control which stems from the growth of the joint stock company. These claimed defects have been tackled from two different viewpoints: first, by the school of managerial economics (Downie, 1958; Baumol, 1959; Marris, 1964); second, by Galbraith (1958, 1963, 1969), who adopted Marris' basic proposition that it was more accurate to regard the economy as operating entirely on a managerial basis

25

than the common practice of treating it as operating in the traditional manner of the theory of the firm. Concomitant with this tenet was the implication for public policy that attempts should not be made to revive artificially traditional forms of competition.

Galbraith, however, departed significantly from managerial economics with his assertion that the large corporation utilizes advertising to control consumer demand, and thereby nullifies consumer sovereignty (there is, for example, a fundamental difference between Marris' explanation of how a new product is introduced to the market, and the assumptions made by Galbraith), and his doctrine that the 'countervailing power' of distributors should be utilized to control the power of the large corporation rather than legislation.

3. That the factors which are taken for granted in traditional theory, i.e. that there is perfect knowledge, that the shape of the demand curve is known, that consumer preferences are known—these are precisely the uncertainties which exist continuously in the real world, and which provide opportunities for firms and create competition. This theory of competition as a process rather than a situation has been expounded most fully by Kirzner (1973), but many of its components have been put forward by other economists as well.

MANAGERIAL ECONOMICS

Managerial economics which describes and predicts the internal decision-making process of a firm is based on propositions which are directly related to two major criticisms of traditional theory. First, firms do not decide how much to produce by equating marginal cost with marginal revenue. As evidence, the difference between the economic concept of cost in the theory has been contrasted with the accounting concept of cost used in actual business firms. Second, because traditional theory does not view the firm as an organization, such factors as management planning, budgets and standard operating procedures are excluded from consideration, although they constitute important factors in a firm's decision-making process. These and other criticisms of managerial economists reflect the emphasis placed in the neoclassical theory to explain, at a general level, the behaviour of firms within a given market, and not the behaviour of individuals within a particular firm.

Baumol provided the first major revision of neoclassical theory to incorporate these criticisms by constructing a mathematical model of a firm growing continuously at a steady rate, and used this model to analyse the implications which followed from it. Baumol suggested that firms do not devote all their energies to maximizing profits, but seek to maximize sales revenue as long as a 'satisfactory' level of profit is maintained. In this theory, therefore, total sales revenue has been substituted for profits, and two decision criteria or objectives have been introduced, namely, a satisfactory level of profit and the maximum sales turnover. The firm, therefore, is no longer viewed as working towards one objective alone, but is attempting to balance two competing but not necessarily consistent goals. From this hypothesis Baumol drew conclusions which are claimed to be more consistent with observed business behaviour: first, that firms faced with an increase in fixed costs will either pass on these costs directly to the consumer in the form of higher prices or will try to reduce an expense over which they have some control (e.g., advertising expenditure); whereas conventional theory asserts that changes in fixed costs should not lead a firm to alter either its output or its prices. Furthermore, he argued that 'sales maximization makes far greater presumption that businessmen will consider non-price competition to be the more advantageous alternative' (1959, p. 76) which signifies that firms will tend to set their prices at the same levels as their competitors, while devoting their competitive energies towards advertising, product differentiation, servicing, etc. This contrasts with the view of neoclassical theory that businessmen will consider price cuts or increases as the primary mechanism for increasing profits.

Although Baumol's theory appears more consistent with observed behaviour, it focuses primarily upon the behaviour of firms in the market-place. It did not consider the analysis and prediction of a firm's decision-making behaviour on such problems as price, output, internal resource allocation. As a consequence, market theories of the firm have been supplemented by behavioural theories of the firm which seek to show how an organization makes decisions on the basis of the information that is available at any given time. It is a theory of decision-making behaviour which has substituted the notion of a satisfactory level of performance for the neoclassical principle of maximization. By abandoning *maximizing* for the *behavioural* principle of satisficing, it is possible to add as many goals or objectives to the theory as is consistent with observed behaviour (see Cyert and March, 1963).

A third strand in managerial economics is heuristic programming which seeks to incorporate into the theoretical model the selective rule of thumb processes that individuals employ in solving complex problems.

The theories of individual or organizational decision-making depict a different working of the price mechanism than is portrayed in traditional theory. If firms only maximize sales revenue subject to a satisfactory profit constraint, or according to the behavioural theory of the firm, then they no longer maximize any criterion function. There is some evidence to support the hypothesis that individuals and organizations make decisions by paying attention to a limited number of objectives and by trying to meet these goals most of the time. In such a situation the setting of prices becomes just one of a number of organizational objectives and, as a consequence, a firm will tend to consider price alterations as one of the possible alternatives facing it at any point in time. A corollary of this conclusion is that changes in the prices of a firm's inputs will also not have the effects on its decision processes that are asserted by conventional theory.

These theories of complex organizations trying to satisfy many competing goals also have repercussions on the theories of market behaviour; for example, oligopolists consider non-price competition to be a more advantageous policy. The behavioural theory of the firm also suggests that large firms, whether or not they are oligopolists, prefer to operate in a stable environment. One way to achieve this is to avoid price competition. Such a theory, therefore, is unlikely to depict the market as a place where firms struggle fiercely to meet price competition, but where competition to a large extent takes place by other means.

Managerial economics theories thus have different implications for economic policy than conventional theory which Clarkson summed up:

'When competitive pricing appears to have vanished and one or two companies dominate an industry, antitrust measures are invoked with the intent of restoring competitive pricing to that particular market. But if, as investigations of business behaviour suggest, the pricing decision is only one of a firm's decision problems, then increasing the number of firms in the market may not have the desired effect. In other words, unless it can be shown that the number of firms in the industry has a direct effect on the prices that are set, it does not make much sense to invoke antitrust measures whose purpose is to increase the number of competing firms.' [1968, p. 66]

Marris provided a more comprehensive theory than that developed by Baumol and Downie by tackling the whole problem of the aims of firms in an era of separation of ownership from control. In particular, he considered the ways in which corporate organizations develop quasi-higher objectives of their own and the means by which they pursue them.

Marris questioned one of the basic assumptions of conventional theory, namely that the firm faces a static demand curve, the shape of which is determined over time by external factors such as changes in tastes or incomes. On this assumption price becomes the only decision-variable capable of influencing the quantity sold, although other variables such as advertising expenditure and/or quality variations were added at a later date. Marris concluded that none of these factors could provide a satisfactory explanation of the existence and growth of the firm over a long period of time.

Marris started from the opposite premise to the assumption of conventional theory, that is, that the distinctive feature of the managerial capitalist corporation is its capacity to initiate its own growth. Furthermore, although growth of demand is created by the individual firm, it is subject to restraints arising from demand, from the need for finance, and from restraints which are not directly economic (e.g., staff training). According to this theory, the rate at which demand expands is dependent on policy decisions relating to diversification, prices and marketing expenditure. These factors, given the production techniques employed, and the general level of internal efficiency, affect profitability. On the other hand, profitability is an essential element in determining growth because there is a close relationship between the rate of return and the maximum sustainable growth rate of capacity.

The Marris model of growth can be divided into management and economic problems. Management problems include the decisions which need to be taken on the rate of diversification, price policy, and other variables affecting demand. Marris, for instance, maintained that the salaried managers of a firm would consider high rates of growth more important than high profits, since they did not benefit directly from the profits. Growth would therefore take place by the mechanism of diversifying into new markets. However, since the cost of introducing new products was expensive this would provide one effective constraint on growth. Another major factor constraining managerial freedom and thus limiting growth would be the threat of a potential takeover bid from another firm if growth was pursued too far to the detriment of profits.

The second part of the model concentrates on the financial aspects of growth to which economists had paid until then little attention. Marris showed how a growth policy of a firm comprises not only an investment policy but also a policy for the financing of that investment which could affect its market valuation and dividends, and be affected by personal and corporate taxation. In early versions of this theory (Marris, 1964) the level of the constraint was exogenous, but in later versions (Williamson, 1966; Marris, 1972; Yarrow, 1973, 1976) it is more endogenous.

This model provides an explanation of why demand can be continued at differential rates indefinitely between individual firms. It also seeks to provide an explanation of why, even if internal efficiency varies between firms, the less efficient may continue in business for a very long time.

MANAGEMENT OF DEMAND (Galbraith)

Although Galbraith agreed with the basic propositions of the economic theory of managerial behaviour he criticized the theory for its continued acceptance of the consumer sovereignty assumption of conventional theory, that is, that firms were still subject to the constraints of the market, particularly the influence of the consumer. He contended that if those who put forward the economic theory of managerial behaviour had been prepared to accept the full significance of the abandonment by the modern corporation of the principle of profit maximization then they would also have realized that it was no longer subordinate to market influences and, consequently, that the concept of consumer sovereignty has become invalid.

Galbraith's main thesis is that since the modern corporation is no longer subordinate to market influences, the concept of consumer sovereignty is no longer a valid assumption in determining the behaviour of the large corporation. 'Consumer sovereignty as a pure case will not do'.

> '. . . the theory of the firm and how it maximises its revenue in the market has undergone endless refinement in recent decades. This theory assumes that the man who maximises the revenue gets the revenue or a compelling share. So he does on a Wisconsin dairy farm. But this is not so in the modern large corporation where the management is on a salary and the beneficiaries are stockholders whom the managers have never seen. Although the large corporation, like the union, is far from new, it has never been assimilated into the main body of economics.' [1969, p. 410]

According to Galbraith the changed situation has been caused by the demands of technology, economies of scale, and the long gestation time of production which have led to the demise of the market; while the separation of ownership from control has caused control in most cases to pass from the entrepreneur to the technostructure. As a consequence, the 'accepted sequence' of traditional economic theory, the flow of instructions by means of purchases from individual consumer via the market to the producer, is no longer valid. The mature corporation has the means to control prices, both of its raw materials and of its products. The producer reaches forward and controls the market and also the behaviour of the consumer, whom he purports to serve. This is what Galbraith calls the 'revised sequence'.

Galbraith, as a result of the above analysis, puts forward three major propositions:

1. The main purpose of large firms is to make themselves larger.
2. Once they have achieved a great size their security is assured.
3. Firms must have sufficient control over their markets in order to reap rewards.

Freedom from risk is ensured by planning, by control of prices, and control of the amount sold. In particular, large size permits advertising, an effective sales organization and careful management of product design—all factors which contribute to bring about the needed customer response. This is furthermore obtained by

'. . . the creation of a compelling image of the product in the mind of the consumer. To this he responds more or less automatically under circumstances where the purchase does not merit a great deal of thought. For building this image, palpable fantasy may be more valuable than circumstantial evidence.' [1969, p. 329]

In Galbraith's view, therefore, the employment of various promotional techniques makes it possible for large firms to be autonomous planning units with sufficient control over their markets to avoid the vagaries of consumer demand and the entry of potential competitors.

It is unrealistic, according to Galbraith, to attempt to break the autonomy of such firms by policies designed to restore competition because these firms operate in industries in which the economies of scale are decisive and where size is a condition for innovation. The strength of such concerns depends ultimately on the advantages to be derived from advanced technology and from the expenditure on research and development needed to promote it. These advantages can be secured only if operations are conducted on a large scale and if there is freedom from risk. Where large distributors confront large manufacturers, we have an illustration of the doctrine of 'countervailing power'. For the defence of the public interest rather than trying to restore old forms of competition in industries one must rely in such circumstances on the bargaining power of large customers.

In the Galbraith model advertising is a major factor in managing consumer demand, and thus in nullifying consumer sovereignty. He believes this situation developed because the industrial system requires a mechanism for making men want what it provides. However, this mechanism would not work—wants would not be subject to manipulation—had not these wants been dulled by sufficiency. In other words, advertising is so effective because the basic needs of consumers have been met.

COMPETITION AS A PROCESS, NOT A SITUATION

A fundamental attack on the neoclassical theory of the firm has been expounded by Kirzner (1973) for its mechanistic and therefore inaccurate analysis of competition.

In this view, the major weakness of traditional theory is the concept of competition as a market situation which means that there is a mechanistic allocation of resources in the market-place. In particular, it is argued that the attempts in traditional theory to incorporate monopolistic and imperfect competition in an equilibrium theory has led to a misleading view of these forms of organization, as well as of advertising. In perfect and imperfect competition, and oligopoly, all three theories focus on the short run and examine *static* competition in which incomes, tastes, technology are assumed unchanged. Kirzner believes that a more accurate picture of economic activity can be obtained by regarding competition as a market process

'which depends on the freedom of those with better ideas or with greater willingness to serve the market to offer better opportunities'. [1973, p. 98]

In this alternative view of competition as a market process the chief departure from conventional theory is in the role of the entrepreneur:

'His [the entrepreneur's] role only becomes somehow identified with movements from one equilibrium position to another with "innovations" and with dynamic changes, but *not* with the dynamics of the equilibrating process itself . . . [Students of price theory] have completely overlooked the role of the entrepreneur in exploiting superior awareness of price discrepancies within the economic system.' [1973, p. 27]

This omission arises, according to Kirzner, because conventional theory deals with equilibrium in which there is no room for the entrepreneur. When the decisions of all market participants dovetail completely, so that each plan correctly assumes the corresponding plans of the other participants and no possibility exists for any altered plans that would be simultaneously preferred by the relevant participants, there is nothing left for the entrepreneur to do.

This view of entrepreneurship and competition has a close similarity with that of another 'Austrian' economist, Schumpeter (see also p. 36). Schumpeter has defined the role of the entrepreneur as:

'. . . to reform or revolutionize the pattern of production by exploiting an invention or, more generally, an untried technological possibility for producing a new commodity or producing an old one in a new way, by opening up a new source of supply of materials or a new outlet for products, by reorganizing an industry.' [1976, p. 132]

Although Kirzner acknowledges the similiarity between his views on the role of the entrepreneur with those of Schumpeter, he also stresses the important difference between them:

'For Schumpeter the entrepreneur is the disruptive disequilibrating force that dislodges the market from the somnolence of equilibrium; for us the entrepreneur is the equilibrating force whose activity responds to the existing tensions and provides those corrections for which the unexploited opportunities have been crying out.' [1973, p. 127]

Kirzner's major criticism of conventional theory is, however, reserved for the theories of monopolistic and imperfect competition which emerged as a result of extensive dissatisfaction with the theory of price as it had developed until the 1920s, and its apparent failure to correspond with characteristics of the real world. For Kirzner, the major weakness of these theories is that they incorporate only minor modifications of perfect competition: they still depict an equilibrium situation, they are still based on given and known demand and supply curves, and they only differ from the theory of perfect competition in the shapes attributed to these curves.

'Thus replacing the old equilibrium theory by a new equilibrium theory preserved the theoretical dissatisfaction of the old theory while failing to offer the simplest explanation of these real-world phenomena it left unaccounted for.' [1973, p. 114]

It has been this failure to change fundamentally the basic assumptions of imperfect competition from those of perfect competition which has led, according to Kirzner, such phenomena as advertising and product differentiation to be invariably identified as monopolistic elements in the market.

'whereas if competition is looked at as a process they would be seen as strategic weapons in the competitive arsenal of rival entrepreneurs.' [1973, p. 210]

3 Replies to the critics of conventional theory

CONVENTIONAL THEORY OF THE FIRM—A TECHNICAL MODEL ONLY

The main response of economists who believe that the theory of the firm has an important role in economic analysis to the criticism that it is divorced from reality is to point out that it is intended as a technical model designed to explain competition, price and the allocation of resources. Consequently, as an abstract model of industry conceived by economists for theoretical reasoning, it is not surprising that it should diverge from reality, and should not, therefore, be taken at its face value. As Johnson put it:

'Some of the things economists talk to each other about are not suitable for airing in public.' [1967, p. 9]

Hallett has pointed out:

'An economic model should not be confused with the reality it seeks to explain.' [1967, p. 8]

And Allen has commented:

'Yet no one believes nowadays in that proposition (consumer sovereignty) in its extreme form except as an analytical device.' [1969, p. 30]

It is also widely recognized that since the only form of competition analysed in perfect competition is price competition, other forms of competition such as sales promotion are automatically excluded from the analysis. It would not, however, be concluded that these other forms of competition are necessarily against the interests of consumers unless perfect competition is a practical alternative.

On the other hand, many supporters of the neoclassical theory of the firm would not regard criticism of the model of perfect competition as damaging, but would argue that it provides a limiting case against which real situations can be compared and evaluated. Thus it could be argued that in a certain industry at a certain time the situation is more competitive (i.e., closer to perfect competition) than in another. Furthermore, it can be said that certain industrial practices are or are not conducive to approaching perfect competition. On such an analysis advertising, for example, would be regarded as 'second best' and only to be tolerated because of imperfections in the market (i.e., imperfect knowledge). Similarly, the emphasis in perfect competition on price competition has led to the conclusion that any other type of competition can only be a poor substitute. It has been argued, for instance, that many types of non-price competition were introduced as a result of resale price maintenance, and that once this was abolished other forms of competition, apart from price, would tend to disappear. An example of this view is that put by Lewis:

> 'Coupon trading is just an adjunct to non-price competition between manufacturers and to manufacturers' advertisements; and the trading stamp is primarily the product of resale price maintenance. If these sources of market imperfection were removed most of this form of trading would disappear.' [1949, p. 149]

In other words, although the model of perfect competition has been devised for theoretical reasoning only it has often been regarded as a goal towards which firms should aim. Yet as Wilson has commented,

> 'Perfect competition is not a norm, and the fact that it has been taken for one is a remarkable example of the way in which we can mislead ourselves with our own emotive terminology. Indeed the expression "perfect competition" has probably done more to darken counsel than any other in modern economic literature . . .' [1962, p. 119]

ORGANIZATION OF THE FIRM INCLUDED IN THE ECONOMICS OF INDUSTRY

Perhaps somewhat surprisingly the literature on the economics of industrial structure and organization which studies the behaviour of the firm in the real world has made little attempt to integrate the main areas of that subject, notably size, entry conditions, concentration, vertical integration and diversification, and decision-making processes with conventional theory. The reason may be that decisions as to the nature and extent of vertical integration and diversification are among the key strategic decisions taken by firms, as are those relating to total size and to rate of growth, whereas these decisions are relatively unimportant in conventional theory since the firm is limited to a single product, and the abstractions introduced into the theory give the firm little freedom for manoeuvre.

Yamey has pointed out how the conventional theory of the firm and the economics of industrial structure coexist:

> 'The omission of strategic decisions from the scope of theoretical formulations is not necessarily a defect from the point of view of the uses to which the

theories are put. But the omission has meant that the body of knowledge and analysis about these decisions has had to find a home in the more applied branch of economics known variously by such names as the economics of industry, the structure of industry, or industrial organisation.' [1973, p. 8]

Although conventional theory therefore appears to be effectively compartmentalized from the economics of industry, many empirical investigations such as those which have been made into the relationship between advertising and competition start from the premises of conventional theory, in particular from a static theoretical framework. As Slater (1980) has explained:

'When we turn to practical work in industrial economics, the dominance of the static framework is . . . apparent. Arguments for and against monopoly power, vertical integration and merger are primarily framed in terms of comparisons of long-run equilibrium positions, as it is only in such terms that welfare implications can be agreed upon.' [Foreword, p. xxiii]

CONCEPT OF 'WORKABLE' COMPETITION

Some specialists in the economics of industrial structure (Allen, 1969, p. 92; Johnson, 1970, p. 5; Yamey, 1973, p. 9) relate the strategic decisions made by firms to explain their actions to the concept of 'workable' competition. This concept of competition has developed parallel with the traditional theory of the firm to explain how under conditions of oligopoly and imperfect competition it is possible for competition to operate effectively.

The concept of 'workable' competition is based on the following precepts:

1. That oligopoly is unavoidable in many industries. It should not therefore be regarded ipso facto as inferior competition because some elements of imperfect competition are inevitable, such as large-scale production, variations in consumer preferences and spatial monopolies, while other elements such as product improvements, and sales promotion and advertising designed to inform or persuade consumers to try new commodities or services may be considered desirable.
2. There is no necessary relationship between a large firm and monopoly. There can be large size without monopoly; there can be monopoly without large size.
3. Competition is wider and more pervasive than those who try to apply the models of perfect and imperfect competition are prepared to concede. This mistake arises from considering competition as existing only between firms in an industry and neglecting the competition between the products of near monopolists; and from taking a short-term view of the economy rather than a dynamic view over time when monopolies are affected sooner or later by new competition.
4. Criticisms of oligopoly and other forms of imperfect competition should be reserved for the avoidable elements, and these should be distinguished clearly from the inevitable elements.

The concept of 'workable' competition was first propounded at the beginning of the century by Clark, who believed that trusts were efficient and inevitable and also that potential rivals were an efficient check upon them:

'When prices are unduly high, owing to the grasping policy of some trust, what happens? New competition usually appears in the field. Capital is seeking outlets, but it has become hard to find them . . . The mill that has never been built is already a power in the market: for if it will surely be built under certain conditions, the effect of this certainty is to keep prices down.' [1901, p. 13]

Potential competition in the background is thus considered the chief constraint on the policies and prices of firms. Clark feared that restrictive practices could effectively frustrate potential competition, and he wanted public policy to be confined to eliminating such practices.

Some decades later Schumpeter stressed that the competition 'which counts' is not traditional price competition but the importance of widening consumer choice and the response to changing consumer preferences by competing firms:

'. . . the competition from the new commodity, the new technology, the new source of supply, the new type of organization . . . competition which commands a decisive cost or quality advantage and which strikes not at the margins of the profits and the output of existing firms but at their foundations and at their very lives.' [1976, p. 84]

Hence, according to Schumpeter, the market was characterized by a 'perennial gale of creative destruction' which a monopoly of the original product could not withstand.

According to Mason the essence of 'workable' competition is

'. . . the availability to both buyer and seller of alternative courses of action.' [1957, pp. 178–179]

To this definition of an imprecise concept, Jewkes has enumerated a number of conditions which provide a means of measuring the degree of competitiveness in the industrial system:

'If firms, otherwise independent, do not make agreements on prices, investment, output or the allocation of markets; if there is an ever-widening range of goods and services to the consumer; if for most products there is a close substitute and fresh substitutes constantly make their appearance; if the consumer is actively exercising his choices, and thereby encouraging the growth of the more efficient suppliers; if in every industry there are enough producers to make it difficult for them to arrange not to compete, but few enough producers to make it clear to each that he has rivals on his tail; and if the firms that lose money decline and those that make profits grow.' [1977, pp. 40–41]

Furthermore, Jewkes maintains that there are two supporting statistical tests which may be applied to determine whether 'workable' competition exists in an oligopolistic industry: first, whether prices are fluid and flexible or 'administered' and rigid, and thus unresponsive to changing demand and supply; second, whether the market shares of the firms remain unchanged.

The processes by which a form of 'workable' competition may come about in practice has been described by Allen:

> 'A monopolistic or oligopolistic organisation may be destroyed by the cheapening of communications, the reduction in barriers to international trade, the standardisation of the product, or the appearance of new sources of supply within the former market area. More generally, with the proliferation of products that accompanies economic progress, the gaps in the chain of substitutes are narrowed, and competition between industries may become keener even if competition within particular industries wanes . . .' [1970, p. 92]

Thus in this broader and more dynamic concept of competition there is the presumption that imperfect competition does not automatically lead to weak competition, higher prices, and higher profits. (Where there are so many alternative choices open to consumers, the concept is also at variance with Galbraithian view that consumer demand can be managed through advertising.)

Furthermore, this concept of competition leads to a rejection of the presumption underlying much public policy that monopolistic behaviour automatically leads to a misallocation of resources.

Part 2

The consumer in the market

4 The theory of the firm and consumer behaviour

Consumer behaviour has been defined by Engel, Blackwell and Kollat as:

'Those acts of individuals directly involved in obtaining and using economic goods and services, including the decision processes that precede and determine these acts.' [1978, p. 3]

In several respects the study of the consumer in the market begins where the conventional theory of the firm ends. The latter, for instance, assumes for the purposes of analysis that tastes and preferences are given. Traditional theory therefore ignores the fundamental question of how product and brand preferences are formed, which is the major problem facing firms, and gives little guidance on how consumers will react to quality variation.

Furthermore, in perfect competition the implicit assumption is made that products are homogeneous, and when product differentiation occurs as under imperfect competition it is assumed to have been caused unnecessarily by advertising and branding. Although in more sophisticated economic theory product differentiation is recognized as a competitive variable, the multidimensional complexity of products precludes viable analysis, and economists have found it necessary to suppress such variables in developing theories of competition. Whereas in theory, therefore, the product is usually considered as homogeneous, in practice products may be differentiated by any one of a number of variables.

Finally, price is a dominant variable in conventional theory, and the degree of elasticity determines the responsiveness of demand to price. Price has achieved a pre-eminent position for two reasons: first, prices are relatively quantitative and unambiguous, whereas it is more difficult to measure non-price variables; second, the theory of the firm is a comprehensive theory of consumer welfare whereby in an economy characterized by flexible prices maximum economic efficiency and welfare may be achieved.

In contrast, in the market, not only are non-price variables of value to consumers and therefore influence demand but, in addition, the effect of price on demand has proved difficult to measure; prices are not always flexible; price is not an unambiguous indicator of value for money; and price changes can cause changes in consumer expectations of product and quality.

5 Consumer behaviour theories

The study of the influences other than price which affect demand has been one starting point for the comparatively new discipline of consumer behaviour which has drawn on a variety of sources, especially the behavioural sciences, in order to develop specific theories of its own. Furthermore, a major purpose of buyer behaviour theory is to increase our understanding of the consumer. Over the last few years emphasis has been placed on consumer decision processes: the problem is to understand what happens in the buyer's mind from the time he first receives impressions about products until he makes his purchasing decisions.

Because consumer behaviour is still a relatively young discipline, all the models so far developed contain considerable scope for revision and development. For the most part buyer behaviour has been studied from a variety of theoretical perspectives which have led to a number of interesting but partial explanations which caused Lunn to stress:

> 'No single theory or model should be expected to be fully comprehensive at this state of our knowledge.' [1974, p. 54]

This situation has resulted not only in an absence of comprehensive laws on consumer behaviour which are generally accepted, but also a wide diversity in the concepts used to describe consumer behaviour.

Buyer behaviour research or consumer models has taken three main forms: *a priori*; *empirical*; and *eclectic*, each of which has contributed in some degree to a greater understanding of consumer behaviour, but each of which has limitations and is the subject of considerable controversy.

A PRIORI RESEARCH

In this approach concepts and theories have been introduced from other disciplines, mainly the behavioural sciences, and explored for their value in understanding the consumer. Since consumer behaviour is a particular aspect of general human behaviour, the strength of the a priori approach lies in its attempt to utilize existing knowledge and insights from other disciplines, and thus to seek explanations by attempting to fit consumer behaviour to previously developed theoretical frameworks. As Kotler has commented,

'Depending upon one's scientific predilection there is the Marshallian buyer, Pavlovian buyer, Freudian buyer, Velblenian buyer and Hobbesian buyer. Less grandiose but equally interesting new breeds of buyers can be formulated, such as the Festinger buyer (Festinger, 1957), Riesman buyer (Riesman, Glazer and Denney, 1956) and Rogerian buyer (Rogers, 1951). It should be recognised that all these models of buyer behaviour are true to some extent, and yet it is incomplete. Buyer behaviour is so complex that theory develops in connection with particular aspects of the phenomena.' [1970, p. 197]

Other well-known examples of the intensive borrowing from the behavioural sciences include Howard's learning theory, perceived risk theory and attitude theories, such as those of Festinger and Fishbein, and several personality theories. The theory of 'cognitive dissonance', for example, put forward by Festinger states that two elements of knowledge are dissonant if they are contradictory, and since dissonance is uncomfortable the individual will actively avoid situations and information which might increase it. Experiments carried out by Festinger and others tested the exposure to information and attitudes held after a decision.

Most buying decisions involve dissonance because the alternative forgone will have had some attractive features, while the product purchased will have had some unattractive features. It was therefore predicted that once a decision is made the attractiveness of the chosen alternative will increase, and the individual will actively seek information justifying the choice. This prediction was borne out by the example of car owners who were found to notice and read advertisements about the cars they had recently purchased more than advertisements about other cars.

Although 'reassurance' may be required in the case of an expensive, infrequently-bought purchase such as a car where the purchaser may feel the need to justify his choice, Lowe Watson has questioned whether

'. . . we [can] so readily assume that the housewife is equally anxious to justify her choice of a brand in a hundred and one relatively unimportant household products?' [1971, p. 322]

and Foxall has questioned whether such a theory can help decision-making:

'No method of generating dissonance that leads to a purchase being made has been put forward to date.' [1976, p. 6]

Although the behavioural sciences have helped to shed valuable light on why consumers behave as they do, the evidence suggests that they are far from perfect even for that purpose, and their limitations have been summed up by Lunn:

'Many of the concepts adopted are still somewhat speculative. They have often been developed in contexts remote from consumer behaviour.' [1974, p. 50]

EMPIRICAL APPROACH

While a priori researchers have sought explanations by attempting to fit consumer behaviour to previously developed theoretical frameworks, empirical research has attempted to derive laws from observations of patterns and regularities in consumer behaviour, for the most part by using consumer panel data.

Brand loyalty, and Brand Share Prediction are two well-known examples of empirical research.

Brand loyalty

There is the widespread assumption in economic theory that advertising can build up durable brand loyalty towards a product, although with no specification of the time element. In marketing, it has until comparatively recently been assumed that advertising could convert users from one brand to another, although the concept of 'brand loyalty' has been imprecise. It has been variously defined in terms of brand choice sequences, proportion of purchases, repeat purchase probabilities, and brand preference over time.

The concept of brand loyalty has been extensively investigated; see Achenbaum (1972), McDonald (1970), Treasure (1975), Joyce (1975), King (1980), and in particular by Ehrenberg et al (1966, 1969, 1972). The general conclusion has been reached using different research techniques that with many consumer goods which are purchased frequently most people have a short list of brands which they find acceptable, and they buy the individual brands from this short list in an irregular way at different intervals of time. In particular, Ehrenberg's analysis of consumer buyer behaviour in a number of stable but heavily advertised markets has produced results which are not consistent with the theory that advertising converts users from one brand to another. He has shown that in such markets people tend to have a very stable multiple brand pattern of purchasing (i.e., they regularly buy a number of brands with different frequencies), and these purchasing patterns are systematic and predictable.

Lowe Watson confirmed Ehrenberg's proposition in one of the markets studied by Ehrenberg, viz. the petrol market. This led him to postulate that while consumers may well be prepared to undertake prolonged search for expensive consumer durables, with frequently purchased consumer goods,

> 'We can interpret Ehrenberg's description of multiple brand purchasing in terms of a series of relationships with the available brands, some frankly experimental, others reflecting varying degrees of acceptance in terms of the purchaser's needs. This would lead to the situation of varying pre-disposition or probabilities of purchase observed by Ehrenberg.' [1971, p. 329]

(However, the validity of Ehrenberg's conclusions have been questioned on the grounds that (1) he does not sufficiently employ the behavioural sciences; (2) that he deals with consumers in general rather than the individual consumer; i.e., consumers who bought certain products in one of his four-week periods may not be the same consumers who are buying in a later period; and (3) one of the major drawbacks of using consumer panel data is that it cannot be considered valid for a period longer than a year because of the changing composition of the panel.)

Joyce suggested that multi-brand purchasing is more likely to be found

> '. . . where the products are physically somewhat different and where they are used to perform different functions (e.g., washing powders, for different types of wash), or where the consumer buys different brands to get variety (e.g., food and drink).' [1975, p. 219]

With these types of products Joyce concludes that advertising can work just as much by persuading people already buying a brand to devote a higher proportion of their total purchase to that brand than simply converting non-buyers into buyers. On the other hand, Joyce pointed out that the multi-brand hypothesis would be unlikely to apply where only one function is performed by the product (e.g., cigarettes).

Treasure used data from the British Market Research Bureau's Target Group Index (a continuous survey of 50 product fields which include food and drink, washing powders, cosmetics, razor blades and analgesics, but *excluding durable consumer products*) to illustrate that purchasing several brands is common in most of these product fields and in many it is the general rule. Treasure agreed with Joyce that purchases made for personal consumption are more likely to be single brand than multi-brand but that

> 'In the kind of markets in which advertising money is spent, consumers typically buy more than one product.' [1975, p. 266]

Treasure, therefore, believes that the most useful picture that one can have of a housewife's purchasing behaviour is that she does not have a passionate devotion to a single brand, but a mental list of several 'purchaseable' brands which meet her requirements. The housewife buys several brands over a period of time (6 to 12 months) for three main reasons: first, to meet differing requirements from within her family; second, because the brands, though similar, are used in slightly different ways; and, third, because she likes to have a choice of brands in stock.

Furthermore, analyses over periods of 6 to 12 months of consumers patterns of brand use collected either from sources such as the Target Group Index or from records of actual purchases over time in consumer diary panels confirm that most alterations in sales turnover occur through changes in the frequency of purchasing of those who have bought before in the preceding period of time, and only a small part through purchases by people buying for the first time. Like Joyce, Treasure therefore concluded that sales of a given brand may be increased not only by 'converting' new consumers to the brand, but by trying to persuade existing users—those who use it at least occasionally—to use it more frequently. This does not require them to increase their total purchases of the product, but to persuade them to devote a larger share of their purchases to this particular brand. According to Treasure, it follows from this analysis that in many product fields advertising is being seen by housewives who already have personal and recent experience of using or consuming the product being advertised.

In a survey undertaken by McDonald (1970) into the relationship between purchasing patterns and exposure to advertising, similar findings about consumer purchasing behaviour emerged. There was, for example, a high degree of regularity in buying behaviour. Previous evidence that most buyers tend to buy only a few brands and repeat them was strongly confirmed; most housewives tended to have one favourite brand and a number of other brands which they bought less frequently; brands of varying size within the product field show similar frequency of purchase distributions; the buyers who buy at the most common frequency for a product field are the regular buyers who buy only one or two brands.

In a further study King (1980) has demonstrated from a survey of 250 households the relatively small degree to which housewives remain loyal to one brand over the short period of three months—even in what is regarded as a conservative market, that of tea (Table 5–1). In order to assess whether the degree of brand loyalty was

Table 5–1 *'Brand loyalty' over three months*

Product	Percentage of purchasing households who bought:		
	1 brand only	*2 brands only*	*3 or more brands*
Tea	50	26	24
Toilet paper	41	26	33
Washing powder	32	33	35
Breakfast cereals	19	33	48

Source: JWT diary study, MEAL, Mintel.

related directly to advertising expenditure, the advertising–sales ratios for these four products in 1977 were ascertained: tea 2.5 per cent, toilet paper 0.5 per cent; washing powder 4 per cent; breakfast cereals 4.5 per cent. At least for these four products there appears to be no particular positive relationship between the advertising–sales ratio and 'brand loyalty'; in these particular examples there appears to be an inverse relationship which depends on the characteristics of the product category.

King further maintains that it is rare for only one brand to be purchased over a long period. Over a one-year period some 10 per cent of the buyers of a brand buy that brand alone; and they tend to be particularly light buyers of the particular product.

Brand share prediction

A conclusion of test marketing research is that consumer purchases of a new product generally build up to a peak and then decline before reaching an equilibrium position. This typical pattern of consumer buying of a new brand has been investigated in order to understand consumer reaction to a new product, and to help firms predict the potential sales of a product at an early stage. This is necessary because of the high failure rate of new products; some 60 to 70 per cent that are tried out in test markets are never introduced nationally, and of those which are many survive only for a short time: for example, of 400 new food products introduced nationally in 1965, 49 per cent had disappeared from the shops by 1969; 69 per cent by 1973, and 78 per cent by 1975 (Kraushar, Andrews and Eassie, 1976).

Davis (1964) showed that in the test marketing of 44 packaged products—groceries and chemists goods—the typical pattern of consumer sales for new brands could be divided into three time periods.

In the first three months, particularly as a result of the growth of distribution as well as advertising and sales promotion, sales rise rapidly as consumers try out the product. During the second period—from approximately the third to the sixth month—sales decline from their initial peak, this decline depending on the degree to which the new brand satisfies buyers. The evidence is that the percentage drop in sales is directly related to the brand itself; for example, it is approximately the same in each area of the country, irrespective of weight of advertising. In the third period, after the sixth month, sales remain more or less stable. Davis derived two 'rule of thumb' guides from his research. First, if at any stage during the initial build-up sales exceed a rate twice as high as the stable sales target level, the probability is about 3:1 in favour of the target being met or exceeded. Second, unless peak sales exceed the target level for stable sales by at least 50 per cent, the probability is about 3:1 that the product will fail to maintain target sales on a long-term basis.

The results of this research were derived from aggregated sales curves. Consumer panel data which record individual patterns of behaviour provide similar results. For example, Parfitt and Collins (1974) used data from analyses of the Attwood Consumer Panel results in Great Britain after 1960. When the progress of two new brands, A and B, was measured in their first two months on the market many households were prepared to try them (in these two examples three million households); then the rate of gaining new triers slows down; finally, after about six months, it becomes a very gradual process, with gains of only about 1 to 2 per cent of households per year.

With these two brands, A was successful while B was a failure. Initially, the launch of the two brands was almost equally successful because after three months 19 per cent of households had bought brand A, and 15 per cent had bought brand B. However, between the third and sixth month only about 2 per cent more households were prepared to try brand B, compared with an extra 6 per cent prepared to try brand A.

However, the factor which determined the eventual success of brand A and the failure of brand B was in their respective repeat-buying rates. Sixteen weeks after the average household which had tried brand B had bought it, it represented only 6 per cent of that household's purchases of the product type. The figure for brand A—16 per cent—was nearly three times as high. A sufficient number of households had therefore tried brand B initially to make it a potential success, but they did not continue to buy it often enough. The permanent success of a brand depends on the willingness of consumers, once having tried it, to continue purchasing it. According to Parfitt and Collins,

'. . . it should be recognised that a substantial proportion of brands do not reach satisfactory share levels and are withdrawn.' [1974, p. 88]

Thus studies of the development of the purchases of new brands show that the ability to sustain repeat buying among those who have tried the brand is often the critical feature in the success or failure of the launch. The evidence from the study of brand failures from many different sources, including Davidson (1976) and Nielsen (1970, 1973), is that the two factors which distinguish success from failure are a product with better performance and distinctiveness, while price is not of such crucial importance. King (1980) wrote:

'Very few new brands are actually disliked; the problem is far more often one of indifference.' [1980, p. 20]

Furthermore, the relative importance of distribution and word-of-mouth as channels of communication which contribute to the success of a new product compared with advertising may be seen in the results of a survey which asked housewives how they had found out about new products they had recently tried (Table 5–2).

Table 5–2 *How young housewives found out about new products recently tried*

Married women between 16 and 43 years saying:	(%)
Saw in shop	43
Recommended	25
Advertising	18
Free sample	9
Other answers	8

Source: JWT New Housewife Survey 1967.

ECLECTIC RESEARCH

Until the middle of the sixties a priori and empirical research formed the basis of consumer behaviour theory. More recently, there has been the emergence of comprehensive theories of buyer behaviour. Basically, these attempt to incorporate the strengths of a priori and empirical research but to avoid their weaknesses. The cornerstone of the eclectic approach is that psychological and sociological concepts should be brought together in a common framework. Its distinguishing feature, therefore, is that it attempts to synthesize those theories, concepts and findings in the various behavioural sciences which appear relevant to consumer behaviour with market research findings, practical and academic (Nicosia, 1966; Engel, Kollat and Blackwell, 1968; Howard and Sheth, 1969; Sheth, 1974). The strength of this approach lies in the comprehensiveness of its perspective, but brings with it the danger of undue complexity (i.e., dealing with too many variables and inter-relationships).

A characteristic feature of the eclectic approach is the emphasis given to decision processes which both precede and follow the purchasing act itself. As one of the pioneers, Nicosia is typical in representing the consumer as purposive, seeking to fulfil certain goals through purchasing behaviour, and going through various decision processes which help him at least to approximate to some optimum solution. Second, he uses the notion of the funnel, that is, that the consumer's predispositions move from generality through the search and evaluation of alternative products, and culminate in the selection of one particular brand. Third, he stresses the importance of the concept of feedback, namely, the effect of the experience of purchase and use upon consumer predispositions towards particular products.

This work has been criticized on the grounds that the search and evaluation process as represented is over-rational, and whilst it may be applicable to infrequently purchased expensive products it is less relevant for low-priced goods which are purchased frequently. A further criticism is that the definitions of attitude and motivation are unsatisfactory.

A second major eclectic work is that of Engel, Kollat and Blackwell who have devised a decision process model similar in many ways to that of Nicosia. A specific criticism of these researchers is that, as with Nicosia, the search and evaluation process is portrayed as highly rational. Finally, Howard and Sheth have developed a comprehensive model of the consumer which includes a wide spectrum of variables and their inter-relationships, and attempts a detailed integration of theoretical positions from several behavioural sciences. Besides focusing on the individual consumer, as in the other models, and seeing the decision process as the matching of products to the consumer's motives, and stressing the importance of feedback, that is, the effects of the purchase act and usage experience upon consumer predispositions towards particular products, they also consider the dynamics of the buying process by distinguishing between different kinds of buying problems—extensive, limited and routine—that the consumer is trying to solve.

This model has already guided research in a variety of product fields and some of its propositions have been rigorously tested. These tests have, on the whole, provided favourable support for the theory, although Farley and Ring (1970) have pointed out certain weaknesses in the measuring instruments. Nicosia regards this weakness as underlining the need to combine concepts and methodology with more accuracy.

At present there is no generally accepted comprehensive eclectic theory of buyer behaviour.

6 Ad hoc market research

Owing to the complexity of human behaviour, the relatively early stage in the development of buyer behaviour theories, and the consequent shortcomings which to date exist in these theories, firms which are considering marketing a new product continue to rely for the most part on ad hoc investigations into consumer behaviour using standard market research techniques, namely product and taste tests, price and promotion tests, and test marketing in order to try to ensure that the product will be acceptable to consumers. During the course of such tests the original product concept will often be modified and adapted as the result of the research findings.

The following case histories of a small range of products which include low-priced convenience goods, an industrial product, a consumer durable, as well as a service, and a retail firm provide examples of the economic and social background conditions which influence the marketing of products, the effect of the competitive environment on marketing and advertising policy, the factors which determine the employment of different types of promotions, and the characteristics of products which influence the selling methods of firms, for example, advertising, sales force, direct mail.

CASE HISTORY   1

Product: Macleans toothpaste

Firm: Beechams

The market

Several distinctive features characterize the toothpaste market. First, it has been dominated by a few firms over a long period of time. Three manufacturers (Beechams, Colgate and Elida Gibbs) had 80 per cent of the total sales in 1955; by 1960 they were responsible for 78 per cent of an enlarged market, and by 1972 their share had reached 88 per cent. With the entry in 1975 of a new competitor for the first time since 1941 (Procter & Gamble with Crest) four firms were in 1978 responsible for 88 per cent of the market. Of the remaining 12 per cent, distributors' own brands (DOBs) (particularly Boots and the Co-operative Societies) accounted for 9 to 10 per cent, and firms selling specialized products such as Sensodyne (Stafford Miller) for the remaining 2 to 3 per cent share of the market.

Although these market shares give the impression of a stable and static market, this is misleading. The entry and exit of many brands occurred throughout the period. This has resulted in significant variations in the shares of surviving brands and companies both from year to year, and over the period as a whole (see Table 6–1 for full details). For example, the share of the market held by Colgate, the brand leader in 1978, has varied from 7.6 per cent in 1941 to 30.4 per cent in 1963, to 42.5 per cent in 1970, and to 31.4 per cent in 1978. Beechams, which in 1941 was the brand leader with Macleans toothpaste with 24.1 per cent share of the market, had a market share of 17.6 per cent in 1963, and in 1978 its market share had reached 25.3 per cent with Macleans and Aquafresh. In 1978, with the third largest share of the toothpaste market, Elida Gibbs' share has ranged from 11.2 per cent in 1941 to brand leader in 1963 with 36.5 per cent market share, and to 21.7 per cent share of the market in 1978.

Moreover, the share of the market held by particular brands during this period has varied widely. The sales of Close-Up (Elida Gibbs), Si-Ko (Danning), and Kolynos (ICC) have all declined dramatically. Three firms—Procter and Gamble, Elida Gibbs and Colgate—introduced fluoride toothpaste in the 1960s but all were unsuccessful. Colgate introduced a new brand, Cherish, in 1975 but withdrew it from the market in 1977.

Second, this market has been continuously associated with a high level of advertising expenditure. Although expenditure still remains high (for instance, in 1977 advertising expenditure amounted to M£4 on a turnover of M£37.5 and each manufacturer spent approximately M£1), between 1973 and 1977 the proportion of advertising revenue to sales declined from more than 18 to 12 per cent.

The relative decline during this period has been caused by several factors: first, price controls which squeezed margins; second, the increasing emphasis on price per se which led to promotional expenditure to be directed to a larger extent than in the past to trade deals and temporary price reductions (TPRs). (TPRs take two forms: price-marked packs where both manufacturer and retailers contribute to the discount; and 'flash' offers—7p off—where the manufacturer offers a discount to shoppers from the recommended resale price.) These two types of promotions constitute the major form of competition between toothpaste manufacturers. Since 1975 TPRs have declined relatively in importance to trade deals which have escalated and become the chief means by which manufacturers gain participation in retailers' promotions, additional shelf space and special displays. To some extent the relative decline of TPRs can be attributed to pressure from retailers for even lower prices, and the uncertainties surrounding the legislation introduced in 1979 on Bargain Offer Claims. Together with other promotions such as competitions, coupons, banded offers and money-back offers, some 7 to 10 per cent of toothpaste net sales revenue in 1978 was estimated to be devoted to promotions. In the economic climate of the 1970s and the changed structure of the retail trade, toothpaste manufacturers believe that expenditure on promotions has been more effective in achieving sales than a similar expenditure on advertising.

This change in the kind of competitive activity prevalent in the toothpaste market is the consequence of increased retail competition and the growing share of the market held by large-scale retailers.

There has been a permanent shift in sales of toothpaste from their traditional outlet, the independent chemist, to the supermarket. The increase in the share of multiples relative to independent chemist shops was already evident in the 1960s but this development accelerated during the 1970s. The 13 largest customers of each of the four major manufacturers are responsible for 50 per cent of toothpaste sales. Boots, in 1979, accounted for 18 to 20 per cent and Co-operative Societies for another 8 per cent. Tesco and Sainsbury together are responsible for 15 per cent of toothpaste sales, and their share of the market is increasing (Table 6–2).

This situation has led to a decline in margins, and lower manufacturer and retailer selling prices. The traditional retail margin on toothpaste was 33.3 per cent, in addition to a wholesaler's margin of 10 to 15 per cent. Because of the change in the type of retail outlets selling toothpaste, sales through wholesalers have continually declined. Moreover, the increased promotional activity by manufacturers, wholesalers and large multiple retailers has reduced gross margins for small retailers to some 20 to 28 per cent during promotions—and the number of promotions has increased in recent years. Retail gross margins on all branded toothpaste, including brands with a small market share, varies between 7 and 28 per cent. Not surprisingly, the gross margins of smaller retailers who carry a wider range of toothpastes are at the upper end of the range, while multiples with far higher turnovers, and selling a more limited range of brands and sizes, take lower margins of between 7 and 12 per cent.

Since 1973 manufacturers have reduced their selling prices in real terms by 7 per cent; at the same time retailers have accepted lower margins through the various special promotions designed to attract the consumer's attention which has reduced retail prices still further.

Table 6–1 Toothpaste market: long-term brand share trend, 1941 to 1978

	1941	1942	1943	1944	1945	1946	1947	1948	1949	1950	1951	1952	1953	1954	1955	1956	1957	1958	1959
Macleans Reg/Freshmint	24.1	17.3	19.3	19.5	22.3	22.3	22.9	23.4	23.1	23.7	26.5	23.0	21.6	20.5	19.7	17.1	16.7	19.3	19.6
Spearmint MWF																			
Total Macleans	24.1	17.3	19.3	19.5	22.3	22.3	22.9	23.4	23.1	23.7	26.5	23.0	21.6	20.5	19.7	17.1	16.7	19.3	19.6
Aquafresh																			
Total Beechams	24.1	17.3	19.3	19.5	22.3	22.3	22.9	23.4	23.1	23.7	26.5	23.0	21.6	20.5	19.7	17.1	16.7	19.3	19.6
Colgate (CDC)	7.6	8.3	9.4	9.9	9.3	8.5	8.9	10.4	10.5	11.9	13.4	17.6	20.5	23.0	26.2	25.6	27.3	27.0	30.5
Ultrabrite																			
Colgate Fluor																			
Cherish																			
Total Colgate	7.6	8.3	9.4	9.9	9.3	8.5	8.9	10.4	10.5	11.9	13.4	17.6	20.5	23.0	26.2	25.6	27.3	27.0	30.5
Gibbs SR	11.2	12.1	11.8	9.7	8.1	13.7	16.9	19.2	19.6	20.2	20.0	18.4	16.6	20.6	22.7	21.4	22.2	23.8	22.5
Signal (Signal 2)																			4.5
Close Up																			
Gibbs Fluoride																			
Total Gibbs	11.2	12.1	11.8	9.7	8.1	13.7	16.9	19.2	19.6	20.2	20.0	18.4	16.6	20.6	22.7	21.4	22.2	23.8	27.0
Gleem																12.1	12.8	9.9	7.9
Crest																			
Other	57.1	61.8	59.5	60.9	60.3	55.5	51.3	47.0	46.8	44.2	40.1	40.1	41.3	35.9	31.4	23.8	21.0	20.0	15.0
Total	100	100	100	100	100	100	100	100	100	100	100	100	100	100	100	100	100	100	100

	1960	1961	1962	1963	1964	1965	1966	1967	1968	1969	1970	1971	1972	1973	1974	1975	1976	1977	1978
Macleans Reg/Freshmint	17.4	19.4	19.3	17.6	19.0	20.0	20.6	19.7	17.9	17.4	17.2	16.3	14.0	13.0	11.5	12.0	10.8	11.8	11.2
Spearmint MWF								1.2	4.6	4.3	4.3	6.5	6.1	6.5	6.5	7.4	7.7	7.5	7.0
Total Macleans	17.4	19.4	19.3	17.6	19.0	20.0	20.6	20.9	22.5	21.7	21.5	22.8	20.1	19.5	18.0	19.4	18.5	19.3	18.2
Aquafresh														1.5	5.2	7.6	6.4	7.5	7.1
Total Beechams	17.4	19.4	19.3	17.6	19.0	20.0	20.6	20.9	22.5	21.7	21.5	22.8	20.1	21.0	23.2	27.0	24.9	26.8	25.3
Colgate (CDC)	26.6	25.7	25.7	21.8	24.5	26.5	27.6	29.0	27.2	26.1	26.0	25.3	25.0	21.9	23.1	21.8	20.8	22.8	23.8
Ultrabrite								1.5	8.8	11.8	13.6	12.8	11.8	10.0	8.1	7.2	5.5	6.6	7.6
Colgate Fluor			0.6	8.6	7.3	5.6	4.9	4.0	3.0				2.2	2.5	2.0	1.5			
Cherish																1.9	4.7	2.0	
Total Colgate	26.6	25.7	26.3	30.4	31.8	32.1	32.5	34.5	39.0	37.9	42.5	40.6	39.0	34.4	33.2	32.3	30.4	31.4	31.4
Gibbs SR	18.3	18.7	16.4	14.0	15.7	15.8	17.4	17.2	15.0	14.8	12.9	12.0	10.9	9.9	10.0	9.4	9.5	9.5	9.9
Signal (Signal 2)	15.1	15.4	13.8	10.6	11.1	12.2	11.7	12.1	10.2	11.2	11.4	10.8	8.9	8.5	9.4	9.6	8.9	8.2	9.2
Close Up												0.4	9.4	12.8	10.9	7.3	6.2	3.9	2.6
Gibbs Fluoride			5.7	11.9	8.0	6.1													
Total Gibbs	33.9	34.1	35.9	36.5	34.8	32.1	33.0	32.5	27.8	26.4	23.8	23.2	29.1	31.4	30.3	26.3	24.6	21.6	21.7
Gleem	6.0	5.4	4.1	3.2	2.5	2.2													
Crest														0.6	0.7	3.8	9.9	9.8	10.1
Other	16.1	15.4	14.4	12.3	11.9	11.6	12.9	12.1	10.7	14.0	12.2	13.4	11.8	12.6	13.3	10.6	10.2	10.4	11.5
Total	100	100	100	100	100	100	100	100	100	100	100	100	100	100	100	100	100	100	100

Source: Trade estimates

Third, compared with some other countries the demand for toothpaste is relatively low. Between 1948 and 1961 the total annual production of toothpaste more than doubled, but despite this expansion consumption was estimated to be only half the amount bought per head in the United States of America and sufficient to provide only one-quarter of the amount the British public might be expected to require for regular use throughout the year. More recent international studies show that the amount of toothpaste purchased per family is still lower in the United Kingdom than in the United States or West Germany: 36 standard packs, United States; 26 standard packs, West Germany; 19 standard packs, United Kingdom.

Fourth, the toothpaste market continues to expand, albeit at a slow rate, at some 1 to 3 per cent per annum. The main reasons for continuing growth are: (1) more

Table 6–2   *Share of toothpaste market of different types of retailers in 1979*

	(%)
Multiple grocers	40
Co-operative Societies	8
Voluntary groups	4
Independent grocers	4
Boots	18
Other chemists (multiple and independent)	5
Discount drugstores	9
Woolworth	5
Other outlets	6

Source: Trade estimates

people are retaining their own teeth (about 29 per cent of the population of England and Wales had no natural teeth in 1978 compared with 37 per cent in 1968, according to *Office of Population Censuses and Surveys*); (2) people brush their teeth slightly more frequently; and (3) people are trading up to a larger size pack which leads them to use more toothpaste.

Fifth, the intense controversy and public debate in the early 1970s concerning the addition of fluoride to drinking water to prevent tooth decay stimulated interest in the inclusion of fluoride in toothpaste to fulfil the same purpose. The subsequent acceptance of fluoride toothpaste by consumers was very rapid. In 1971 some 15 per cent of toothpaste contained fluoride; by 1978 it was almost universally included in toothpaste. This development had two major effects on the toothpaste market: (1) it stimulated the entry of a new competitor. In 1975 Procter & Gamble launched its fluoride toothpaste, Crest, and this is now the fourth largest brand in the United Kingdom; (2) it changed the theme of manufacturers' advertising from emphasis on the function of toothpaste to keep teeth white and clean and freshen breath, to the therapeutic advertising theme of helping to prevent tooth decay, particularly among children.

There are other distinctive features of the toothpaste market, namely, although the total demand for toothpaste is relatively inelastic, the demand for individual brands is very elastic. Furthermore, the major companies spend large sums of money on research and development amounting to an average for United Kingdom manufacturing industry of 2.5 per cent of sales, compared with an average for United Kingdom manufacturing industry of 1.5 per cent. In addition, the Price Commission Report on Toothpaste (HC 125, 1978, p. 47) suggested that manufacturing costs per ton were considerably smaller for the major brands compared with the minor brands, pointing to noticeable economies of scale.

Finally, specialized toothpastes which appeal to particular segments of consumers (e.g., children, smokers) have been introduced and established successfully and profitably alongside the brands of the four major manufacturers. The market share of Sensodyne, for instance, which caters for a semi-clinical condition of sensitive teeth is increasing; sales depend more on the personal recommendation of dentists than on advertising. In these specialized sectors of the market brands are less affected by price competition and the need to respond to it than in the main sector of the market.

With regard to DOBs, their share of the market appears to have stabilized around 10 per cent with one multiple retailer, Boots, responsible for 6 per cent of the toothpaste market. Two factors would seem to account for the relatively small market share held by DOBs compared with some other product fields: (1) the relative decline in the price of manufacturer branded toothpaste has increased its value to consumers and inhibited the entry of additional DOBs; (2) the constant and aggressive advertising and sales promotion schemes of the major manufacturers provide consumers with a series of attractive offers and price reductions at the point of sale.

The product

Macleans toothpaste was introduced in 1928. Before that, the firm supplied toothpaste to chemists with the name of the chemist printed on the tube and carton. Although there was no fixed retail price, Macleans toothpaste sold at 6d for the small size (originally designed for sale at Woolworth) and 1s for the larger size. These prices were similar to those of other proprietary brands but yielded retail margins between 33 and 50 per cent which were higher than was general. Small-scale point-of-sale advertising accompanied the introduction. The first advertising campaign started in 1930 with posters and display cards on the London Underground.

When in 1938 Macleans was acquired by the Beecham Group, retail prices were reduced: the large tube was 10½d and the extra large 1s 6d. The effect was to narrow trade margins to between 24 and 27 per cent but retailers could increase their earnings by sharing in the larger volume of sales that had followed advertising of the national brand. Thus a virtuous circle had been created; growing output encouraged the company to invest in production methods that reduced costs; the higher rate of sales stimulated by advertising enabled retail margins to be reduced; and lower prices in turn stimulated sales. In the immediate postwar period sales of Macleans toothpaste doubled whilst advertising expenditure trebled; but after that increased competition, including the establishment of new brands, caused advertising expenditure to rise more steeply than sales (Table 6–3).

Table 6–3   *Macleans toothpaste: index of sales and advertising, 1931 to 1979*

Year	Index of sales	Index of advertising
1931	100	100
1938	600	450
1946	1150	300
1952	1850	1150
1959	2800	2350
1961	3350	2650
1965	3852	4213
1970	3785	2941
1973	5259	6068
1975	7068	3392
1978	11 825	9699

Source: Beechams.

The competition

Between the 1930s and 1950s Macleans was the brand leader in a market dominated by three firms (see Table 6–1). In 1954 Colgate became the brand leader, a position it has since maintained (Table 6–4). Table 6–4 shows that Beechams had a market share of 20 per cent in 1954, and has since hovered around 20 to 25 per cent. This share has been maintained by the introduction of variants of the main brand: a new brand (Aquafresh); advertising, and a continuous programme of promotions which have pre-empted a proportion of the expenditure formerly spent on advertising.

Table 6–4   *Toothpaste manufacturers: share of market, 1954 to 1978*

Firms	Years (%)		
	1954	1967	1978
Beechams	20.5	20.9	25.7
Colgate	23.5	34.5	31.4
Gibbs	20.6	32.5	21.7
Procter & Gamble	—	—	10.0
Others	35.9	12.1	11.5

Source: trade estimates.

Product development

In 1967 Beechams introduced a second flavour of Macleans toothpaste—spearmint—to their original mild mint flavour to appeal to the section of the market which preferred toothpastes with a mild flavour. These two variants of the main brand helped to stabilize Beecham's share of the market around 20 per cent but were unable to expand it. At the beginning of the 1970s the firm concluded from its research findings that further expansion of the Macleans brand would be achieved only by high, and probably unprofitable, expenditure.

As a result the decision was taken to introduce a second brand as a more economic method of increasing the firm's share of the toothpaste market. In 1973 the development work which had been carried out on a blue and white striped gel led to the launch of Aquafresh, designed to appeal to mouth freshness. The introduction of this second brand raised the firm's total share of the market to 25 per cent by 1978 despite the heavy promotional expenditure which accompanied the entry of Procter & Gamble's Crest fluoride toothpaste in 1975 (Table 6–5). Although the company has undertaken trade research to discover how the sales of a new brand are built up, no consistent pattern has become apparent. On the whole it appears that some sales are drawn from all the existing brands, particularly the weakest. Experience has shown that the introduction of a third brand by a manufacturer has not proved a successful method of expanding market share; for example, Colgate's Fluor introduced in 1962 achieved 8.6 per cent of the market the following year, but thereafter its share declined drastically and it was withdrawn in 1975; this is probably due to the difficulty of differentiating brands sufficiently in the mass market, and the high cost of promoting a brand adequately in a competitive market.

Table 6–5 *Beecham's share of toothpaste market by brand (%)*

	1963	1967	1973	1976	1978
Macleans Fresh Mint	17.6	19.7	13.0	10.8	11.2
Macleans Spearmint	—	1.2	6.5	7.7	7.0
Aquafresh	—	—	1.5	6.4	7.1
Total	17.6	20.9	21.0	24.9	25.3

Source: trade estimates.

In 1975 both the variants of Macleans toothpaste and Aquafresh were re-introduced on the market with the inclusion of fluoride in response to the entry of Procter & Gamble's Crest. Although Aquafresh had contained fluoride from the outset, this feature of the brand had not been stressed, because there was little consumer interest in fluoride at the time of its introduction.

Besides meeting the competition from Crest by introducing a fluoride toothpaste, Beechams competed against this newcomer in four ways: by reducing the price; by a consumer promotion in 1976 (i.e., a twin-pack offer which by providing a 40 per cent discount is an effective, if expensive, promotion); by increased advertising; and by increased sales effort from the sales force who were provided with additional incentives.

Advertising

Two significant changes have taken place over the past decade in advertising policy. First, the proportion of advertising expenditure has declined in relation to expenditure on promotions. Whereas the ratio of advertising to promotions was formerly 60:40, it is more often now in the ratio of 40:60 because of the growing emphasis on price competition combined with the need to attract the attention of the shopper at the point of sale, and provide her with an immediate reason for purchasing a particular brand. Despite this relative decline in advertising expenditure the chief medium for advertising Beecham's toothpastes is still on television, which means that less advertising is undertaken than formerly. (This decline in television advertising has been accentuated still further by the cost of advertising which has risen faster than the rate of inflation.)

Second, during the 1970s along with most other toothpaste firms, the advertising theme of Beechams toothpastes was changed from the cosmetic to the therapeutic. Whereas the emphasis in the advertising of Macleans toothpaste had in the 1950s been on the benefit of cleaning teeth with toothpaste, leading to healthy teeth and white teeth, and in the 1960s the stress was almost entirely on whiteness; with the inclusion of fluoride in Macleans toothpaste and Aquafresh the emphasis changed to the value of toothpaste in preventing tooth decay. In 1980, however, since the value of fluoride is generally accepted and included in all toothpastes, Aquafresh is once more being promoted on a freshness claim, while Macleans toothpaste has been re-introduced with an improved fluoride (which has been patented) that gives more protection against decay and helps to remove plaque, which is of concern to consumers.

Promotions

As has been seen, Beechams spend relatively more on promotions than on advertising than in the past. This is due to the changed structure and competitive nature of the retail trade; it is also due to Macleans' position in the toothpaste market as the second brand. Under these two conditions, the firm believes that a given expenditure on a promotion can be more effective than a similar expenditure on advertising.

On average, consumers buy toothpaste twice a month. Shoppers, therefore, have 26 opportunities annually to switch from one brand to another. Since Macleans has a smaller share of the market than the brand leader, Colgate, it has by definition a smaller number of 'loyal' customers, and this fact influences the number and type of promotions it employs. Macleans, like Colgate, places heavy reliance on trade deals with retailers in order to ensure that it is price competitive, and gains participation in retailers' own promotions. In addition, the firm promotes more frequently and more intensively than Colgate on the pack to provide shoppers with an additional incentive to purchase its brand in preference to those of its rivals, and to sustain the loyalty of existing customers.

Many of these on-pack offers are designed to encourage the shoppers to buy more than one pack of Macleans toothpaste: two packs for the price of one; '7p off' this pack, and then a coupon worth 7p off the next pack purchased; send in tops of three packs and receive 50p in cash. Because these particular promotions are expensive, although effective in increasing sales, they are interspersed with lighter and less costly promotions, such as the offer of a 'free' magic painting book. Such an offer may nevertheless be sufficient to achieve a display in the supermarket and thus help to attract attention to the product.

These promotions are an integral part of the firm's promotional policy which is based on negotiating a trade deal with retailers on price and/or temporary price reductions (TPRs), and then supporting the deal by advertising and promotions so that it may make the maximum effect in retail outlets. Three promotions a year are run on Macleans toothpaste, and each of these is alternated with a promotion on Aquafresh; these six promotions annually enable the sales force to promote intensively one or other of the toothpaste brands throughout the year. However, the firm finds it less easy than in the past to determine the timing of a promotion, because it is increasingly required to fit in with the promotional calendar of retailers. A recent development has been the pressure exerted on the firm for a price-marked pack to be made available for one retailer only.

CASE HISTORY 2

Service: Golden Rail

Industry: British Rail

The service

Golden Rail (GR) began in 1971. Since then it has been adapted and extended in several respects, notably by the introduction of short-stay and self-catering

Table 6–6   *Golden Rail bookings, 1971 to 1979*

Year	Total holidays[a]	Breathers[b]	Self-catering
1971	30 000	—	—
1972	27 000	—	—
1973	60 000	1800	—
1974	98 000	5000	—
1975	114 300	12 300	—
1976	94 300	12 000	—
1977	111 000	16 400	1600
1978	141 000	19 800	5600
1979	159 000	22 000	14 100

Source: British Rail.

[a] More than 5 per cent of main holidays are now outside the peak season.
[b] Golden Rail has not so far offered Breather holidays to London; these are organized by Stardust, another sector of British Rail.

holidays, and the introduction of additional resorts including the Channel Islands and Stratford-upon-Avon. The number of holidays booked has grown from 27 000 in 1972, to 98 000 in 1974, to 141 000 by 1978 and 160 000 by 1979 (Table 6–6). However, the basic characteristics of the scheme have remained virtually unchanged; an inclusive holiday comprising accommodation with either half or full board available from a wide choice of hotels and resorts; 2nd class rail travel (or 1st class on payment of a small supplement); all transport from traveller's local station to holiday address and return and, where appropriate (across London, Manchester and Glasgow), by pre-booked taxi; seat reservations on Inter-City services— individually labelled wherever possible; service of GR couriers at main stations and at resorts/inland centres; a voucher giving a 50 per cent reduction on a rail day trip within a radius of 100 miles; and holiday cancellation and curtailment insurance.

The objectives

A major objective of British Rail is to attract additional passengers at off-peak periods of the week and year in order to minimize the spare capacity which exists even during the summer season, apart from a few Saturdays. High fixed costs are generated by the need to meet the short-lived peak demand of commuters and businessmen; running extra trains and filling empty seats off-peak involves only marginal costs. Hence over the past decade BR has introduced a wide range of services designed to appeal to specific subsections of potential customers— shoppers, senior citizens, students, families, holidaymakers—in order to open up additional markets which would make a contribution to rail passenger receipts.

The introduction of GR as an inclusive holiday package in the United Kingdom is part of this general objective. The contribution of GR to rail receipts rose from under 4 per cent in 1974 to 14 per cent in 1979. Other objectives of GR were:

1. To help counteract the decline in holiday travel by train which had fallen between the late 1940s and late 1960s from around 50 per cent to 11 per cent due to the rapid expansion of car ownership and foreign holidays, particularly package tours. A GR holiday would have the advantage of combining to some degree the convenience of car travel with that of a packaged holiday.
2. The introduction of GR was regarded as a suitable means of enabling British Rail to capture a sizeable proportion of the *domestic* packaged holiday market which at that time was practically non-existent. Although in 1970 packaged holidays amounted to only some 5 to 6 per cent of holidays in this country, and were dominated by coach operators, both coach and tour operators were beginning to promote this market energetically, based mainly on coaches.
3. To attract a proportion of that segment of the market who do not take holidays away from home[1] but who might be persuaded to do so by the reassurance and convenience offered by an inclusive holiday.

---

[1] In 1970 the British Travel Association had estimated that 20 million people did not take holidays away from home.

Finally, but by no means least, it was anticipated (and has now proved) that GR could simply be a profitable arm of British Rail in generating extra revenue.

Organization

In the first year of operation British Rail undertook the marketing and funding of GR. However, in order to benefit from the expertise of an experienced tour operator, administration and booking were contracted out, and these functions were incorporated into the tour operator's own business. Under this arrangement, one- and two-week holidays were offered throughout the year.

Furthermore, in order to utilize the railway network to the fullest extent, the conventional tour operator procedure of block bookings at reduced rates in a limited number of hotels was not adopted; instead the knowledge of the Resort Officers of the resorts which were to be featured in the GR brochure was enlisted.[2] A policy was evolved by which these officers helped to recruit and screen a large number of hotels and guest houses where GR could place customers without any prior commitment on either side. This arrangement helped minimize the financial commitment, since British Rail's role was confined to that of broker placing business it had created with a large number of loosely affiliated hotels. Furthermore, it enabled GR to offer its customers a large number of resorts, and a wide choice of prices and standards of hotels and guest houses. It was recognized that the major weakness of this policy could be the difficulty of ensuring room reservations, and could result in a slow booking procedure. Besides cooperating in the selection of hotels and guest houses, the resorts which participated in GR also agreed to publicize the scheme in their holiday guides.

At the end of the first year which had been beset by a postal strike as well as the not unexpected difficulties associated with a new venture, 30 000 holidays had been sold. Several valuable lessons were drawn from GR's entry into packaged holidays:

1. GR holidays, for the most part, had been purchased by summer holidaymakers. This market suffered from two major disadvantages for the future: (a) it had been static for several years and therefore offered little scope in the long run; (b) it could not contribute towards BR's objectives of attracting extra passengers during off-peak periods.
2. Despite an additional supplementary charge for Saturday travel during the peak holiday season, a high percentage of GR holidaymakers had travelled on that day, partly as the result of the reluctance of hotels to change their booking days.
3. GR had not attracted to any extent that segment of the market that does not take holidays away from home; it had become evident that it required a price below that which would make GR economically viable to attract them.

---

[2] Hotels and guest houses had to comply with the minimum standards of local authorities.

4. Despite initial teething troubles, which included a shortage of hotel rooms, particularly in the summer months that had resulted in 'frustrated' sales, the potential did exist for packaged holidays by rail in this country, and GR had achieved a foothold in this market from which it could build a range of holidays that would meet satisfactorily its marketing objectives. (The apprehensive comments and verbal attacks by competitors which accompanied the launch and operation of GR were also regarded as confirmation that it had become an effective competitor in the domestic holiday market!)

After the outside tour operator had withdrawn from the administration and booking of GR, in 1972 British Rail took over these functions. Since then, GR has been based on cooperation between three interests: British Rail, hotels, and resort tourist boards. The operation and administration of GR are, however, the sole responsibility of BR.

Short-stay holidays—Breathers

Experience had shown that the original type of holiday offered by GR required to be broadened if large-scale sales were to be generated, and if off-peak travel was to be encouraged. A pilot small-scale scheme confirmed that this would be achieved if, in addition to its main scheme, GR diversified into short-stay holidays during off-peak periods which would appeal to people seeking a second holiday outside the traditional holiday period.

As a result, GR began to issue two brochures: the first offered one- and two-week holidays between April and October; the second brochure offered short out-of-season holidays covering, with a small overlap, the remainder of the year. 'Breathers', as these holidays were named, were for a minimum of three nights which could be extended, if required, up to five nights, and would include all the standard elements of the main holidays, apart from insurance. There were, however, several distinguishing features of Breathers: holidaymakers could travel on any day of the week[3] (excluding Sunday) compared with the Wednesday and Saturday travelling days stipulated in the main scheme; fewer resorts were available compared with the main scheme, but these included several inland holiday centres designed to appeal to those taking holidays outside the summer period.

Pricing structure

Although the main programme of GR continued to offer a wide range of prices and selection of hotels, the pricing structure was simplified in two directions. First, Easter was abolished as a pricing period, which reduced their number from four to three: the low season; the shoulder (mid-September to end of October, mid-May to end June); and summer. Second, whereas the original pricing structure had been

---

[3] This feature distinguished it from its competitors.

based on zones this was replaced by a system of inclusive prices from 53 charging stations to groups of resorts (and subsequently reduced drastically still further).

GR becomes financially more advantageous to holidaymakers compared with a do-it-yourself holiday the longer the distance travelled and the more out-of-season the holiday. Hotels also contribute to this financial advantage compared with a 'do-it-yourself' holiday by reducing prices below those otherwise charged during the shoulder and winter periods. On the other hand, short-stay holidays offer the most financial benefit to British Rail because the rail element constitutes a higher percentage of total price than on longer holidays. Although this pricing policy means that holidaymakers who take high season holidays and short journeys benefit least financially, they nevertheless obtain the convenience of GR's assuming responsibility for booking and travel arrangements, and they reduce the risk of choosing an unsatisfactory hotel/guest house.

Sales promotion

In 1973 £100 000 was expended on a sales and advertising campaign. A large part of this expenditure went on printing half a million brochures. Advertising was divided among the following: national newspapers and magazines, including the *Radio Times*, *Reader's Digest*, and women's magazines, which incorporated coupons for interested readers to send off for the brochure; television, which also encouraged viewers to telephone or write off for a brochure; and posters displayed at railway stations. The inquiries made through advertising media were monitored. Other promotions included the provision of 'resort leaflets' at cost to resort authorities for distribution with local hotel guides. In addition, participating tourist authorities and hotels contributed towards the cost of publicity and promotions, especially out-of-season short holidays. Advertising for Breather holidays was limited to the press and posters.

As a result of the changes made to the original scheme, in 1973 GR holidays doubled to 60 000, of which 97 per cent were for the main holiday scheme, and 3 per cent[4] were Breathers. Although the 45+ age group predominated in both schemes, constituting more than 65 per cent of the total, their socio-economic composition differed significantly. Whereas Breathers attracted ABC1s,[5] the main scheme appealed principally to C1, C2, Ds. Similarly, the geographical background of the participants varied widely in the two schemes. Holidaymakers taking Breathers came mainly from London and the South-east; the main scheme appealed most to people living north of the River Trent who tend to take holidays on the East and South coasts. Furthermore, a higher proportion of those taking Breathers owned cars compared with people taking holidays in the main scheme. Many people who take a Breather holiday apparently welcome it as a change from driving.

Further research into the operation of GR showed that two-thirds of the business

---

[4] The number of Breather holidays is detailed in Table 6–6.
[5] Socio-economic groups as defined in IPA Readership Survey.

had been taken away from other means of transport, principally coach and car, and that the proportion of repeat business was higher than that achieved by other inclusive tour operators. This was taken as a measure of customer satisfaction and 'loyalty'. In addition, research into customers' attitudes showed that 95 per cent of respondents enjoyed their holiday. 'Convenience' was considered the most valuable attribute of GR in association with the provision of a personalized service. The elements in the scheme which contributed towards these attitudes were: the personal booking procedure; the comprehensive information provided in the travel wallet; reserved seats; the services of GR representatives in transit; provision of taxis to connect major railway stations, and to transport holidaymakers to and from the hotel to the railway station. Thus the impression of GR emerged from this research as a caring operator, offering quality holidays, which seemed to be confirmed by the high proportion of passengers who paid a small supplement in order to travel first class. Research also suggested that it was misleading to describe GR as a packaged holiday because its customers appreciated the absence of organized travel, and therefore another description would be more accurate and appropriate.

These market research findings, however, faced GR with a dilemma. Although the favourable attitudes of customers towards GR suggested that rapid expansion would be possible, it was feared that a too rapid expansion might outstrip the available handling capacity and thereby destroy the very attitudes which had contributed to its successful development so far. Consequently, for 1974, the aim was to increase bookings by 25 per cent. Two new resorts were added to the scheme, and the 50 per cent reduced rail voucher was continued in view of its popularity.

Furthermore, it was recognized that successful expansion would depend more on the ability of GR to satisfy potential holidaymakers who sent in completed booking applications which could not be confirmed through the unavailability of hotel rooms, particularly in the summer season. The need to reduce such 'frustrated' sales led to organizational changes in two inter-related aspects of GR: (1) the selection of hotels and (2) the booking system. These changes have resulted in a more highly controlled operation in place of the former voluntary system.

Hotel selection

Originally GR offered a wide selection of hotels in each holiday centre. This policy has been reversed, although the number of resorts has continued to expand. The radical contraction of the number of hotels per resort has had two effects: first, it has raised the general standard of hotels in the scheme because these must now conform to the English Tourist Board's voluntary standards introduced in 1974, as well as to strict fire regulations. Since 1977, no hotels have been accepted without inspection. Second, with fewer hotels GR has a closer relationship with hoteliers, and has become a more important customer to them. A pre-reservation system has been introduced since 1974 in place of the former voluntary allocation of rooms by hotels which had not proved satisfactory. In the peak season in the more popular resorts a deposit reserves a high percentage of rooms on behalf of GR, and a penalty is incurred if they are not taken up. This system will be extended to all resorts in the main programme from 1981. In the off-peak season GR reserves a certain number of rooms in each hotel according to anticipated demand. By concentrating their business in fewer hotels, GR is now responsible for a substantial proportion of a hotel's turnover, which can amount to 50 per cent throughout the year. The growing importance of GR to a hotel out of season has been an important contributory factor in persuading hotels to allocate rooms to GR during the high season.

Booking system

Until 1975 bookings could only be made by post, and although telephone inquiries were dealt with this facility was not publicized. The installation of a computer to undertake pricing and billing speeded up the booking procedure. More recently, the installation of a new computer has released sufficient staff time to undertake telephone bookings for Breather holidays, low-season bookings for holidays in the main scheme, and bookings for high-season holidays after mid-March, as part of an overall planned improvement in the booking system. (To some degree GR still operates an open-ended booking scheme by inquiring whether a hotel has other rooms available once its allocation has been taken.)

The reduction in the number of hotels per resort, combined with the introduction of a computerized booking scheme, helped to lower the 'frustrated' rate of sales from 35 per cent in 1974 to 13 per cent in 1978. These changed operating methods were doubtless one factor in contributing in 1977 to the reversal in the fall in sales (contrary to the national trend) which resulted from the economic recession of 1976.

Sales outlets

Bookings for GR holidays are made through three channels; direct by post or telephone to York, the headquarters of GR; through 300 selected railway stations; and through the 1700 appointed agents who sell British Rail tickets. Hitherto, sales strategy has been biased towards direct sales, although the facility of booking through travel agents is mentioned in advertisements. However, bookings through travel agents have risen steadily, averaging around 40 per cent for holidays in the main scheme, and more emphasis will be given to this sales outlet in future.

Developments in sales promotion

The relatively high proportion of repeat bookings which was a feature of GR holidaymakers in its early days has persisted during the 1970s as a measure of customer satisfaction. The dispatch of the annual brochure automatically to former customers comprises, therefore, an important component of sales promotion policy. In 1978, 26 per cent of GR holidays were sold to former customers via the mailing list. The value of customer satisfaction in generating additional business is also evident from research which shows that personal recommendation is more important than the media in generating awareness, and probably bookings. Research has shown that half of those who booked GR holidays in 1978 first heard of them by word-of-mouth, whereas half of those who did not book a holiday had been made initially aware of GR by the media. A coupon is therefore provided in the brochure to enable people to request GR to send a copy to their friends.

In view of the high proportion of GR bookings which emanate from the Midlands and the North, television advertising has been discontinued in the London area and concentrated in those areas of the country where it has been found to be cost effective; commercial radio continues to be widely used in the London area. The original division of total sales promotion expenditure in the ratio of 50 per cent on brochures and 50 per cent on advertising has continued.

The competition

Two factors have increased the competitiveness of the domestic holiday market for GR. First, the number of firms offering rail package tours has grown. Besides Saga (principally senior citizens), other firms such as Cosmos, Eden Vale, Galleon and Co-Operative Travel have entered this market. The National Bus Company and other coach operators have introduced package coach holidays. GR also faces direct competition from the many hotel groups (e.g., Grand Metropolitan) which organize short-stay holidays and which have negotiated inclusive tour fares with British Rail, and indirect competition from other sectors of British Rail such as Sealink and Stardust, which specializes in short holidays to London.

Second, the economic situation from 1974 onwards adversely affected the domestic holiday trade. Besides reducing the total number of those going on holiday, many holidaymakers have traded down in order to continue taking holidays. This has led them to choose lower priced hotels, or reduce the length of their annual holiday, or switch to self-catering holidays.

Demand for holidays is therefore very susceptible to price, and GR have responded to this situation in several different ways. In particular, in 1980, pricing policy was made more flexible than formerly by the introduction of much smaller price changes between pricing periods by means of a 'mid-season' between low and high season. There are now fewer abrupt price changes, for instance, on either side of the peak holiday period in order to encourage an expansion of business between mid-September and the end of October. In the main scheme, too, additional reductions at many hotels were made available for holders of Senior Citizens Railcards during the very low season weeks, after the successful completion of a pilot scheme in 1978.

On Breather holidays, since 1979, the minimum period has been reduced from three nights to two to counter the effect of inflation and the policies of competitors.

Widening the market

As a means of increasing turnover, the number of resorts included in GR has been continuously increased. Among the most recent additions have been the Channel Islands and Stratford-upon-Avon. Furthermore, to widen its appeal to holiday-makers with children in 1977, GR introduced self-catering holidays in chalets, suites or caravans, in cooperation with leading holiday camp operators. Families naturally constitute the major part of the self-catering market which is the fastest growing sector of a static *domestic* holiday market. It comprises some 28 per cent of the total market, and 14 per cent of self-catering holidays are taken in holiday camps. By 1979 GR self-catering holiday bookings had risen to approximately 14 000, of which approximately half were for children. Because the average size of the self-catering party is four to five persons, these holidays generate more revenue than either holidays in the main scheme with 2.38 passengers per booking, or Breathers with two people per booking.

CASE HISTORY 3

Product: Superfry

Firm: Van den Berghs

Superfry was a gelled vegetable oil suitable for shallow and deep frying. Its distinguishing characteristics were its high performance for frying, and that it was a cooking oil with the advantages of cooking fat, in that it melted when heated, and reverted to a jelly-like solid state when cold. Furthermore, it was packed in a tub which acted as a storage container after the product had been used.

Between 1972 and 1974 a comprehensive series of market research tests was carried out into every aspect of the product, namely, pricing, packaging, and advertising, and consumer attitudes towards the concept and the product and towards existing cooking oils and fats. In 1974 it was first marketed in a town which, although not representative of a national launch, enabled the firm to test the operation of their production and distribution facilities in the market-place. When this small-scale test had proved satisfactory, towards the end of 1974, the product was put into an area test market which duplicates in miniature the national marketing situation without incurring the expenditure and risks of a national launch. However, although sales were initially satisfactory, after six to eight months they were failing to reach their predicted levels. After post-launch investigations to try to discover the causes for the lower-than-anticipated sales, and further tests of a modified product, the brand was finally withdrawn from the market in 1976.

The market

Superfry would have comprised part of the White Fats/Oil market, that is, lard, compounds, such as White Cap and Cookeen, and cooking oils which are used primarily by housewives for shallow and deep frying and roasting, and also, to a lesser extent, for pastry and cakes. During the period when Superfry was being developed and tested, this market remained fairly static; sales volume declined by around 4 per cent; the relative share of the three products which constitute this market also remained relatively stable, the variations which did take place resulting from changes which occurred in the price of cooking oil (Table 6–7).

Table 6–7 *White Fats/Oil market: product share and price, 1972 to 1976*

	1972 % Price (p/lb)		1973 % Price (p/lb)		1974 % Price (p/lb)		1975 % Price (p/lb)		1976 % Price (p/lb)	
Lard	63	8.2	60	9.9	61	16.7	63	19.0	61	18.4
Compounds	15	13.9	15	14.3	15	22.3	16	23.1	16	23.5
Oil	22	18.2	25	18.2	24	26.7	21	24.8	23	30.8

Source: trade estimates.

A feature of this market is the high share of distributors' own brands (DOBs) of cooking oil which amounts to some 50 per cent. In the compounds market, there are three main brands: White Cap, Cookeen, and Trex (Table 6–8).

Table 6–8 *Compounds brand share, 1972 to 1976*

	(%)
White Cap	39
Cookeen	33
Trex	14
DOBs	14

Source: trade estimates.

The product

In 1972 Van den Berghs had developed three new cooking fats, each of which had certain advantages over existing products on the market. When each of these was tested by a representative sample of housewives, Superfry received the most favourable response. At the same time as these products were being tested by housewives, their cooking habits regarding grilling, frying and roasting were also ascertained, and found to be very similar; that is, the majority used oil and lard for deep frying, but lard, white fat, and occasionally oil for shallow frying; many used their own dripping or lard for roasting, and a few cooked vegetables, omelettes, scrambled eggs and onions in butter or margarine; not many added fats to grilled food, but when they did, it was frequently butter or margarine and occasionally oil or lard; although some women chose cooking fats on the basis of health, for many it was not a very important factor. It was also evident that while oil users may choose oil because of its health advantages, those who do not use oil seldom consider the health or purity advantages of a cooking fat.

Once Superfry emerged as the most favoured product tested, there were group discussions with the housewives to analyse the product in detail. A very large number of women intimated that for a variety of reasons they would like to buy Superfry, with the proviso that it was in the same price bracket as the cooking oil or fat they currently purchased. The main advantage of Superfry was considered to be that it did not spit or splash, nor did it burn. Another desirable feature of the product was its neutral flavour and, in contrast to lard or oil, few of the women noticed any smell; but they did notice that it left food crisp and dry and it was not absorbed by food. A further asset was seen to be its versatility; because it combined many of the properties of lard, white fats and oil, Superfry could be used as a substitute for them. Other favourable characteristics were considered to be its convenience compared with lard because it melts quickly, and compared with cooking oil because it hardens and does not require to be poured back into a bottle; that packaging in a tub was preferable to paper wrapping and provided a means of storage; that the product gave good cooking results even when reused several times, and that food cooked with the product was easy to digest even by people with indigestion problems.

On the other hand, some of the features of the product were disliked by the group, principally its appearance and texture, and the quality of the tub. There was a general dislike of the product because it looked like 'hardened oil', and it did not look fresh, clean or new. It was generally agreed that a matt finish would be preferred. The texture of the product was also criticized although this varied according to where it was stored. Despite some disagreement over its texture, the women all maintained that Superfry should have a 'whipped soft texture' like soft margarine. The tubs were criticized because they broke easily and melted when hot fat was poured into them. It was suggested by the groups that the container should be brick-shaped instead of round so that (1) the housewife can 'judge an ounce'; (2) the tub would take up less room; and (3) the tub would be easier to store and stack.

The anticipated price of a pound of Superfry was estimated to be somewhere between the prevailing prices for lard and oil respectively.

Several suggestions were put forward for improving the product: instructions should be given on the quantity required for different types of cooking; the colour should be a creamy off-white. The group members wanted reassurance that the product was suitable for baking as well as shallow and deep frying and suggested that the texture should be the consistency of solid margarine, that would be easy to store, would not spill, and would melt quickly. The product should revert to this consistency after use.

Three main conclusions emanated from these group discussions: first, that the chief merit of the product was that it combined the best qualities of lard and oil, and if it could be used for deep and shallow frying, roasting and pastry making, it would offer the housewife the opportunity of buying only one product for all these purposes; second, that many housewives who use lard for deep frying would prefer to use oil, but do not want to struggle pouring it back into a bottle. This product eliminated the problem, and finally, that many women who buy lard and cheaper cooking fats would be reluctant to spend money on fats, although they admitted that Superfry had advantages over lard.

In March 1972, while this representative sample of housewives was choosing between three cooking fats, and giving their detailed comments on them as above, another piece of research was being undertaken into the attitudes of housewives towards cooking fats (including butter and margarine) in general for frying, grilling and roasting in order to discover the relative strengths and weaknesses of these products. An analysis of the product categories combined with the general attitudes of the respondents towards each product made it possible to build up a composite picture of the cooking fats market. For instance, all the respondents used more than one fat in their cooking. Only some housewives used cooking oil for health reasons. It proved difficult, however, to give a relative weight to the strengths and weaknesses of each product because while a housewife may be well aware of the deficiencies of a particular cooking fat, she continues to buy it because the positive features outweigh the negative (e.g., economy or versatility). As an example, lard is frequently criticized for its flavour or smell but is purchased by a large number of respondents.

Then in June 1972, to supplement the research into the attitudes of housewives towards the concept and their reactions to the product, a qualitative study was undertaken to discover, if possible, how to describe and name the product. This involved group discussions with two groups of housewives restricted to the younger age group as these are more likely to be willing to try new products than are older housewives.

The study concluded that the word or description 'jelly' was an inadequate and incorrect description of the product, because it suggests a wobbly but more solid consistency than Superfry, and is generally associated with greater transparency. The report therefore concluded that it was premature to try to find an acceptable description of the product until it could be made slightly more solid and far more transparent. The study furthermore suggested that while housewives appeared to appreciate and often welcome a product that can perform the function of both oils and fats, many housewives experience conceptual difficulties in changing their current habits of employing the former for frying and the latter for making pastry and cakes. As a result of this report, further product formulation work was undertaken, and concepts pursued that would make it easier for housewives to understand the specific assets of Superfry.

Testing the marketing mix

The aims of the next piece of research, undertaken in May 1973, were threefold: first, to assess the relative acceptability of the various parts of the brand—the concept, the advertising, the product and the packaging—as used in the total package; second, to identify strengths and weaknesses in these four areas; and finally, to establish whether Superfry was as acceptable to the projected market, namely, purchasers of white fats and cooking oil, as their present products.

Because of the newness of the product concept and lack of consumer knowledge for such a product a short pilot study was undertaken in the north and south of the country, half among those who use distributors' own brands (DOBs) of oil, and half among those using white fats before the recruitment of a full-scale sample, who were then asked to test the product at home, shown TV commercials, and asked to complete a questionnaire on their views of the product, and their reactions to the advertising.

Since it was only through the advertising copy that the idea behind the product could be communicated, it proved impossible to separate the housewives' assessment of the concept from that of the advertising. However, the research did reveal that these two elements generated a high initial interest in the product, a high propensity to purchase and a high level of expectations of the performance and quality of the product. Furthermore, the advertising had managed to communicate successfully, first, the nature of the product, that is, that it had the qualities of cooking oil to a greater or lesser extent than those of cooking fat, but was equally suitable for the uses generally associated with both products, and second, had presented it in a manner which appealed to housewives who purchase DOB white fat and cooking oil.

The research identified three minor but nevertheless important weaknesses in these areas: first, only 43 per cent of those who were shown the advertisements spontaneously recalled the brand name which suggested that it required more emphasis; second, the initial communication did not describe Superfry adequately enough since a majority of the sample thought that the product was something other than a 'type' of cooking oil, and many thought it was a margarine; finally, housewives tended to identify convenience as the product's basic claim rather than its main asset of high-quality performance in deep and shallow frying.

When the in-home trials had been completed, it was found that the product had achieved a satisfactory level of response measured against the 'action standards',[6] with packaging identified as the only weakness. On the whole, the housewives in the sample were satisfied with their experience of the product, and that it came up to the expectations created by advertising. However, after the product had been tried the propensity to purchase was disappointing.

Housewives could be divided into two groups: acceptors and rejectors. The acceptors were prepared to purchase after they had watched the TV commercials, and after they had tried the product. The rejectors, on the other hand, found that although the product performed well in trial it did not reach the expectations generated by the advertising. It appeared that, on balance, the rejectors think that Superfry is a good product but one which they cannot integrate into their traditional patterns of usage. Whether Superfry was accepted or rejected bore no relation to existing product usage (i.e., cooking oil or white fat) or to any other specific characteristic that could be identified in this research.

---

[6] 'Action standards' are generally set before a test commences and then scores must reach those levels to be acceptable.

The packaging

As anticipated, the packaging did not reach the expectations of housewives. The company had been aware of the defects in the packaging before the test, and an investigation into tub design was therefore instituted.

The other major factor that emerged from the in-home trial was that larger sales (pro rata) would be achieved of the product in the north of the country than in the south. In Lancashire, for instance, housewives were more favourably disposed towards the product than in London after trial, although this had not been evident at the post-advertising stage of the research.

Following the results of testing the advertising, a modified and shortened version of the original advertisement was devised to overcome some of the weaknesses which had been revealed. This revised advertisement was pre-tested in June 1974 to establish whether it adequately explained the product, and whether it made viewers sufficiently interested in it.

The new version of the advertisement appeared to communicate satisfactorily the basic features of the product, and these were understood by housewives. Unfortunately, just as in the original advertisement, the main claim was still perceived as convenience rather than the high level of performance which could be achieved in deep and shallow frying. However, despite the continued tendency to judge the product for convenience primarily, its other attributes were also appreciated. In addition, the research showed that the advertisement generated a high level of interest in purchasing the product in the future, among both the purchasers of white fats, and the users of DOB cooking oils (i.e., the lowest-price product).

Before the company proceeded to test market the product in October 1974 in the Harlech/Westward TV area, earlier that year, in May, two further tests were carried out so that any deficiencies in the product, production techniques and distribution which might otherwise emerge during the test market could be rectified as early as possible. First, the product was test marketed in a town—Haverford West—which was clearly on a smaller scale than the proposed test area, for the purpose of verifying that Superfry could be produced and distributed satisfactorily under actual market conditions.

Second, a further evaluation of the product was undertaken, albeit on a limited scale, to test production from a pilot plant. To date, Superfry had been produced in the firm's development laboratories; production on a pilot plant involves a trial time in the factory. The products from the pilot plant were used in the town test, and by a small sample of the company's staff who had been recruited because they were deep fryers of food. This panel of 44 employees tried out Superfry at home for a fortnight, kept a usage diary and completed a questionnaire.

Superfry was eventually launched in the test market area in October 1974. It was available in a tub pack in two sizes, 1 lb and 2 lb, selling at 28p and 56p respectively. The brand was advertised in the test market area with 45-second and 30-second television commercials which told consumers about the brand as follows: simple awareness of its market presence; that it is a vegetable oil; that it has setting properties; that it is suitable for shallow as well as deep frying. In addition, money-off coupons were distributed to encourage trial of the brand: 900 000 6p coupons were distributed in Harlech TV area and 300 000 10p coupons in Westward TV area (100 000 of the former and all the latter coupons requested the redeemer to provide their names and addresses on the coupons so that they could be contacted and interviewed about the product.)

Post-launch research

Two pieces of research were commissioned to examine the launch of Superfry into the test area:

1. In January 1975 qualitative research on the progress of Superfry was undertaken. This consisted of six group discussions to examine consumer attitudes towards the brand. The majority of women in each group undertook shallow and deep frying of food.

    Many housewives had experienced difficulty in finding Superfry in the shops after their interest had been aroused by advertising and coupons. They also complained that even where it was stocked, it was difficult to find because of lack of displays and promotion. There was the additional difficulty that whereas many housewives expected to find Superfry next to cooking oil, it was stocked alongside cooking fats. Furthermore, some housewives had difficulty in translating the pound weights into liquid equivalents so that it could be compared in quantity and price with their present products. In particular, oil users wanted reassurance that Superfry was no more expensive than cooking oil; the housewife who used cooking fats needed to understand that Superfry was not much more expensive than her usual product. The suggestion was made in this qualitative research that Superfry might be better value if it could also be used for baking, roasting, and perhaps other forms of cooking. The group members also expressed a wish for more information on the time interval before Superfry can be poured back into the container (i.e., was it necessary to wait as long as suggested?). Related to the last point was the suggestion that a stronger container that could withstand a higher temperature oil would be preferable. Finally, information was requested on the amount of Superfry required for shallow frying to avoid waste.

2. In February 1975 another study took place among users and non-users of Superfry to establish the extent to which it was being used for deep frying and for shallow frying and therefore how far it had replaced cooking oil and white fat respectively; to determine how far housewives in general were aware of Superfry and understood its qualities; and finally to assess how those who had tried Superfry understood its qualities, particularly in relation to white fat and cooking oil.

The main facts which emerged from this research were: most housewives who purchased Superfry used it for deep and shallow frying; that it appealed more to housewives who used cooking oil than to those who used white fat, and that the product concept was also more favourably received by housewives who used cooking oil; those housewives who had tried the brand thought that it was superior to other frying agents because it could be reused, caused less mess, was convenient, and attractively packaged. Among all Superfry purchasers there was an objection to the price; the test market showed an encouraging level of usership of the product and also favourable opinions of the brand.

Lapsed usage check

During the early weeks of the launch of Superfry into the test market area deliveries were extremely encouraging, but by the summer months of 1975 they had begun to fall to a very low level which caused concern about the development of the brand in the market. As a result, in August 1975 a survey was initiated to search for the reasons for the decline, and to re-evaluate the likely repeat purchase level for the brand. The results of the survey showed that the level of interest in the product remained high; however, problems relating to taste and price accounted for a substantial proportion of the reasons for rejecting the brand. At this time an estimate of the likely long-term share of the brand, admittedly subject to a considerable degree of error, showed that if brand loyalty of 50 per cent was assumed this would result in a 4 per cent share of the market.

Previous research into Superfry had indicated that a certain proportion of purchasers had complained that the product had a 'peppery' taste although it had not appeared to be a major problem.[7] Since this could have been caused by a setting agent in the product, it was thought that an alternative hydroxystearic acid might help to eliminate the problem. Accordingly, research was undertaken among samples of housewives who use lard and cheap cooking oil for deep frying with the original version of Superfry, and with an alternative version using a different acid. In the in-home tests that took place there was no evidence that this alternative version of the product would reduce any of the adverse taste effects. On the contrary, there was a suggestion that housewives who use cooking oil found the adverse taste effect worse than the original version.

As a result of this research the company decided not to proceed with the product.

---

[7] It is probable that the change in taste could have been the result of a slight product reformulation due to raw material costs which took place at a very advanced stage of development of the product, that is, when the pilot plant was established and that early product research had therefore been investigating a slightly different product.

CASE HISTORY 4

Product: Persil Automatic

Firm: Lever Bros.

The washing powder market has several distinctive features.

Purchases of washing powder used almost exclusively for washing clothes have risen over the past 20 years to 347 000 tonnes per annum, M£224 at 1979 retail prices. Between 1976 and 1979, for example, the market grew by an average of 5 per cent annually, reflecting the higher consumption of powder by the owners of automatic washing machines which have made washing clothes an easier task, and the predominance of materials which require little or no ironing. Furthermore, purchases have been somewhat higher than these figures suggest because washing powder was formerly used for dishwashing and household cleaning. With the development of specialist products for these purposes, they no longer form part of the washing powder market.

The market is dominated by two major manufacturers plus a number of distributors' own brands (DOBs), none of which are manufactured by Lever Bros. or Procter & Gamble. Besides these two companies and the 'own name' brands of multiple and supermarket chains, there are several international organizations which have the technical potential to develop branded products for the United Kingdom market, that is, Colgate–Palmolive, Henkel, BP (who have acquired Robert McBride (Middleton) Limited) and Teneco (who have bought up Allbright & Wilson, the manufacturers of distributors' own brands).

Furthermore, this market has been characterized by product innovation (synthetic detergents, powders with enzyme additives, solvent-based detergents, and low-suds washing powders), and by frequent reformulations of existing products to keep pace with developments in washing-machine technology, in types of fabrics, and in the washing powder market.

Two major factors have affected consumers' preferences for different types of washing powder: (1) the growing ownership of washing machines, in particular the purchase of front-loading automatic washing machines (see Table 6–9a), and (2) changes in types of fabrics (see Table 6–9b). Moreover, the temperature at which clothes are washed has declined because of the predominance of man-made fabrics and the tendency to mix loads of different types of washing.

Washing powders can be divided into two broad categories: heavy and light duty. The heavy duty sector predominates. The light duty sector consists of such products as Stergene, Dreft, and Lux Flakes, specifically designed for washing delicate clothes and fabrics. The share of the heavy duty market held by each manufacturer has changed over the past decade (Table 6–10).

The most significant change in the heavy duty market over the past decade has been the introduction of low-suds washing powders (Persil Automatic and Surf Automatic by Lever Bros., and Bold and Daz Automatic by Procter & Gamble) for use in front-loading automatic washing machines at the expense of other types of washing powders (Table 6–11).

Table 6–9a *Ownership of washing machines*

	1962 (%)	1975 (%)	1978 (%)
Total home ownership	47	74	76
Type:			
Single tub	34	18	14
Twin tub	12	31	30
Automatic[a]	1	25	32

Source: Lever Bros.

[a] Of the 1.06 million automatic washing machines sold in 1978 over 90 per cent were front-loading.

Table 6–9b *Shirt materials*

Type:	1962	1975	1977
Man-made fibres	7	31	10
Cotton	90	23	28
Mixture	3	56	60
Colour:			
Coloured	20	80	88
White	80	20	12

Source: Lever Bros.

Table 6–10 *Share of heavy duty washing powder market*

	1969 (%)	1973 (%)	1979 (%)
Lever Bros.	43	47	51
Procter & Gamble	50	44	40
DOBs and others	7	9	9

Source: trade estimates.

The tonnage of low-suds washing powder doubled between 1975 and 1979. By 1979 sales of low-suds washing powder comprised 34 per cent (see Table 6–11) of the heavy duty washing powder market, that is M£75. Lever Bros.' larger share of this market is the major factor accounting for their higher share of the *total* washing powder market in 1979, compared with 1969 (i.e., 43 per cent in 1969 and 51 per cent in 1979; see Table 6–10).

Table 6–11 *Share of market of different types of heavy duty washing powder, 1969 to 1979*

	1969	1970	1971	1972	1973	1974	1975	1976	1977	1978	1979
Lever Bros.:											
Persil	21	20	20	20	18	19	18	19	18	16	15
Radiant	9	11	9	7	6	6	4	2	2	2	1
Omo	8	9	7	6	5	5	4	2	1	1	1
Surf	5	6	8	9	10	10	9	8	8	8	7
Drive					1	2	6	7	6	4	4
Low suds:											
Persil Auto	1	2	3	4	6	8	10	12	14	19	23
Surf Auto										1	1
Procter & Gamble:											
Daz	12	13	13	14	12	10	9	9	9	7	6
Fairy Snow	10	9	9	9	8	6	6	7	7	6	6
Ariel	22	18	18	17	15	14	14	15	14	13	12
Tide	6	6	6	6	6	6	6	6	5	5	4
Low suds:											
Bold					4	5	6	6	6	6	9
Daz Auto										1	1

Source: trade estimates.

The product

Persil Automatic was the first washing powder in this country especially formulated to have a low-lather performance to make it suitable for front-loading washing machines. Conventional high-suds washing powders are unsuitable for these machines because the rotation of the drum causes excessive foaming which may lead either to clothes' being washed inadequately or the machine's becoming clogged and/or foam spilling on to the kitchen floor. If, in order to avoid the risk of foaming, only a small amount of high-suds washing powder is used then clothes do not get washed properly.

Low-suds washing powder differs significantly from other washing powders and has different performance characteristics: the powder must be able to dispense and disperse automatically, and when combined with the smaller amount of water used in a front-loading automatic washing machine it must not clog up the pipes of the machine. As a result of these requirements, low-suds washing powder is technically a more complex product.

Persil Automatic was introduced in 1968. At that time (see Table 6–9a) the United Kingdom market comprised a minority of housewives who owned front-loading washing machines but who were unable to purchase a product made by either of the major detergent manufacturers specifically to fulfil their needs. The only suitable product then available, Pat, was poorly distributed and little advertised; as a result it was neither well known nor readily obtainable.

A new opportunity clearly existed in the washing powder market for the introduction of a new product. Although this would not be immediately economically viable because of the restricted market, if it was successful sales could be expected to rise as the ownership of front-loading machines expanded. However, one particular disadvantage of entering the market so early was the difficulty of forecasting the rate at which the ownership of these machines would grow. Although on the continent front-loading machines had quickly become established as the predominant type, it was not certain that this would necessarily occur in this country because the ownership of twin-tub machines had become firmly established (see Table 6–9a), a development which had not occurred on the same scale elsewhere. Furthermore, because of the specific product characteristics of a low-suds washing powder, it was not found possible to modify the formulation of Lever Bros.' major brand, Persil. In order to avoid the major expenditure of technical, marketing and financial resources that would be necessary to develop a new brand it was decided to adapt to British requirements work already carried out by other Unilever companies in Europe into the technical formulation, packaging and advertising policy of a low-suds washing powder. Then the major decision had to be made whether to market the new product with a new name and pack which would distinguish it from other Lever Bros. washing powders, or whether to market it as a variant of an existing brand. Both these courses had advantages and disadvantages.

The advantages of an independent brand would be a greater degree of flexibility in designing all aspects of that brand to meet established consumer needs. No aspect of the brand would have to be compromised to avoid conflict with the parent brand. However, experience indicated that this course of action might well prove unsuccessful because the initial small size of the market and the limited promotional resources consequently available would make it difficult to build up adequate levels of awareness and understanding of the brand. In addition, it might prove difficult to achieve adequate distribution of a new brand with limited promotional resources.

The alternative case for launching the variant of an existing brand was that, if successful, there would be major economies in advertising and presentation. For example, the use of an existing brand name with some modification would help to create an image for the product without heavy investment advertising. However, this course of action had two important disadvantages: first, consumers might be confused by two brands with similar names which ran the risk that most of the sales of the new product might be at the expense of the established brand; second, some degree of flexibility would be lost as the existing consumer attitude to the basic brand would need to be taken into account in deciding the presentation approach for the new variant.

Test marketing the name

A decision between these alternatives (an independent brand or a variant of an existing brand) was clearly difficult to make without the accumulation of further evidence. It was therefore decided that both approaches would have to be developed and tested. Since management resources were limited, the approach which offered the chance of the greater return if successful, and with fewer long-term difficulties, was selected to be examined first—the independent brand. Under the name 'Skip' the product was test marketed in the Yorkshire area which constitutes about 10 per cent of the United Kingdom population. Since the number of potential customers was very small, advertising was confined to a few publications with comparatively low circulations which were, however, read by a substantial proportion of the target group. Unfortunately, no similar coherent pattern about the target group's shopping habits could be deduced. Since little investment was available to secure widespread distribution through the grocery trade, it was possible only to aim for a low level of distribution and anticipate that the brand's success would stimulate a slow growth in distribution in the area.

The preliminary results of test marketing Skip in 1966 were disappointing. The 'low-key' approach was clearly unsuccessful; awareness of the product among its target group was lower than expected and distribution through the grocery trade failed to attain the predicted level. Before abandoning the test market altogether it was decided to discover whether higher levels of investment in advertising would take the brand through some sort of threshold of consumer awareness and thereby raise sales to an acceptable level. This entailed advertising on television for the first time, and introducing special trade activities in order to stimulate distribution. Both these measures improved awareness and availability of the product, and subsequently the level of sales; but the degree of improvement did not justify the extra investment cost.

As a consequence, the firm withdrew from the test market, and decided to test a variant of an existing brand, Persil Automatic. Persil was chosen in preference to other Lever Bros. lines for several reasons. It was a long established brand with an equally long-established reputation for washing clothes at all temperatures. Its association with washing machines was very strong, dating from the early 1950s when washing machine manufacturers found it particularly suitable for use in washing machines and recommended it for this purpose. Because it was soap-based, Persil could also be used in front-loading washing machines, although it was a high-suds powder. Frequent reformulations to incorporate technical developments had enabled Persil to keep pace with changes in washing machine technology and in washing powders, with the result that despite the widespread penetration of synthetic detergents in the middle of the 1960s it still accounted for over 25 per cent of the total washing powder market. It was this direct relationship with washing machines which made Persil a suitable vehicle for the introduction of a variant specifically aimed at fulfilling the market need for a low-lather powder which gave a better performance than existing products in these front-loading machines.

The major concern about the new brand was its possible detrimental effect on the image and sales of Persil. Furthermore, as the performance characteristics of Persil Automatic were different, this confusion could result in dissatisfaction and even withdrawal by Persil users. On the other hand, if the new brand was successful, it would help improve Persil's image by demonstrating that the parent brand had become more modern and up to date. The Persil name could also continue to be recommended by washing machine manufacturers for all types of machines.

The choice of test market was determined by two considerations: first, the risk to Persil had to be minimized, and therefore the test market had to be fairly small and preferably in an area in which Persil was relatively weak; second, since Persil Automatic had in the short term a very limited potential market because of the relatively few lather-intolerant machines in use, it was important that ownership of these machines in the area chosen should be as high as, if not higher than, the national average. Southern Television area best met these criteria.

Before test marketing Persil Automatic, market research had been carried out on the package design, since packaging would be an important factor in emphasizing the difference between the two products. However, how far consumers were likely to be confused by the two brands, and their attitude towards the new brand were questions which could be resolved only in the market-place and not in an artificial test situation.

The price to be asked for Persil Automatic was higher than for standard Persil for two reasons: first, the formulation for a low-lather product was more expensive, and second, the small size of the market would not allow the benefits of the economies of scale which were enjoyed by the higher tonnage powders.

The brand was advertised on television with a straightforward educational approach. The difference between Persil and Persil Automatic was clearly explained; it was also stressed that Persil was keeping up to date with new washing machine developments, and that leading manufacturers now recommended Persil for both front-loading washing machines as well as for other types.

Distribution was obtained very quickly, an important advantage of using the Persil name. Sales built up rapidly, and the previous concern about the brand's possible adverse effects on Persil was dispelled by the results of a market research investigation carried out after the launch. Although the brand was taking sales away from Persil, this was not due to the similarity of name but because Persil had been the brand most used in front-loaders because of its relatively low lather and its association with washing machines. It was found that there was little confusion between Persil and Persil Automatic; non-owners of front-loading washing machines were mostly unaware of the existence of Persil Automatic.

These favourable results stimulated the firm to extend Persil Automatic rapidly into national distribution. It was anxious that Persil Automatic should be accepted in the market as the brand of washing powder suitable for front-loading washing machines before the anticipated introduction of a competitive product by its major rival. It was also keen to see Persil Automatic become firmly established before the rapid growth of suds-intolerant washing machines weakened the close link, that had been built up over several years, between Persil and washing machines. In addition, it was considered important to obtain the endorsement by washing machine manufacturers of Persil Automatic as more compatible for front-loading automatic washing machines than any other washing powder.

Once Persil Automatic had been launched nationally the emphasis in the advertising continued to be educational, explaining why it was the brand of washing powder most suitable for front-loading machines, and the pack also continued to be used for educational purposes. At the same time, in order to safeguard the future position of Persil Automatic to some degree, a contract was negotiated with washing machine manufacturers to supply a sample with every front-loading machine. This was to ensure that it would be the first brand tried by the housewife in her newly acquired machine as the market expanded and encouraged the entry of competitive products. By the end of 1970 Persil Automatic had become established as the brand recommended by manufacturers and electrical dealers. It had also from the outset been a commercial proposition because until 1971 it was sold with very little expenditure on advertising.

Competition 1970 to 1979

As Lever had anticipated, it was not long before their major competitor, Procter & Gamble, entered the low-suds washing powder market. In 1970, Procter & Gamble's brand, Bold, was test marketed in the Southern Television area. Unlike Persil Automatic, it had been formulated for all types of washing machines (suds intolerant and tolerant), doubtless because the front-loading washing machine market was still considered too small to justify a specific washing powder. This version of Bold was withdrawn once it became apparent that housewives were uncertain for which type of washing machine it was intended. By the time Bold was relaunched nationally in 1973 specifically for suds-intolerant washing machines, sales of Persil Automatic amounted to 24 000 tons annually, some 6 to 7 per cent of the heavy-duty washing powder market. The major difference in the formulation of the two brands was the addition of enzymes to Bold.

Since the establishment of a second major brand, competition in the low-suds washing powder market has become intense as each firm has sought to secure a larger share of an expanding market. Competition was further intensified in 1974 to 1975 by the introduction of DOBs of low-suds washing powders which quickly gained a 12 per cent share of this segment of the washing powder market. In 1978 another competitive product, Dynamo, a low-suds washing liquid, was introduced by Colgate–Palmolive. This product was technically a simpler product than the washing powders. A liquid, however, did not prove entirely compatible with the dispensing mechanism of front-loading automatic washing machines although it was suitable for twin-tub washing machines. Dynamo was withdrawn from the market after 18 months. Then in 1978 Procter & Gamble introduced a new brand, Daz Automatic, and in 1979 Lever Bros. introduced Surf Automatic.

A combination of marketing devices, including advertising, samples, trade discounts, consumer promotions, and, in particular, temporary price reductions, has been deployed in order to build up the sales volume of Persil Automatic to achieve economies of scale, and lower unit costs, and profit from an increasing share of a still-expanding market. In 1979, for example, the market for front-loading washing machines had increased by 10 per cent, compared with the previous year.

During the period 1971 to 1979, advertising expenditure as a percentage of sales turnover has remained constant, but an increasing proportion of the total promotional budget has been devoted to promotions. Advertising is seen primarily as a means of stimulating demand over the long term by informing the consumer what the brand offers, and how it can be used most effectively. The advertising theme has become less educational as front-loading washing machines have become commoner, and increasing emphasis has been placed on the performance of the brand in achieving good washing results at all temperatures. In addition, the brand name has been included increasingly in the advertisements of washing machine manufacturers who recommend Persil Automatic for their washing machines.

Closely related to the long-term purpose of advertising, the value of samples has been recognized in encouraging housewives to try Persil Automatic from the time they purchase a new washing machine. As a consequence, negotiations have continued with all washing machine manufacturers for full-size packs of Persil Automatic to be included in the drum of their front-loading washing machines—a policy also actively pursued by their major competitor.

The role of short-term promotions

As a complement to advertising, and to serve another obective, short-term promotions are employed. Their purpose is to provide the consumer with an additional incentive to purchase Persil Automatic at the point of sale. They also aim to generate interest among retailers to feature the brand which may involve providing a prime display spot in the store or the provision of additional display space, and/or inclusion in the retailer's own advertising and promotions. Some six to seven promotions are organized annually to focus trade interest on the brand, and encourage purchase at the point of sale. Promotions have included competitions and 'free offers'. Competitions sometimes feature as prizes the products of firms who also manufacture washing machines, thus emphasizing the close link between Persil Automatic and front-loading washing machines. A promotion may be undertaken jointly with another organization (e.g., British Rail, the Post Office). The promotion organized with British Rail, for example, offered a 'free' rail ticket voucher in exchange for three tokens collected from one or more of six Lever Bros. products, including Persil Automatic. In the 1979 to 1980 promotion 1.2 million British Rail vouchers were issued. This voucher enabled the recipient when he purchased a rail ticket to obtain another one to the same destination free of charge. In the following year, 1980 to 1981, an estimated 3.5 to 4 million vouchers were issued. Both these promotions were widely featured in supermarkets. Another joint promotion in 1981 with the Post Office and RCA offered a 'free' record, plus a poster calendar giving a reminder of 'special' occasion days and anniversaries, in return for vouchers collected from specified Lever Bros. products, including Persil Automatic. Applications for this promotion reached 250 000. Apart from expenditure on advertising the promotion, the cost of the offer may be negligible; for example, in a high fixed cost industry such as British Rail the marginal cost of filling an empty seat is very low, and the extra revenue generated very high.

Promotions are also frequently tailored to a specific retail firm. The intense competition prevailing in food retailing means that many traders prefer to participate in a promotion with a manufacturer which is exclusive to them. In this arrangement the retailer will include Persil Automatic in its own promotional schemes and advertising. In such promotions there is usually joint funding of the prizes, price reductions and advertising.

Trade bonuses are also negotiated with retailers as a means of focusing trade interest on the brand, and thus achieving shelf and floor space in the store, and being featured in retailer advertising.

However, the major proportion of promotional expenditure on Persil Automatic is in the form of temporary price reductions (TPRs), either 'money off' or 'price-marked' packs. These have been deployed on a larger scale to encourage trial and retrial of the product, as the consumer has become more price sensitive, and as competition between retailers has intensified, and concentration of retail trade has accelerated (e.g., 50 per cent of sales of Persil Automatic are made through four distributors). TPRs have been found to be effective in encouraging the most price-sensitive consumer, namely the purchaser of DOBs, and the shopper who shows little loyalty to any manufacturer brand, to try Persil Automatic.

The cumulative effect of advertising and promotions, combined with the general strength of the company's sales force, have helped to ensure a widespread distribution penetration of Persil Automatic (Table 6–12).

Table 6–12 *Distribution penetration[a] of low-suds washing powders, 1977 to 1980*

Year	Persil Automatic (%)	Bold (%)
Jan 1977	63	47
July 1977	66	48
Jan 1978	70	52
July 1978	70	55
Jan 1979	60	47
July 1979	70	53
Jan 1980	73	55

Source: trade estimates.

[a] Distribution penetration is the percentage of individual retail outlets which normally stock a product.

When Bold entered the market in 1973, sales of Persil Automatic were affected temporarily by its advertising and sales promotion campaign. Between 1975 and 1978, however, by the deployment of its 'mix' of sales promotion techniques and, in particular, by offering TPRs more frequently than Bold and with deeper price reductions, sales of Persil Automatic expanded by 100 per cent, whereas those of Bold increased by 15 per cent. This deliberate policy of reducing margins to achieve volume was pursued still further in 1978 to 1979 because it was discovered from

Table 6–13 *Brand shares of low-suds washing powder market (volume), 1977 to 1979*

Brand	Year 1977 (%)	1978 (%)	1979 (%)
Persil Automatic	58	60	59
Bold	25	21	24
Daz Automatic	0.2	3.1	6.0
Surf Automatic		1.8	2.0
DOBs	15.4	13.0	8.0
Others	1.4	1.4	1.0

Source: trade estimates.

research that many consumers were still using heavy-duty washing powders although they had purchased front-loading washing machines. The following table shows the changes in market share which took place between 1977 and 1979, and also the impact of the introduction of two further brands by the major manufacturers (Daz Automatic, Procter & Gamble; Surf Automatic, Lever Bros.) which seem principally to have reduced the market share of DOBs (Table 6–13).

The effect of the intense competitive activity in this market has culminated in a relative decline in the price of low-suds washing powders compared with the retail price index, and also in relation to the price of heavy-duty washing powders (Table 6–14).

Table 6–14a   *Price index of low-suds washing powder in relation to retail price index*

	1973	1979
Retail price index	100	240
Raw materials index	100	276
Low-suds washing powder index	100	211

Source: trade estimates.

Table 6–14b   *Price index of low-suds washing powder in relation to heavy duty washing powders index: based on £/tonne*

	1976	1977	1978	1979
Total heavy duty	432.6	484	524.7	567.7
Persil Automatic	447.4	500.6	527.3	566.4
Price index	103.4	103.4	100.5	99.8
Bold	440.1	491.3	528.6	559.8
Price index	101.7	101.5	100.7	98.6

Source: trade estimates.

CASE HISTORY 5

Product: Quick Custard

Firm: Batchelors Foods Ltd

In March 1978 two competing brands of instant custard—Batchelors and Brown & Polson—were introduced almost simultaneously into the old established custard market. In April 1979, Birds (General Foods), a famous name in this market, also introduced an instant custard powder.

Batchelors Quick Custard is a mixture of custard powder, sugar and dried milk packed in a foil sachet. When boiling water is added to this mixture and stirred it reconstitutes to liquid custard. The product is both time- and labour-saving because the need for saucepans and washing-up is eliminated. Furthermore, unlike traditional custard powder, the addition of milk and sugar is not required, and this guarantees greater consistency of end result.

The product

Since its introduction in 1839 the custard market has been dominated by Bird's, an instance of a brand name which has become synonymous with a product. Originally, custard was served as a cold pudding. Its modern history dates from the interwar period when it was taken increasingly as a hot pouring sauce; and it is still used predominantly in this way. Furthermore, research carried out by Batchelors into this market in 1976 revealed that over 63 per cent of housewives served custard; it is served up to three times a week; and most of these housewives have stocks in their larders at most times.

The market

The custard market was in slow long-term decline from at least 1952 until 1969 when the first convenience custard was introduced in cans. During this period efforts to stem this decline were made by Bird's with the introduction in 1958 of a number of flavoured custards which stimulated the market temporarily by 7 per cent and restored it to its 1956 level. This expansion in sales was short-lived, however, and not sufficient to stabilize the market against the long-term contraction. During the latter period of slow contraction during the 1960s, there was little or no advertising in this market as there seemed little prospect of growth; sales nevertheless totalled some M£13 (at 1977 prices).

Several factors had combined to intensify the competition facing custard powder. Among these were the wider choice of 'afters' on the market, the tendency for many housewives at work and with rising incomes to prefer convenience desserts, and the change in taste towards lighter sweets.

The introduction of canned custard (which became possible as the result of a technical advance—aseptic canning) first by Ambrosia and Heinz and then followed several years later by Bird's in 1975, stimulated the expansion of the total market, although the slow decline of custard powder persisted (Table 6–15).

Table 6–15 *Value of custard market, 1969 to 1977 (at 1977 prices)*

Year	M£	Powder (%)	Canned (%)
1969	13	90	10
1977	16	66	34

Source: trade estimates.

Thus in 1977 custard powder still retained the predominant share of the market; some of the expansion in canned custard sales had been the consequence of intensive price cutting. The relative importance of canned and powder custard by value, packs and servings is outlined in Table 6–16.

Table 6–16 *Custard market, 1977, by value, packs and servings*

	Powder (M£)	(%)	Canned (M£)	(%)
Value	10.6	(66)	5.4	(34)
Packs/cans	50.0	(60)	33.0	(40)
Servings (pints)	573.0	(96)	25.0	(4)

Source: trade estimates.

It can therefore be seen that whereas canned custard in 1977 accounted for more than one-third of total sales in value, the overwhelming proportion of servings was still from custard powder.

In the two sectors of the custard market in 1977, the shares of the various brands were as shown in Table 6–17.

Table 6–17 *Custard market brand share (value), 1977*

Powder	(%)	Canned	(%)
Bird's	61	Ambrosia	36
Own labels	28	Heinz	30
Others	11	Bird's	27

Source: trade estimates.

It was into this market situation that Batchelors decided to introduce Quick Custard, which had several advantages over canned custard: a lower price; no saucepan required to make hot custard; lighter packaging; the housewife could still be involved in the preparation of the custard and determine the degree of thickness required by varying the quantity of water added.

Although the company was entering a market with which it was unfamiliar, it nevertheless believed that it possessed several important assets which would ensure success: first, it had the technical expertise in producing dried products (e.g., soups and vegetables) and packaging them successfully; second, it had an efficient handling and distribution organization geared to the grocery trade; finally, and just as important, the company was confident that the formulation of this product was a technical advance which could not easily be imitated by competitors. It was, however, aware that at some subsequent, if speculative, date, other firms, particularly Bird's, would develop a similar product, and that this factor would need to be taken into account in setting financial targets and strategy. Nevertheless, because of the prevailing conditions in food manufacturing and retailing a technical advance can often be the decisive factor in determining whether a firm's financial target can be attained. On the one hand, the intense competition in food manufacturing caused by excess capacity and a consequent tendency for marginal costing leads—when products are technically simple to copy—to their speedy introduction by competitors, followed by severe price discounting. On the other hand, the increasing homogeneity of supermarkets and the competitive pressures on distributive margins stimulate grocery multiples to seek out·distributors' own brands (DOBs). When new products can be copied easily retailers find it easier to introduce DOBs which are then sold more cheaply than the manufacturer's brand, but at a higher retail margin.

New products emanate from a variety of sources, not least a fortuitous technical development. The company's first version of a quick custard in 1970, for instance, was a spin-off from the general research being undertaken into dried foods by the firm's laboratories. It was not proceeded with because the custard mix needed to be added to hot milk, and the taste proved unacceptable when tested among a sample of housewives.

In 1977 the present and significantly different version of Quick Custard was the result of a technical development which had been applied to the firm's instant soup product—'Cup-a-Soup'. Although the new product had no direct link with the earlier research, the marketing department no doubt recalled its previous experience with a quick custard product, and therefore quickly recognized the significance of the new process.

In 1977, therefore, before the product was marketed the company undertook its standard market research tests with large samples of housewives to discover how far Quick Custard was acceptable for formulation, taste, texture and price, and to what extent these factors required modification.

In the product tests the potential market for Quick Custard was evaluated by asking samples of housewives to compare the relative merits of powder, canned and quick custard for a variety of attributes, namely quick and easy to prepare; no messy pans; no milk needed; familiar form; consistent end result; good quality; thickness can be varied; inexpensive. On all these attributes Quick Custard scored highly. For instance, after the samples of housewives had tested the product at home for a stipulated period, the respondents considered that Quick Custard was highly comparable in taste and texture to the usual custard that was served; that it was quick and easy to prepare; and that the respondents would be prepared to serve Quick Custard more frequently than they served traditional custard. Research also suggested that the preferred quantity of Quick Custard per pack was three-quarters of a pint—the same as the contents of canned custard.

As part of the company's standard market research tests a comparison and evaluation of Quick Custard were undertaken against two competitive products— Heinz Canned Custard, and Brown & Polson Instant Custard which since September 1977 had been on sale in a test market area. The results showed that Batchelors was liked equally with Heinz canned custard; but preferred to Brown & Polson. In addition, preparing Quick Custard was easier and quicker because it did not need whisking in a bowl, and its notional price was lower. This routine evaluation led to some small changes in the colour and flavour of Quick Custard.

Despite the knowledge that Brown & Polson (a firm already well known in the dessert market for custard powder and blancmanges) were also preparing to launch an instant custard, Batchelors were confident from this research that they had a technological lead and would be maintaining product superiority in the market for some time. Batchelors were also aware from their own development work that the technical process on which Quick Custard was based had become considerably simplified, a factor which would stimulate the entry of competitors.

The next stage in the marketing process was to move away from the controlled conditions of testing, and discover how the product performed in the market-place, where circumstances are invariably different from the unavoidably artificial testing methods which are used to forecast the acceptability of a product in the first instance.[8]

Test marketing in a television area is the conventional method of assessing the performance of a product in a real-life situation before the larger expense of the national launch is incurred. As is well known, however, test marketing is a long and laborious process which may last up to nine months or a year, and which has several important drawbacks. In particular, it enables competitors to find out about the forthcoming national launch of a product, as had occurred in this instance, enabling them to intensify their promotional activities in the particular area, and buy up the product. These competitive tactics often effectively invalidate the test market findings. In addition, it may be difficult to achieve adequate distribution in a test market because national multiples often refuse to stock a product in only a selection of their branches, etc. Despite these acknowledged disadvantages of test marketing, it persists because firms are anxious to use any method, even if imperfect, in order to reduce the risks of a full-scale launch.

In place of the normal procedure of test marketing in a television area Batchelors employed an alternative method of making a preliminary judgement of Quick Custard under more realistic conditions—the Mini-van test[9]—operated by Forecast Market Research Ltd. Although this method diverges in many important respects from an area test market, nevertheless experience has shown over a number of years that its results provide a reliable guide to a national launch. Besides being comparable in predictability to a test market area the Mini-van test has the advantages of speed, economy and confidentiality. These assets were particularly valuable to Batchelors with their knowledge that a competitor was about to introduce a similar product. In the Mini-van test, Quick Custard expanded the total custard market by over 10 per cent. Moreover, the brand was purchased by 23 per cent of housewives in only 11 weeks and, most important, a high level of repeat sales was achieved. In view of these encouraging signs from the Mini-van test, the firm decided to introduce the product nationally in order to be first in the shops. This took place in March 1978. Brown & Polson followed with their launch of

---

[8] Batchelors, however, also undertakes the marketing mix test which is an intermediary stage of research between the individual tests undertaken on formulation, pack, name, price, advertising and so on, and testing in the market-place. It has been designed to test consumer response to the whole marketing mix rather than the individual elements. See K. Clarke (Marketing Services Manager, Batchelors) and M. Roe (1977) 'Marketing mix test' for further details.

[9] The major features of a Mini-van test are: (1) sales are made from a van and not via shops; (2) a panel of 1000 housewives is utilized instead of the random selection of shoppers in a test market area; (3) these housewives see details of a new product for the first time by means of magazine advertising in *The Home Shoppers Gazette*, sent to every panel member each month; (4) test is usually completed in 16 weeks.

Instant Custard three weeks later which Batchelors believed was earlier than had been planned in their original test marketing programme.

Firms are eager to be ahead of their rivals in the market with a new product because of the quicker trade distribution and consumer trial this normally ensures. This factor alone, however, is unlikely to sustain sales unless the product itself has also proved satisfactory to consumers.

Promotion

Between March 1978 when Batchelors Quick Custard was launched nationally and December 1978 some £600 000 was expended on promotion and marketing. Sixty per cent of this sum was spent on television advertising, 20 per cent on price reductions to the trade, and 20 per cent on consumer promotions. The consumer promotions comprised flash offers of '2p off' on the pack and coupons in advertisements which enabled consumers to buy at a reduced price. In addition, trade press advertising, display material and in-store demonstrations amounted to some £4000 to £5000. To encourage smaller retailers to stock Quick Custard, a promotion designed specifically for voluntary groups and independent grocers included samples of the product, and a leaflet which gave details of the sales promotion campaign and incorporated a 25p-off coupon to encourage trial purchase.

Once Quick Custard was launched nationally sales expanded very rapidly, particularly in the second half of 1978 (see Table 6–18). Its major effect was to expand the total custard market. The entry into the market of two brands of instant custard almost simultaneously had little effect on the sales of custard powder; canned custard sales have, however, been adversely affected, and both Heinz and General Foods have withdrawn from the market.

Table 6–18 *Share of custard market (value), July to December 1978*

	(%)
Custard powder	53
Canned custard	22
Quick + Instant Custard	25
	100

Source: trade estimates.

In early 1979 the predicted entry of Bird's into the instant custard market took place, and immediately sparked off intensive price cutting by all the brands in the market. This situation was accentuated further by the introduction of some lower-priced brands, some of slightly lower quality, as well as distributors' own brands. This competitive situation has led to increasing emphasis by all the major manufacturers on promotional expenditure at the expense of advertising, particularly trade deals and consumer promotions. At the end of 1979, for instance, Batchelors offered a marked pack promotion with 2p off, with the purpose of maintaining competitive prices in smaller accounts and also the independent sector of the grocery trade.

By the beginning of 1980 the total custard market declined in volume, compared with 1979, as did sales of canned and traditional powder custard. Thus the continued growth of the instant custard sector was not sufficient to offset the decline of the traditional powders (Table 6–19).

Table 6–19 *Volume performance of custard market, first quarter of 1980 v. first quarter of 1979*

	Index 1st Quarter 1979 = 100
Total custard	88
Instant custard powder	154
Canned custard	82
Traditional powder	84

Source: trade estimates.

Over the same period the relative share of the different types of custard on a servings basis were: powdered custard 85 per cent; instant custard 12 per cent; and canned custard 3 per cent. This would seem to suggest that there still exists ample scope for the expansion of instant custard powder.

As at March 1980, within the instant custard market, each of the three leading brands—Batchelors, Bird's, and Brown & Polson—had some 20 to 25 per cent share of the market; while Bird's had an additional 25 per cent share through its segmentation into flavoured instant custards. The remaining 10 per cent of the market was divided between the smaller brands and DOBs. The relatively small share of the market held by DOBs to date is hardly surprising in view of the severe competition which has occurred between the major manufacturer brands, particularly in trade discounts to individual retailers. In this marketing situation, the low prices of manufacturer brands have not provided the opportunity for multiple organizations to introduce their own brands with a worthwhile price differential.

CASE HISTORY 6

Product: Mr. Kipling Cakes

Firm: Manor Bakeries Ltd

The background

The development and concept of Mr. Kipling cakes date back to 1960; the brand was launched regionally in 1967 and nationally in 1970 by Manor Bakeries.

In the early 1950s the Joseph Rank business was in flour milling, and it faced strong competition in a slowly declining market. As a result, British Bakeries was formed to build up a bakery chain, partly to guarantee outlets for flour, and partly to gain the economies of a more vertically integrated business. By 1960 British Bakeries had acquired a large number of regional and local bakery businesses. Most of these bakeries were selling cakes, though the type, quality, and degree of packing varied widely: some were almost wholly selling 'tray confectionary' (daily delivery unwrapped cakes), some were making high quality, standard packaged cakes for Marks & Spencer. During the 1960s British Bakeries concentrated on rationalizing this very diverse operation, but it was a gradual and difficult process because the nature of the business required local control. Although two small unadvertised brands of packaged cakes were being marketed, these had achieved only limited distribution regionally.

In view of the continued slow decline in the volume of bread sales, the company needed to generate new sources of turnover and profit. An investigation conducted into the strengths and weaknesses of the company's production facilities, marketing advantages, and financial position revealed clearly that any new product should be related closely to its existing products. Although the company possessed considerable production facilities, for instance, they specialized in flour, and flour-based products. Furthermore, the main marketing assets of the company comprised: a large van sales force which is essential for the distribution of a short-shelf-life product such as cake; experience in the daily delivery of products; and close connections with a section of the grocery retail trade. All these factors were equally necessary for the marketing of packaged cake which has a shelf life of no more than two to three weeks. This basic characteristic of cake marketing requires the operation of a carefully controlled and expensive van selling system, and an efficient stock rotation system. A further marketing advantage which stemmed from the company's experience of short-shelf-life products was a detailed knowledge of consumers' tastes. On the other hand, because this operation had been on a local basis, little market research had been undertaken either into the cake market or into the attitudes of consumers towards branded cakes.

The financial position of the company also pointed towards the introduction of a product which could make use of existing production facilities, because although investment capital was available there were many competing demands in the company for investment plant. A further factor which emphasized the value of introducing a product which could utilize existing resources was that the company owned one of the food industry's biggest basic food research facilities, and some of the individual bakeries which had been acquired had undertaken a certain amount of process development work.

The cake market

Since all the preliminary investigations indicated that a future product should be flour-based, a short list of potential products was drawn up which included cakes.

In the early 1960s the available published data and trade sources revealed that cakes were a large and expanding market; that is, at that time it was worth more than M£100 per annum and had been growing in value at about 5 per cent annually. Packaged cakes were the fastest expanding sector of the cake market, and grocers were becoming more important as distribution outlets. In general the quality of the products was low, although firms like Marks & Spencer had helped to raise standards. The market was very fragmented, and included a number of distributors' own brands. The two best-known firms in this market were Lyons and Marks & Spencer.

Several important conclusions were reached about the basic requirements of the proposed new product from the economic analysis which had revealed the growing importance of cake sales through grocers, particularly through multiple grocers and supermarkets. Since this distributive sector pursued a merchandise policy of limiting the number of brands stocked in any particular product field to avoid product duplication, this implied that supermarkets would be more prepared to stock a brand of cakes if it included a complete range of cake types. Furthermore, the short shelf life of cakes would make a large and efficient distribution system essential. The ability to provide both these requirements seemed to be factors which favoured British Bakeries more than, say, Cadbury, who had entered the cake market on a test basis in 1963.

The predominant position occupied by distributors' own brands (DOBs) and supermarkets also suggested that the lower prices of DOBs compared with national brands would lead to pressure on profit margins, and this pressure would be further accentuated by the buying power of the supermarket groups. This feature of the market suggested the need to build up a strong national brand which could rely on continuous consumer demand to persuade retailers to stock it.

If the policy was adopted of establishing a national brand this would be a departure from the firm's traditional daily delivery of cakes, both tray confectionery and packaged cakes, tied to bread distribution. Although the latter had certain advantages over a national brand—greater flexibility, shorter production runs, closer personal links with retailers—it suffered from the major disadvantage of higher distribution costs. Besides economies of distribution, a national brand had several other advantages over daily delivery of cakes, namely a larger number of stockists, and economies of large-scale production which would enable consistent production to higher quality standards, better quality control, improved packaging and more advertising. Perhaps, of most importance, a national brand would provide the opportunity to build up profit margins in the long run based on consumer demand.

In the early 1960s several significant developments took place in the packaged cake business which helped to intensify the competition in an already competitive, although expanding market:

1. DOBs were expanding their share of the market.
2. The Bakery Division of Lyons, the brand leader, was restructured and this led to the introduction of aggressive sales promotion techniques, and a vigorous drive for improved distribution.
3. After test marketing their range of cakes in 1963, Cadburys expanded into

national distribution in 1965, and supported this launch with substantial advertising expenditure. This range was deliberately priced higher than the Lyons range of cakes; promotion was based on product quality through the claim that all the products were made with butter.

4. The McVities division of United Biscuits introduced a range of cakes into the market in 1965 with very little advertising, but a large expenditure on merchandising at trade level. By 1967 the claimed turnover had reached M£8 per annum.

In view of these competitive developments, plus the fact that many other large grocery companies appeared to be considering diversifying into the packaged cake market, attracted by its present and potential size and a relative absence of brand loyalty, the decision was taken that the company should introduce a new brand on a worthwhile scale nationally as quickly as possible.

Taking into account the analysis of the market, and of the company's assets, when in 1965 the decision was made to introduce a national brand of higher quality packaged cakes suitable for display it seemed inevitable. Entry into this market offered more opportunities for product differentiation than bread. The company could capitalize on its existing skills and advantages. The data suggested, moreover, that this market could provide many opportunities for expansion, especially if economies of scale could be made in production. Entry into this market at this stage could enable the brand to get established, particularly in multiple grocers, before it became dominated by a few large brands.

The product

The consumer research findings—published and commissioned— helped to form a picture of the cake market, and the consumers' attitudes towards cakes.

Attwood panel data revealed the breakdown of buying by product types, shop type and brand. Swiss rolls, for instance, constituted only a modest section of the market and was dominated by Lyons. On the other hand, 'small cakes' were the largest as well as the most fragmented section of the market, with no major brand specializing in it.

Survey data, including the National Food Survey and an Odhams Survey, provided some basic facts on who eats cakes and at what meals. Perhaps somewhat surprisingly, it emerged that adults were responsible for a larger share of this market than were children, and that appreciable quantities are eaten as the last course of the meal.

Large-scale research into cooking attitudes, carried out by British Market Research Bureau in 1961, revealed how housewives viewed cakes, and the kind of competition that packaged cakes would face from home-made cakes. The research showed that home-baking, more than other forms of cooking, appealed to the pride and creativity of housewives, and was particularly linked with prestige and hospitality. There was also evidence of a trend to lighter, fancier cakes, usually made from recipes, whose visual appeal was particularly important. There was a very strong feeling that home-made cakes—baked by one's parents or grand-parents—are the ideal! As a result, bought cakes were considered as dull, and there were misgivings about putting a bought cake on the table if friends came to tea.

Small-scale attitude research, group discussions and individual interviews plus observation added to this information.

Prejudice still existed against bought cakes even from regular purchasers ('dry', 'stale', 'too long in shops'). Cakes are appreciated more for their appearance and taste than for their food value. Group discussions also revealed strong feelings about cakes as a treat rather than a food, and cakes from the local baker were preferred to those from the large manufacturer. A distinction was also made by consumers between 'modern' and 'traditional' cakes. The latter referred to the kind of cakes that could easily be made at home and had been for many years (e.g., sponge cakes, fruit cakes, jam tarts). 'Modern' referred to fancier, more unusual cakes, especially those unlikely to be made at home (e.g., almond slices, mini-rolls, battenburg). Although this distinction was not very precise, it did again denote the preference for home-made cakes rather than those made in a factory.

The research further emphasized the importance of the visual senses in judging cakes, and that they appeared to be judged in a visual sequence. First, the top of the cake symbolized the home-made cake—it must not be too regular. Second, a cut is made into the cake in order to judge its texture and freshness. Finally, a second cut is made into the cake, and this produces the first piece of cake which is placed on the plate, ready to be picked up and eaten. If all these stages are negotiated satisfactorily the cake tastes good before it reaches the mouth.

When this research into consumer attitudes was combined with the initial research into the market, it was possible to outline the essential features of the new brand, and the marketing policy required to launch it.

Marketing policy

The brand should comprise a complete range of cakes available nationally. At that time, Lyons were selling 70 lines; and there were at least 35 lines which had a reasonable level of sales. Some 20 lines were considered to be the minimum feasible number for a full cake range.

The cakes should be of higher than average quality. Within the product range, there should be concentration on small cakes for several reasons: they held a large share of the market; they were popular with 'heavy' cake buyers; they offered scope for innovation, process development and brand specialization; and this segment of the market had been neglected by its competitors and was still dominated by bakers' cakes. Furthermore, efforts should be made to produce 'non-standard' rather than the 'standard' cakes included in virtually all manufacturers' ranges (e.g., cherry cake, jam and cream sponge), since this policy would avoid direct competition with other firms' ranges. (When they were launched initially, Almond Slices and Manor House cake were unique to Mr. Kipling.)

Production should be concentrated into a small number of units to gain the economies of scale.

On pricing policy, this would, to a large extent, be determined by the price leader, Lyons. Although Lyons' prices were above those of most minor local brands, they were extremely competitive. The prices of Cadbury's cakes were higher than those of Lyons; the firm was selling a quality product, backed by the Cadbury name and heavy advertising. It was decided that initially Mr. Kipling's prices should be comparable to those of their competitors, although eventually they might justify a marginally higher price than Lyons on some lines through a quality appeal.

On distribution, the maximum use should be made of the company's distribution facilities (1) by utilizing the existing bread delivery system, and (2) by establishing a specialized sales force based on the company's existing cake sales force. This would be necessary to ensure that the economic advantages (i.e., larger drops) of selling to larger stores would be achieved, because distributing through such retail outlets required van salesmen to merchandise the cakes.

Finally, the economies of distribution and production, plus somewhat higher prices, should be utilized to finance higher quality cakes, advertising, and improved packaging that would help to extend the shelf life.

Product quality, packaging, advertising

In order to satisfy the basic conditions of the cake market (that it was competitive, that a range of diverse products was required, that it would be difficult to demonstrate easily the difference between the brand and its competitors, even if new types of cakes were introduced) it was decided that the brand would succeed only if it could be made distinctive. As a result, product quality, packaging, advertising and display material were employed in a variety of ways, but with the one objective of conveying to consumers that the brand provided better value for money than other brands.

Product quality was enhanced by improving the consistency of quality by modifying recipes and introducing new machinery; new materials and/or new types of sealing were used to improve the shelf-life and protection of cakes; and new products were introduced to fill the gap which existed in the market between puddings and cakes.

Although the company believed that product quality would be the basic factor in ensuring consumer acceptance, the importance of the visual aspects of cakes required to be reflected in the name of the product, the design of the pack, and the advertising. The company also wished to convey the distinctive features of the brand, that is, that it was made by a specialist cake firm as opposed to a manufacturer, that it was made by traditional methods but on up-to-date machinery, and that it contained high quality ingredients.

The name of the product was also required to be suitable for a range of cakes partly because there is a rapid rate of change in cake types since people like variety, and partly because no single line would justify sufficient advertising expenditure to establish it. The name finally chosen—Mr. Kipling— apparently 'came in the bath' because it suggested a specialist company, somewhat traditional, giving personal attention. Research confirmed that housewives were ready to believe that a man could make cakes better than they did, as long as he was doing it as a full-time job, and they thought the name intriguing and different.

Besides the basic requirement of packaging that it should protect and preserve the product, the pack was designed with lettering and with an appearance that would distinguish the brand from its competitors; an unusual feature was the handle intended to convey the idea of cake as a treat or a gift rather than food; a large picture on the pack showed a cake with sections cut from it already for picking up and eating, and showing the inside of the cake to demonstrate its texture and moisture; and tear strips for ease of opening.

Finally, the major aim of advertising was to reinforce the theme of the name and pack. As a result television was selected as the most appropriate medium because it could best express the characteristics of the brand, and especially the visual appeal of cake; for example, the advertising film showed close-up pictures of cakes being cut into sections ready for eating, and a voice-over talking about 'Mr. Kipling' made the point that he was a specialist cake-maker. Thus all the aspects of the presentation of the brand, including pack design, display material, letter headings, van livery, and salesmen's uniforms, were integrated in order to create a consistent and cumulative symbol. The vans, for instance, provide a valuable moving poster advertisement.

The regional launch

In 1967 the regional launch took place with the setting-up of a new company, Manor Bakeries, a new brand, Mr. Kipling, and a new range of 21 cakes. This was a compromise between a national launch which would have required fundamental changes in the organization and operation of the company, and a small test market which was an unrealistic alternative in view of the company's commitment to market entry as soon as possible. As a result, London and the South-east were chosen as the starting point for a national rolling launch which would establish the brand and forestall potential competitors. After a short period in London it should be possible to correct any major faults that came to light and utilize the London experience in other areas.

The regional launch of Mr. Kipling was accompanied by television, press and poster advertising, and trade promotional activity. It stimulated vigorous competitive opposition from its competitors, particularly in the form of price cutting; opposition was very intense from McVities which was now the second brand in the market.

Although sales started to grow quite rapidly as distribution was achieved, it was evident from an early stage that things were not going according to plan. Sales volume per van were below target, and the company was not meeting its financial objectives. In view of the elaborate logistical exercise which had been involved in making the launch, perhaps this was not altogether surprising. An immediate reappraisal of the situation took place, and it became clear that the difficulties that were being experienced in making the most efficient use of capital investment in plant, equipment and vehicles had been underestimated, as well as some of the start-up costs. In addition, ingredient costs were higher than had been forecast.

Steps were taken to remedy these weaknesses: several lines that were completely uneconomic were withdrawn; improved production techniques were introduced; packaging costs were reduced by simplifying packaging and packaging material (e.g., handles on packs were eliminated from some products, and film introduced in place of board on others in order to remain competitive); and formulae were modified on some cakes to reduce ingredient costs.

Retail audit data on distribution had been bought at intervals since the launch and showed an unsatisfactory state of affairs. In an area of the country dominated by multiple grocers, the distribution of Mr. Kipling cakes showed a relatively marked bias towards independent outlets. This was due to the refusal of some retail grocery chains to stock the brand because they found regional operations an inconvenience; other chains showed little interest in stocking cakes. An analysis of the van-selling operation revealed that drops below a certain level were uneconomic, and in the regional launch area a high proportion of drops were unacceptable.

Two key factors needed to be corrected: the relatively low level of sales due to the above factors meant that plant was working well below capacity with consequent disproportionately high overheads. To overcome this problem sales were increased by extending the launch area in 1968 to Lancashire, and a limited area of the north Midlands. This was done with minimal advertising support, and resulted in a valuable addition to sales. The second key factor was distribution. Journeys were realigned, field supervision tightened and numbers of salesmen increased. Intensive efforts were made to obtain better distribution in multiple stores in order to increase the size of the average drop.

Perhaps most important, it became clear that a more pragmatic approach was needed in the relative deployment of the specialized delivery system and the firm's bread vans. Bread vans, for example, were successfully used for distributing Mr. Kipling when the launch was extended in January 1969 to the South-west, a region notoriously difficult for van sales of many products owing to the few major population centres and extended communications. As a result, local bakeries bread vans began to account for a substantial share of sales once administrative and inter-company problems had been solved.

Finally, significant improvements in manufacturing techniques occurred when Mr. Kipling moved from its original factory which had proved uneconomic to three highly automated factories.

Early in 1970 distribution was extended by stages into the rest of the country. As the competitive situation in the cake market intensified and multiple grocers appeared increasingly reluctant to stock additional brands of cakes, it was considered essential to extend distribution as quickly as possible in order to gain entry into those major multiples who had refused to handle the brand as long as it was distributed only regionally.

The planned expansion of Mr. Kipling was slower than had been anticipated due to the changes and modifications, already noted, which the firm had been compelled to make in the operation of its business in response to tight retail margins and intense competitive activity. However, by 1972—five years after entering the market—Mr. Kipling had become well established. During this period Mr. Kipling had become the brand leader in the small cakes section of the market, and had also expanded its number of lines from 20 to around 40, with more in various stages of development. More important, its financial objectives were being achieved.

During the 1970s the marketing situation in the cake market changed in several respects (see Table 6–20):

1. An increasing percentage of cake sales was being sold through grocers, and particularly through large grocers.

Table 6–20 *Cake market: changing pattern of distribution, 1961 to 1976*

Type of outlet	1961 (%)	Year 1966 (%)	1976 (%)
Grocers	33	39	47
Bakeries	54	46	35
Marks & Spencer	6	6	7
All other outlets	7	9	11

Source: trade estimates.

2. While the cake market was relatively static during the 1960s, during the 1970s cake consumption declined by some 38 per cent. The decline from 4.58 oz per head in 1969 to 2.85 oz per head in 1976 has been due to a combination of factors, including the growing emphasis on slimness; the changing social pattern of life which has eliminated to a large extent the formal high tea; a revival in home baking of cakes due to relative increases in cake prices based on fluctuations in flour prices.

3. Competition in the cake market has intensified from two main sources: the introduction of frozen cream cakes which by 1978 held 6 per cent of the total cake market; and the stabilization in sales of baker's sales. The latter had declined by some 10 per cent between 1966 and 1971, but the share stabilized by the mid-1970s through the active promotion of the sale of fresh cream cakes in conjunction with the Milk Marketing Board. (On the other hand, the share of the market held by DOBs has declined chiefly through the fall in sales of Co-operative Societies' own brands, and the tendency of several other multiples to give more emphasis to branded cakes; Table 6–21.)

Table 6–21 *Share of cake market of different kinds of cakes*

	1978 (%)
Frozen cakes	6
Fresh catering packs	2
Loose cake (bakers' own)	32
Own label cakes	15
Branded cakes	45

Source: Mintel.

Within this declining and competitive market the sales of packaged cakes have continued to grow, and the sector of that market—small cakes—in which Mr. Kipling has specialized has also continued to expand (contrary to the experience of cut cake and sponges) as they are often eaten as snacks or desserts.

In 1976 Mr. Kipling became brand leader, and by 1978 it had one-third of the manufacturer branded packaged cake market (Table 6–22).

Table 6–22 *Manufacturer brand shares in packaged cake market[a]*

	1972 (%)	1978 (%)
Lyons	26	24
Mr. Kipling	12	30
McVities[b]	13	6
Cadbury	11	6
Hales	7	7
Memory Lane	—	4
All others	31	24

Source: trade estimates.
[a] These market shares exclude distributors' own brands.
[b] The cake sections of McVities and Cadburys merged in 1970.

Just as important as its large market share has been the profitability that has been achieved under very competitive conditions. Retailer brands, for instance, which were already firmly established in the 1960s, are still more important in this market than in many other packaged goods markets despite the inroads made into their share by Mr. Kipling and other manufacturer brands.

The leading position established by Mr. Kipling cakes appears to have been due to the successful implementation of the marketing policies it has pursued: concentration in the expanding small cakes sector of the packaged cake market; emphasis on distribution to larger grocery outlets where turnover is usually faster, which helps to minimize the ever-increasing cost of van selling; combining, where appropriate, bread and van sales, again in order to make distribution more economic; and basing the operation of the business on the original consumer research which had revealed the physical and psychological qualities consumers associate with cakes, and presenting these in an integrated and consistent form.

CASE HISTORY 7

Product: Catalogue showroom shopping

Firm: Argos Distributors Ltd

The background

Argos introduced catalogue showroom shopping in 17 showrooms in 1973, a method of retailing new to this country but already well established in the United States and Canada where jewellery accounts for some 30 per cent of the turnover. The raison d'être of this system of distribution is to offer a wide range of branded merchandise at competitive prices by effecting economies in distribution costs.

The idea of catalogue showroom shopping had been brought back from across the Atlantic by Richard Tompkins (the founder of Argos' then associated company, the Green Shield Trading Stamp Co. Ltd) who was seeking ways of expanding the original business. This method of shopping appeared to have two major assets: it would be attractive to consumers in the price competitive environment which had become a dominant feature of retail distribution in the 1970s; at the same time, it would permit the company to utilize and build on its existing strengths (i.e., the expertise it possesses in producing catalogues; the skills it had developed in acquiring retail property, in buying, and in operating warehouses and retail establishments).

The time of launching the company was both propitious and unpropitious. After the Resale Prices Act 1964 had abolished the individual enforcement of resale price maintenance (RPM), price competition had been introduced in one type of merchandise after another. In the early 1970s there were, however, still a number of trades in which price competition remained weak or non-existent (e.g., toys, gardening equipment, jewellery, some sports equipment) because such merchandise was being sold mainly through traditional retail outlets. The opportunity therefore existed not only to sell products in which price competition was already widely prevalent, and to compete with well-entrenched well-known retail firms, but also to enter product fields where price competition had hitherto been negligible.

Less fortunately, the launching of the company coincided with the oil crisis of 1973. The company was gratified that initial sales were higher than had been anticipated, which indicated that the new shopping concept was appreciated by the public; but it was less than happy that the prevailing economic conditions resulted in stock shortages and led to rancour with the public and the press.

Two significant changes have occurred since the company began. First, in 1978, the resources of Argos were combined with those of its then associated company. This had two consequences: eighteen of Green Shield's showrooms were converted to Argos showrooms in 16 weeks, which increased the firm's outlets by 40 per cent; Green Shield stamps could be exchanged at any of the Argos showrooms, with each filled saver book qualifying for an additional discount of 50p off the Argos discount price.

Second, in 1979 Argos was acquired by BAT Industries Ltd, and became a wholly-owned subsidiary of BAT Stores Holdings. By the end of 1980 the number of showrooms situated throughout the country had grown to 102, and turnover had reached M£140 per annum.

The operation

The major economies in this method of distribution are fourfold: first, the shopping system occupies less space than traditional retailing, with a consequent saving in rent and rates; second, computerized stock control reduces the number of staff required; third, large-scale sales enable bulk orders to be placed with manufacturers, which ensures that maximum discounts are obtained; and last, displaying products in showcases reduces pilferage. In addition, staff costs are lower than in traditional retailing because the catalogue replaces assistants to some extent, and merchandise does not require to be wrapped. Storage costs are also lower because many items are flat-packed (e.g., wheelbarrows and furniture) to enable customers to transport them home easily.

The basis of the operation is that the customer obtains a catalogue which can be taken home and studied at leisure from the showroom, or browses through one of the catalogues available on the special counters in the showroom. When the customer has decided on an item a selection form is completed by giving details of the product, number and quantity required. The customer then proceeds to one of the service points where staff check that the order form has been completed accurately, and that the requested item is in stock. Then at the cash register the purchase is paid for by cash, cheque, or credit card. The customer finally moves to the despatch counter, where the item purchased is ready to be taken home.

The four-sequence procedure can be completed in as little as three minutes because the purchasing system in the showroom is computerized, and in the latest showrooms when the customer's order form is checked at the service point an electronic stock-verification system confirms that the entered price is accurate, that the item on order is in stock, and indicates how many of that item is in stock in case the customer requires more than one. The facility of providing an instant stock balance simplifies the re-ordering of stock. The service operator's mini-television screen also indicates whether any items ordered are supplied with batteries. When the sale is confirmed a ticket is automatically produced from equipment in the stockroom and a member of the stockroom staff immediately picks the item from the stocking shelves and sends it to the dispatch counter by conveyor belt. Depending on the age or size of the showroom, other systems for stock verification are based on the Plessey lightpen system or a manual stock board.

The catalogue

The catalogue is the major communication vehicle of this method of retailing. The 1800+ to 2000 lines available in the showrooms are illustrated in the catalogue in colour, fully described, and include the code number for ordering. In addition, the shopping procedure as well as the methods of payment is described, and emphasis is given to the money-back guarantee which enables the customer to return a purchase within 14 days if it is not exactly suitable. (This guarantee is over and above the customer's statutory rights.)

Double-pricing—the chief promotional tool of catalogue showroom selling—is also explained in the catalogue. Where a manufacturer has a recommended retail price (RRP) the lower Argos price is quoted alongside. In those instances where no RRP exists then Argos' suppliers are asked to supply a suggested national retail selling price which is based on the traditional retail margins of that product, and the retail price at which the product is generally being sold. Similarly, the lower Argos price is quoted against the comparative retail price.

The catalogue is published twice a year, in February and August. The print run is more than two million copies an issue, of some 230-plus pages. It is distributed free to customers through the showrooms. That a new catalogue has become available is publicized by window display and by advertising in the national press.

The showroom

The average size of a showroom is 10 000 to 12 000 sq ft, which is divided in the ratio of 2:1 between stockroom and the selling area, providing a smaller public area than in traditional retailing. In the early showrooms very few products were placed on display; reliance was placed on the illustrations in the catalogue. However, it was soon discovered that many customers wanted to see the merchandise before deciding to buy. In addition, many people living near a showroom, as well as passers-by, visit the showroom on impulse and choose from the displays. As a consequence, all Argos showrooms now display merchandise in their windows, and in glass cabinets, while large items are displayed on island sites. Up to 75 per cent of merchandise can now be viewed on display. (It is estimated that 10 per cent of purchases are made as a result of consulting displays.)

Originally, too, it was believed that showrooms could be sited off main shopping centres because shoppers would have selected their purchases before they visited the showroom. In view of the importance of passing trade, however, showrooms are now sited wherever possible in prime shopping sites alongside major multiples. Other important factors which determine showroom location are convenient parking facilities, and that shopping centres should serve catchment areas of more than 130 000 people.

Merchandise

The Argos catalogue offers a wide range of merchandise: textiles, including bedding; toys and cycles; electrical products; auto equipment; furniture, including garden and office; sports goods; hardware; cameras and photographic equipment; do-it-yourself equipment; jewellery and gifts.

Since the first catalogue in 1973, changes have taken place in the number and type of products stocked. Whereas initially 4000 lines were stocked, these now number some 1800 to 2000, a reduction which has been facilitated by the introduction of two catalogues a year compared with the original annual catalogue.

The following are the main factors which determine the inclusion of a product in the catalogue: the rate at which it sells, and the gross profit generated; the amount of space that it occupies; whether it can be handled easily (e.g., white goods—see also below); whether sufficient supplies can be obtained to last the six months' life of the catalogue; whether it is a well-known manufacturer brand; and whether manufacturers are willing to supply.

After the first two years of operation the number of lines was revised drastically in four product groups: jewellery, audio equipment, photographic equipment, and white goods (e.g., refrigerators, freezers and washing machines).

With audio and photographic equipment experience had shown that at the higher price level of these products consumers preferred a specialist shop with trained and knowledgeable staff, and where demonstrations could be provided. With expensive jewellery, it was evident that consumers preferred to compare a selection of rings, and to purchase in more traditional surroundings! As a consequence, the firm reduced the number of lines of these products stocked, and traded down to a lower price range. This change in stock assortment has proved successful: jewellery and fancy goods now account for one-quarter of total sales turnover. However, once a study of the psychology of customers buying jewellery was completed Argos began again selling more expensive jewellery, separating this from the remainder of the sales area, and providing service and carpeting in what is now the Elizabeth Duke 'boutique-in-a-showroom', thus overcoming a basic difficulty of selling jewellery at reduced prices: customers being unable easily to judge the value of such lines.

In 1977 the decision was taken to withdraw white goods (washing machines, refrigerators, freezers) from the catalogue because sales were not reaching their anticipated levels on account of delivery and servicing problems. In 1980 a selection of white goods was once more introduced solely from Hotpoint, with delivery being made direct by the manufacturer, instead of via the showroom. But this second experiment was discontinued six months later. Credit facilities were also re-introduced in 1980 on all purchases above £55. Other products which have been dropped from the product range include such products as rotovators which Argos customers regard as the province of the specialist retailer only.

At the same time as certain lines have been dropped from the catalogue for various reasons, other lines have been excluded because of the refusal of certain manufacturers to supply a discount operation by claiming that they are entitled to do this under the Resale Prices Act because Argos would not be prepared to stock their full range, or that it would not be able to provide the necessary after-sales service. As a result, the company has been unable to obtain supplies of certain sports goods, audio lines and watches from certain firms, and have never been able to purchase well-known brands of cosmetics. On the other hand, although Argos sells Citizen, Omega, Seiko and Tissot watches, supplies are obtained from indirect sources, and not directly from the manufacturers.

What could be a significant development in the firm's efforts to stock additional lines was the decision by the Office of Fair Trading in February 1981 to refer the refusal of T.I. Raleigh to supply discount retailers to the Monopolies and Mergers

Commission under Section 5 of the Competition Act 1980 as being an anti-competitive practice.

Promotional policy

The main promotional expenditure is devoted to the catalogue, supplemented by advertising in the press to announce the opening of a new showroom, and the publication of a new catalogue.

Since the company is anxious that customers should be alerted as quickly as possible to the publication of the new catalogue, advertisements take two forms: first, illustrations of a number of products compare the recommended price with the lower Argos price; second, combined with the announcement of a new catalogue, the advertisements include vouchers of certain values (e.g., £3 off an item costing more than £45). Some of these vouchers are valid for the first six weeks of the catalogue; the remaining vouchers are valid for the following six weeks. These vouchers are therefore intended to encourage potential customers to visit their nearest showroom and obtain the new catalogue. Local press and radio are also used to announce the opening of a new showroom.

The major drawback of catalogue selling is its inflexibility. Prices must be decided three months before the catalogue is issued to allow for printing and binding. Then when the catalogue has appeared, competitors are in a position to adjust their own prices accordingly whereas the catalogue prices are fixed for the next six months. (To some extent this drawback has been overcome by marking those products which have been reduced in price for a limited period, or constitute a special offer, with a red 'Star Value' badge in the showroom, and advising customers to look out for these products in the catalogue.)

However, under rapidly-changing market conditions (e.g., VAT increases), the drawback of inflexibility has been exacerbated still further. Since 1979, therefore, in order to demonstrate to competitors that Argos can respond quickly to changing conditions and reduce prices in order to stimulate volume, the firm has issued supplements during the life of a catalogue, giving details of products which are available at reduced prices for a limited period.

Supplements are issued midway and towards the end of the life of the catalogue in the same way that a traditional retailer holds a sale at the end of the Summer and Winter seasons. Three million copies of these supplements are made available in the showrooms and sometimes publicized in the daily press. The first supplement in May 1979 was also designed as a market research exercise to discover the potential popularity of electronic toys before the decision was taken to include them in the Autumn Catalogue. An additional supplement at Christmas 1979 substantially reduced prices of 130 out of 250 toy lines which were selling slowly following the ITV strike that autumn. The mini-catalogue issued in June 1980 had two distinctive features: almost two million copies were delivered to homes in the neighbourhood of Argos showrooms, and a further 300 000 were available at the showrooms; unlike previous supplements which have reduced prices for a limited period, the merchandise will be sold cheaply until stocks are cleared.

Pricing policy and competition

The practice of discounting from the manufacturer's recommended price has been the major factor in the rapid expansion of Argos. By 1978, for instance, *Retail Business* (June 1979, No. 256, p. 23) estimated that discount houses, principally Argos and Comet, held almost 20 per cent share of the trade in electrical appliances. Although it is not always easy to define a market, and in some product fields Argos may only sell two or three lines, nevertheless in electrical appliances the firm has achieved a relatively high penetration in many products, for example, electric knives 13 per cent; food mixers 13 per cent; deep fat fryers 12 per cent; coffee makers 11 per cent; slow cookers 10 per cent.

The success of Argos and other discount firms naturally provoked a price response from their major competitors, multiple electrical appliance retailers, and this has led to a general lowering of retail margins. In the Price Commission's Report (1976, No. 18, p. 10) the gross margins on electrical appliances in different types of retail outlets were as shown in Table 6–23.

Table 6–23   *Gross margins on domestic electrical appliances, 1975*

	Small appliances (%)	Large appliances (%)
Mail order houses	36.4	32.0
Electricity Boards	28.8	26.9
Multiple electrical retailers	24.4	21.7
Independent electrical retailers		
retail margins	24.0	19.8
wholesale margins	15.0	11.1
Department stores	19.4	14.8
Retail cooperatives	21.1	16.8
Discount houses and catalogue showrooms	18.2	15.4

Source: Price Commission.

As a result of the increase in price competition, *Retail Business* (1979, No. 256, p. 23) estimated that by 1979 the gross margins of multiple electrical retailers had declined to the level of those of department and discount stores. The expansion of sales through Argos and other discount stores has been mainly at the expense of independent electrical retailers whose market share has consequently been eroded.

Discounting from the manufacturer's recommended price has been instrumental in expanding Argos sales of domestic electrical appliances. It has probably proved an even more valuable marketing technique in making consumers aware of the introduction of price competition in product fields where it had previously been very weak or absent (e.g., toys, some sports equipment, watches). The comparison with a recommended price has provided an effective and shorthand way of publicizing price reductions, and stimulating traditional retailers to respond to this competition more quickly than they might otherwise have done.

CASE HISTORY 8

Product: Materials and Storage Handling Equipment

Firm: Lansing Ltd[10]

The market

Fork lift trucks constitute a relatively new and a relatively small industry. It is at the same time an international and fragmented industry. In 1980 sales turnover reached some M£400, which included imports and exports.

The industry dates effectively from the end of the Second World War. The first fork lift trucks were first seen and employed in this country during the last war as part of the Lease–Lend arrangements. After the war a number of British companies and a few American companies set up in business in the United Kingdom. Since that time the number of companies has proliferated, and there are now some 80 companies marketing fork lift trucks of which Lansing is the largest. Many of these companies are foreign—American, Japanese, Italian, German, Polish. Some companies export directly to this country; others manufacture here; while still others use the services of importers. Up to 10 years ago imports constituted some 10 to 15 per cent of United Kingdom sales; this figure now amounts to some 30 per cent, largely due to the influx of Japanese trucks. Conversely, a high proportion of the output manufactured in this country is exported.

Lansing, a private company, is responsible for about 25 per cent share of the United Kingdom market, and exports some 40 per cent of its production. The firm, together with four other major companies, accounts for 50 per cent of the market.

Fork lift trucks are a production tool designed to facilitate efficient and economic handling and storage of materials and products. In order to operate effectively they must be suitable for their purpose. Since they are a key factor in production and distribution they require a reliable and speedy after-sales service.

As a part of the capital equipment market, fork lift trucks have many characteristics common to that market which influence marketing and promotional policy: longevity—fork lift trucks have a life of some 10 to 15 years; high cost—fork lift trucks cost between £5000 and £10 000 each; the decision which types of trucks to purchase and the quantity involves a number of people at different levels of authority in a firm; fork lift trucks are sold direct to buyers because customers have variable needs, and relatively small quantities are sold compared with consumer

---

[10] Lansing Ltd is the marketing division of the Kaye Group of Companies which sell electric powered trucks manufactured by Lansing Bagnall and engine powered trucks manufactured by Lansing Henley. Bonser, whilst part of the Lansing Group, is not advertised as such and markets its trucks through distributors.

goods; and they are purchased on behalf of a company and the decision can thus affect profits.

In addition, the fork lift trucks industry has some specific characteristics. Although like many other types of capital equipment sales are closely related to the general economic climate, because its sales are so widely spread (almost every trade and industry is a potential user of materials handling equipment) a decline in the economy has not hitherto affected this industry as adversely as those which supply a narrow range of firms. As a result, until the very severe recession of 1980 to 1981 the industry had expanded steadily and had been both profitable and highly competitive. In view of the numerous markets which are open to fork lift trucks, advertising and marketing have an important role in supporting the sales force to enable prospective customers to be reached economically. There is also a wide variation in the size of customers; while some may require only two or three trucks, or even one, other customers may be placing orders for 50 to 100, and operating fleets of up to 500 trucks as a group. Furthermore, whereas in the early years of the introduction of fork lift trucks a series of technical advances enabled a manufacturer to gain a substantial product advantage over its rivals, the stage has now been reached in the product's development where improvements tend to be only marginal. Finally, as the first models of fork lift trucks have come to the end of their useful life, there has developed a large business in secondhand trucks.

The firm

The origins of the firm date back to 1920 when a Mr F. E. Bagnall, representing the Lansing Company of Michigan, opened an office in London to distribute mechanical handling equipment. However, when in 1930 the Lansing Company ceased to make trucks and tractors Mr Bagnall secured the right to manufacture their designs in this country. Shortly afterwards the petrol-engined 'Imp' touring tractor was developed and became very successful, particularly on the railways.

The Lansing–Bagnall Company was acquired in 1943 by Emmanuel Kaye (the present Chairman and Governing Director) and the late John Sharp, who were convinced that although the company's sales at that time were declining there would nevertheless be a promising future for the company and its products after the war. During the following years the new company concentrated increasingly on the development of prototypes for postwar production. These included a new industrial towing truck introduced in 1945 to supersede the 'Imp', and which remained in continuous production for 20 years. During 1946 export markets were opened up and overseas agents appointed. In 1949, by which time expansion had caused the company to move to a much larger site at Basingstoke, production started on the first powered pallet truck to be designed and built in Britain. This included a patented regenerative braking system which became an important selling feature of the truck in the future. Soon afterwards fork trucks were introduced for the first time which enabled unit loads to be stacked on pallets. Subsequent expansion of productive capacity took place due to increased business, and the desire of the firm to become more self-sufficient by manufacturing truck components.

The continual process of technical improvement and innovation led to the introduction of two new models: in 1951, the pedestrian controlled fork lift truck, capable
of working in extremely confined space due to its compactness, and in 1954 the
stand-on reach truck, designed to stack 1016 × 1016 mm pallets in an aisle only
1829 mm wide, which was the forerunner of the present range of such trucks. Some
time later, in 1958, a rider controlled fork truck with tilting mast appeared, to
augment the first pedestrian fork lift trucks, and a two-ton reach truck with a
sideways-sitting driving position.

Product developments

Three product developments have provided the foundation of the firm's growth.
First, in the 1960s Lansing–Bagnall made the decision to stop production of
engine-powered trucks which had hitherto been the most prevalent truck in
the market, and decided instead to concentrate on manufacturing battery-
electric powered trucks which are cheaper to run, cleaner and quieter. Whereas
engine-powered trucks had formerly dominated the market compared with electric-
powered trucks in the ratio of 70:30, that ratio has changed to 40:60. Lansing–
Bagnall are now the largest manufacturers of electric lift trucks in Europe.

Second, Lansing introduced a range of trucks that saved space; for example, the
current truck was designed to meet demands for intensive storage facilities in the
narrowest possible aisles. As a result of application experience and design
modifications this truck can achieve lift heights up to 12 m, and then rotate its load
through 180 degrees. It later received the Queen's Award for Technological
Innovation and a Design Council Award.

Third, Lansing has introduced a number of specialist trucks such as the reach
truck, and is responsible for supplying 80 per cent of this market in the United
Kingdom.

Throughout its existence Lansing has undertaken a large and intensive programme of research and development, although by the nature of the product and
the advanced stage reached in its development most changes tend to be minor
improvements, as has already been pointed out. Nevertheless, the incorporation of
electronic devices and the application of electronic-magnetic techniques, which
provide a smoother and progressive speed control while eliminating power
wastage, have contributed to better performance.

From its inception, Lansing's product policy has been to provide a wide range of
trucks which, together with their design variations and optional attachments, will
meet most industrial needs. (Trucks can also be manufactured to specific orders.)
As part of this policy to provide a comprehensive range of trucks, the firm's own
range was supplemented in 1976 by the acquisition of what is now called the
Lansing–Henley range of engine powered trucks which is giving the Lansing
Group entrée into the engine powered market with trucks covering all capacities
from one to 40 tonnes. Then in 1978 Bonser Engineering, which has a range of
products complementary to those of Lansing–Bagnall and Lansing–Henley—
principally industrial and rough terrain fork lift trucks—was acquired. (The
decision to purchase Bonser Engineering followed the recommendation of the
NEDO Industrial Trucks Sector Working Party which had expressed concern about

the fragmentation of the United Kingdom Industrial truck industry, particularly in view of the increasing competition from foreign importers.)

Since its formation the company has also actively promoted sales in overseas markets. At present 40 per cent of the company's production is exported. Between 1969 and 1972 Lansing received four awards for export achievement, and received this award again in 1980 for its export performance between 1976 and 1978. Lansing–Henley has also won three Queen's Awards for exports. The establishment of a world-wide distribution system has been an important factor in sustaining and expanding sales abroad. In addition, subsidiary companies are situated in Australia, Canada, France, Holland, Germany and Switzerland.

Sales and promotional policy

The direction and proportions in which Lansing combines sales and promotional activities are determined by the particular characteristics of the product: direct contact with customers essential; the breadth of the market; the difficulty of identifying and contacting decision-makers; that 80 per cent of turnover comes from 20 per cent of customers; that 80 per cent of turnover is repeat business; and that an integral part of a sale is the provision of reliable and prompt after-sales service.

As is customary with industrial products, the sales force comprises the company's chief marketing effort. This consists of about 120 men—a larger number proportionately than their rivals employ—who spend most of their time discussing the particular materials handling problems of existing and potential customers. As part of the policy to ensure that customers obtain the correct fork lift truck for their purpose, Lansing do not supply a truck until it has been demonstrated in action, and until a full discussion and perhaps an application investigation have determined the most appropriate method of dealing with the specific materials handling problem. In addition Lansing offer a rental service which enables a trial to be undertaken before a large investment is incurred.

Once a sale has been made the firm has a team of more than 600 service engineers sited in 15 service depots throughout the country to provide an after-sales service and spare parts. To enable this service to be undertaken promptly the firm employs more service engineers proportionately than its competitors, which means that they each cover a smaller geographical area. Thus a Lansing service engineer may be covering only half a county rather than four or five counties, so that, by these means, customers have quick and direct access to service engineers, which provides the reassurance that such a service will ensure that their fork lift trucks will be in continuous action throughout their working life.

The basic purpose of the promotional policy of the firm is to back up and reinforce the efforts of the sales force. Promotions consist of a combination of advertising, direct mail, public relations and exhibitions. Perhaps somewhat unusual for an industrial goods firm Lansing has, from its early days, displayed a flair for publicity alongside its product, and research and development abilities.

Furthermore, it has appreciated the value of promotions in reaching potential customers and, as a result, it has always been prepared to spend more pro rata than its competitors on publicity, and still continues to do so. Currently, Lansing spends

1.5 per cent of its turnover on all forms of publicity (i.e., M£1.5). This is divided equally among (1) advertising; (2) print (i.e., leaflets); (3) exhibitions and demonstrations; and (4) films, public relations and direct mail.

This distinguishing feature of Lansing, compared with its competitors, to give more attention to, and place more emphasis on, promotional activities led in its early days to the introduction of publicity methods which were then unusual in industrial goods marketing. For example, in the formative years of the firm, when the concept of fork lift trucks was still novel, advertisements were placed in the national press, a technique more familiar in the field of consumer goods than in industrial products. Again, in its early years the firm was in the vanguard of on-the-spot demonstrations which took place in hired drill halls and on customers' premises as well as on a train which was hired for the purpose. Furthermore, when 20 of the company's fork lift trucks were used in the film 'I'm All Right Jack' it derived a great deal of favourable publicity from this unlikely source; displays of Lansing trucks were arranged in the foyers of leading cinemas throughout the provinces while the film was showing.

Advertising

Advertising does not sell fork lift trucks. It is, however, a valuable method of generating inquiries which it is then the task of the sales force to follow up and try to convert into sales. Furthermore, advertising is an aid in familiarizing the name of the firm to prospective customers so that when they come to consider the purchase of materials handling equipment they will at least be aware of Lansing in this field. This function of advertising is essential to a company with a potential market which encompasses practically every industry and trade, and for whose sales force it would be too time-consuming and costly to visit all prospective customers regularly. Furthermore, since a product such as mechanical handling equipment is purchased infrequently, advertising helps to serve as a reminder of the firm's continuing presence in the market.

Other features of Lansing's advertising themes are also closely related to the characteristics of the product. It is important, for instance, that firms contemplating the large investment entailed in the purchase of fork lift trucks should have confidence in the product and the company supplying it. Advertisements therefore give examples to illustrate the leading position of Lansing in the market; provide details of its nationwide service centres as evidence of a large well-established company which can supply a reliable after-sales service; stress the many years the firm has been in existence and hence its accumulated experience and expertise in dealing with a wide variety of mechanical handling problems under diverse conditions; and provide data showing the firm's proven ability to compete over many years in 79 foreign markets, often against indigenous and thriving truck industries.

However, whilst deploying advertising to build up the confidence of potential customers in Lansing on account of its age, size, expertise and experience, advertising is also employed to try to reassure the small prospective customer that

Lansing welcomes and is sufficiently flexible to deal with small orders at its local depots which are organized to deal with local requirements.

Finally, but by no means least, advertising is employed as the most effective method of reaching the various levels of decision-making for fork lift trucks.

Initially, advertising and publicity concentrated on educating potential customers about the functions and attributes of trucks rather than selling to them because the product was not familiar to many firms. Over the years as the product has become an accepted production tool the emphasis of the advertising copy has shifted towards selling, although the educational theme is still continued to a lesser degree because new firms are always setting up in industry.

However, unlike their competitors Lansing seldom use advertising to try to sell a fork lift truck per se. Advertising is regarded as a means of informing possible customers that the firm can help to solve their materials handling problems. There are occasions when an advertisement does deal more specifically with the sale of the product; this is usually when a new truck is being introduced or when the firm is attempting to boost sales of a particular range. Nevertheless, in these instances the emphasis is still on the benefits which can accrue from the purchase of a fork lift truck, rather than on extolling the virtues of a piece of machinery.

During the current recession Lansing has used advertising to tell existing and prospective customers that it appreciates that the ability to pinpoint and overcome any materials handling weaknesses within a firm has become even more crucial than in the past, and that on account of its size, range and experience Lansing is in a good position to assist them.

Media selected for advertising are those which will provide the largest coverage of the target audience at the least cost. Four departments are primarily concerned with the purchase of fork lift trucks: materials handling, storage, production, and purchasing. In order to reach these decision-makers effectively research is carried out into advertising and promotion. (This is part of a comprehensive market research investigation commissioned by the firm at some three yearly intervals to check on its position in the market, to test advertising campaigns and strategies, and to determine where its advertising is being noted.)

Promotion research investigates the readership habits of the main decision-makers. From the results of this research, and those of independent Businessmen's Readership Surveys, a small list of journals is selected which provide a cost effective coverage of the target audience from a quantitative and qualitative viewpoint.

As a consequence of this promotion research the firm has tended to move away from advertising in the national quality press (apart from an occasional front page advertisement in the *Financial Times*) and the specialized trade press, and instead to advertise in the horizontal trade press in such journals as *The Engineer*; *Management Today*; *Works Management*; *Freight Management* and *Industrial Equipment News* which are read by potential decision-makers in many different trades and industries. Ninety per cent of the advertising budget is now spent in such journals. The remainder of the advertising expenditure is used to reach potential customers in very specialized fields such as freight handling, and in these instances advertisements are placed in the specialized trade press.

Advertising for the firm's overseas subsidiaries and for exports is not carried out from the United Kingdom because a corporate advertising policy would not be sufficiently flexible to take into account the variations in the needs and requirements of different markets. As a result, advertising in overseas markets is handled either by the firm's subsidiary companies or by its agents. However, manuals are supplied from the United Kingdom, and the firm publishes a quarterly journal, *Handling and Storage*, which has a circulation of over 100 000, 60 000 of which are sent overseas.

Direct mail

Advertising informs existing and prospective customers of Lansing's marketing policy, and reaches all decision-makers through selected media. In this way advertising helps to create a favourable climate for the firm's direct mail efforts. Direct mail has the same objective as advertising, namely, to prepare the ground for the sales force by keeping customers aware of the company, and by raising inquiries from specialized sales shots. It is, however, a more selective weapon than advertising because it can be directed at specific individuals, firms and industries. By means of letters and brochures, as well as invitations to demonstrations, prospective firms can be provided with far more detailed information about the firm's products than is possible in the relatively small space of an advertisement. Not perhaps surprisingly, more inquiries are achieved as a result of the selectivity of direct mail compared with the general coverage of the whole market by advertising. Direct mail is therefore very economical in reaching a specific market, where 0.5 to 1 per cent response to a mailing is considered satisfactory.

The compilation of the mailing list, and the extent to which it is kept up to date, determine to a large degree the response to direct mail campaigns. The success of direct mail is therefore very dependent on encouraging the sales force continuously to report changes in the names and addresses on the mailing list.

An integral part of direct mail promotion is the distribution of the company's quarterly publication *Handling and Storage*, referred to earlier. This is posted directly to existing and prospective customers. It includes case studies describing applications of Lansing's trucks in particular markets, and general information on the firm's activities and achievements, in order to reassure customers that it is keeping up with the latest developments. Responses from readers to its Reader Inquiry Service are monitored to ensure that the contents are relevant to reader requirements.

Exhibitions and demonstrations

Exhibitions and demonstrations form a further contribution to the firm's promotional policy. Again their basic purpose is to support the sales force in its task of obtaining orders. Both provide an economical method of reaching specific industries (e.g., agricultural, print). Stands are taken at general trade shows in many different industries and trades to provide the opportunity of meeting and discussing the firm's fork lift truck range with prospective customers on a personal basis. In addition, special demonstrations are organized, to which a specific audience is invited to a site which is convenient for them. At these demonstrations films are shown which explain the benefits of materials handling equipment and this obviates the need to shift trucks around the country.

CASE HISTORY 9

Product: *Accounting and Finance* by Alan Pizzey

Firm: Holt-Saunders (Holt, Rinehart and Winston)

The market

The market for books on accountancy is large, expanding and very competitive. The number of students taking accountancy courses has continued to grow because of the good career prospects available to those with accountancy qualifications. Besides students studying the subject at universities, polytechnics and colleges of further education who number more than 70 000 at any one time, a large number of students from overseas (Hong Kong, Malaysia, Nigeria, Caribbean) is also studying for British accountancy qualifications and these students therefore constitute part of the market for accountancy textbooks.

The establishment and validation of accountancy courses are closely associated with both academic and professional bodies. In recent years two trends have become discernible in such courses. First, a technician qualification (Institute of Accountancy Staff—IAS) has been introduced for students who do not progress beyond foundation level. This has necessitated a broadening of the introductory accountancy course to incorporate the range of tasks expected of a technician in both private accounting practice and commercial or service firms. Second, in recognition of the growing importance of the role of the accountant in business, management accountancy syllabuses have been broadened on degree courses as well as on those of the Business Educational Council (BEC) to provide a multidisciplinary approach to business studies. Hence on these courses accountancy forms part of a comprehensive study of the business environment, and includes economics, law, organizational behaviour, and quantitative methods.

This shift in the emphasis in the syllabus of accountancy courses had stimulated the demand for a new kind of textbook which, while not neglecting the study of basic techniques and underlying concepts of accountancy, would place the subject in the wider context of the business world by including the related disciplines of law, economics and business organization and thus reflect the more versatile and comprehensive role of the accountant.

Holt-Saunders specialize in books on medicine, biological science, education, and economics, marketing and management—all aimed at students in higher education. Their catalogue lists several books on finance and accountancy which are well known for their rigour and excellence. However, until recently virtually all these books were imported from Holt-Saunders' American company. As a consequence, despite their high reputation, most of them were not entirely relevant to the needs of British students. Holt-Saunders were aware that a gap existed in the market for an accountancy textbook that would meet the needs of the changed syllabuses of accountancy courses, and this led them in 1978 to approach Alan Pizzey to be part of the team to adapt an American book on Management Finance for the British market. In the discussions which ensued it emerged that Alan Pizzey had himself almost completed a textbook written specifically for introductory and foundation accountancy courses. His main reason for writing the book was that his experience as a practising lecturer in accountancy had made him aware that the available textbooks for introductory courses were not wholly satisfactory. The main aim of his manuscript, therefore, had been to prepare students for the foundation stage of their studies in both methodology and concepts by a balanced 'mix' of theory and practice. (Once the student has passed this stage he chooses which professional body to join.) Furthermore, he wished to demonstrate that accounting does not operate in a vacuum but is interfaced with such disciplines as economics, law and business systems. Another aim of the book was to provide plenty of examples and 'Question and Answer' practice for students overseas who might be out of touch with a teacher. Finally, the book had been written to meet the requirements of the six accountancy bodies.

Several features characterize the market for accountancy textbooks in higher education. First, recommendation of a book by lecturers to their students is the chief factor which determines sales turnover. Second, copies of textbooks must be readily available in bookshops in or near institutions of higher education once a book has been recommended by a lecturer—this is particularly important in overseas markets. Third, books do not appear to rate very highly in the list of spending priorities of students; there is in any event the alternative of either borrowing from a library or buying books, at much reduced prices, which are no longer required by their predecessors. As a result of this high elasticity of demand the price must be kept as low as possible, consistent with achieving an adequate return on sales. This is usually attained by publishing in soft, rather than hard, covers which also helps to make the book more competitive. Fourth, the overseas demand for such textbooks is an appreciable proportion of the total. Finally, sales are dependent to a large extent on a book's being selected for the reading list of a professional examination syllabus.

Since the basic requisite of the successful sales of a textbook is that it must meet the needs and preferences of the lecturers who will use it, when Alan Pizzey's manuscript was received specimen chapters were sent to two well-known accountancy lecturers to obtain their initial reaction to it. This proved favourable, and a contract was subsequently drawn up with the author.

Market research

In order to gain the maximum benefit from this potentially large market, the publisher proceeded to carry out an intensive market survey to determine the views of accountancy lecturers on (1) the contents of an ideal introductory and foundation textbook; (2) the suitability of the existing textbooks which they used; and, finally, to gain an estimation of the number of students on different types of courses, and hence their distribution among different courses.

The survey was carried out by means of a questionnaire (devised in conjunction with the author), and sent out with an accompanying letter which explained that the purpose of the questionnaire was to make certain that the publisher's proposed new introductory book would fulfil the requirements of potential users. The questionnaire and letter were sent to 500 lecturers on introductory accounting courses at degree or diploma level, and those teaching students on professional courses for the ACA and Institute of Accounting Staff examinations, BEC National and Higher National Level and similar courses. It was estimated that this list comprised almost the total number of lecturers on such courses. The high response rate of 24 per cent of questionnaires returned completed was in part a reflection of the eagerness of a large proportion of lecturers to see their opinions incorporated in a textbook for their course; in part a reflection of the degree of dissatisfaction with existing textbooks; and in part a reflection of the publishers' offer to send a complimentary copy of the book on publication to those who completed the questionnaire!

An analysis of the questionnaires confirmed some well-established views on accountancy textbooks, and provided useful background data for the marketing of the proposed book: many existing textbooks were considered to be too theoretical; others were criticized for the provision of too much numerical work. There was dislike of American terms in accountancy textbooks from the United States. There was a request for 'more analytical rigour' in textbooks used for degree accountancy courses. Books that attempted to be comprehensive often only succeeded, it was claimed, in being superficial. The questionnaires also revealed that two major British accountancy textbooks were widely recommended, and their strengths and weaknesses were analysed. It appeared that the potential market for a first-year introductory textbook was approximately 10 000 copies annually.

The final stage in the investigation to ascertain the most appropriate contents for an introductory accountancy textbook was a further approach to the two reviewers who had originally read specimen chapters of the manuscript, requesting them to provide a very detailed review of it. Once these had been received the author added some of their comments to the alterations and modifications which he had been continuously making to the manuscript ever since its completion as part of an on-going task to incorporate the market research findings and his own changing thoughts into the book which is essentially a live and developing process. For instance, four of the original chapters were omitted, the sequence of others were rearranged, and additions were made to parts of other chapters.

Towards the end of 1979, almost a year after the manuscript had been received, it was ready to be transmitted into production. Publication date was arranged for May 1980. Several factors influenced the decision to price the paperback edition at

£3.95: the cost of production; the anticipated volume of sales which could continue over a number of years; the degree of elasticity of demand; and the prices of competing books.

Distribution

As with the other books on their list, the publisher's main selling effort for *Accounting and Finance* was concentrated through the specialist academic bookshops which stock books for students in higher education. Holt-Saunders' sales representatives called on these booksellers to encourage them to place orders for the book in advance of publication, and especially when it became known that a lecturer had recommended the book and had informed his local bookseller that he required copies to be made available for students to purchase.

While the sales force is considered the major influence in stimulating sales through close coordination of promotions, lecturers' recommendations, bookseller ordering and student purchases, nevertheless the level of sales depends also on the publisher's ability to supply promptly. In the United Kingdom and Northern Europe, which provide 70 per cent of the College book turnover of this publisher, books are sent direct from the publisher's warehouse. By means of strict managerial controls and systems, and the allocation of adequate financial resources to this task, orders received in the morning are invoiced by lunchtime; 70 per cent of these orders are dispatched by the same afternoon, and the remainder by the following morning. The publisher also liaises very closely with its contracted carriers who deliver in the United Kingdom. The effectiveness of this operation may perhaps be gauged by the firm's high position (sixth and fourth respectively) over the last three years in the Booksellers' Association's Publishers Delivery League Table where in each year they were the highest placed academic publisher. This reputation for speedy delivery gives booksellers confidence to order, and also sometimes influences the recommendations of academic staff. In addition, availability may be the key factor in conjunction with price, etc., in making a sale to the consumer—in this instance the student who tends on the whole to be passive and reacts only when a lecturer has put pressure on him to consider the purchase of a book.

Promotional policy

The final task facing the publisher was to analyse how the potential market for a textbook which could be used in all types of higher education could best be reached. This led to an investigation of the most efficient promotional channels for this first-year textbook. In the meantime, the publisher's sales representatives were asked on their regular visits to colleges to discuss this forthcoming publication with accountancy staff, and feed back their reactions to it to the firm. In addition, the book appeared in Holt-Saunders' catalogues from January 1980.

It became clear from the investigation of promotional channels that the marketing strategy necessary to optimize sales would involve a multi-pronged attack on the market which should include: dissemination of complimentary copies to the major lecturers in this discipline; the offer of inspection copies of the book on 30-day approval (approximately 20 per cent of lecturers would have obtained a copy in this manner); sending the book for review to the journals of professional bodies and to other important journals such as *Accountancy*, *Times Higher Education Supplement*, and the Journal of the National Association of Teachers in Further and Higher Education, and to professional bodies for possible adoption on reading lists; advertising in relevant accounting, educational and bookseller journals; sending review copies to and advertising in student accounting publications; informing the American, Australian and Canadian associate companies of Holt-Saunders of the forthcoming publication of the book and encouraging them to order copies; and displaying the book at major and a few small exhibitions.

As had been previously arranged, complimentary copies of the book were sent automatically to the reviewers of the manuscript, and the respondents of the market research questionnaire.

The main emphasis in the promotional campaign was to reach accountancy lecturers and offer them copies to study. This was achieved in two ways. The publisher's sales representatives undertook extensive sampling of the book, particularly in Polytechnics. Secondly, a large-scale direct mail campaign was directed at accountancy lecturers who had been previously contacted in the original market survey, the accounting departments in colleges of the old Commonwealth and other overseas countries, and professional accounting bodies. All these potential users of the book received a leaflet describing its contents, a sales letter from the author, and a response card. In addition, organizations such as the British Council and the Technical Education and Training Organisation for Overseas Countries also received details of the book.

This mailing took place during April and May 1980, immediately before publication. Advertisements also started appearing in professional and management journals from March onwards to reinforce the direct-mail campaign and act as a reminder of the publication of the book, particularly to lecturers who had been informed about a proposed textbook a year earlier. The textbook was also advertised in the Spring and Autumn Export Numbers of the *Bookseller*.

A further impetus to sales was given to the book when it was displayed on the publisher's stand in April 1980 at the London Academic Bookfair, and in October 1980 at the Frankfurt Book Fair, as well as at a number of smaller exhibitions attended by academic staff and booksellers. On these occasions the publisher has the opportunity to discuss the book informally with potential users. In the summer of 1980, too, the leaflet and response card were also distributed at a conference of the Association of University Teachers in Accountancy held at Loughborough University.

The Certified Accountants Students Newsletter is an influential publication. Alan Pizzey was already known to its readers through articles which had appeared in the Newsletter, and from the publisher's advertisements which had been inserted in it. In the November 1980 issue of the Newsletter *Accounting and Finance* was listed on the recommended reading list for foundation accounting and for advanced accounting practice for the examinations syllabuses of ACA. This recommendation was regarded by the publishers as an important contribution towards the acceptance of the book by lecturers and students.

Between May and October 1980, sales amounted to 2500 copies. It is estimated that by October 1981 total sales will be in excess of 7000, by which time the book will have become a viable proposition.

The outstanding problem which still remains is the penetration of the overseas market from the United Kingdom. In many countries (e.g., Italy, Greece, Middle East and Africa), the publisher has a number of exclusive and non-exclusive agencies through whom local booksellers can place orders, although they also deal to a large extent with direct accounts. In these areas the availability of a book locally may well be as important a factor in generating sales as recommendation from a lecturer: viz. if book 'A' is recommended but book 'B' is available then book 'B' is often purchased. Availability and recommendation are thus equally important in overseas markets, and the publisher is trying to ensure that both these requirements are being met in the case of *Accounting and Finance*. Booksellers have been contacted in the relevant overseas countries, and 1000 copies were sold abroad in the first year of publication. Once the book is fully established, it is anticipated that 20 per cent of sales will eventually consist of exports. Distribution overseas is, however, more complex than in the home market, and it takes time for information from the various accountancy bodies and publications to percolate through to export markets.

Promotional expenditure on the book has amounted to an estimated £1000, the major portion of which was spent on complimentary copies. These amount to £500, and leaflets and postage to £300. Advertising space cost £200, and was employed chiefly to supplement the direct mail campaign and advise booksellers of the appearance of the book. Since exhibition stands and sales representatives represent a fixed overhead cost for the publishers a share of their operating costs was not attributed to the accountancy textbook.

Part 3

A comparison of advertising and competition in theory, practice and public policy

7 Market factors affecting advertising and competition

In Part 1 the literature in economic theory concerned with advertising and competition (theory of value, concept of consumer sovereignty, theory of the firm, and the theories and empirical studies on the effects of advertising and competition) was outlined and discussed, together with the literature of critics of the theory of the firm.

The major findings of conventional theory on advertising and competition are compared in this final section with examples from the case histories (CH) of the operation of advertising and competition in the market place, and the findings of the empirical research outlined in Part 2. In addition, examples are included from the publications of official bodies, notably the Monopolies and Mergers Commission (MMC), Price Commission (PC), National Consumer Council (NCC), and Office of Fair Trading (OFT) to illustrate the attitude of public policy towards advertising and competition.

The following aspects of advertising and competition will be considered:

1. *The effect of advertising in practice on*
   (a) barriers to entry and prices;
   (b) product differentiation and brand loyalty;
   (c) retailers' brands and competition;
   (d) information.
2. *Competition under oligopoly*
   (a) oligopoly and prices;
   (b) non-price competition and oligopoly.

It is not suggested that the case histories in Part 2 represent a balanced cross-section of products and services. Nevertheless, they do include examples of the main forms of competition prevalent in industry, ranging from a statutory monopoly (British Rail) and a duopoly (Persil Automatic) to oligopoly (Macleans Toothpaste, Batchelors Quick Custard) and monopolistic competition (Mr. Kipling Cakes, Argos Distributors, Holt-Saunders' accountancy textbook).

The case histories also include a range of product areas in which advertising varies in significance. Some case histories, for instance, consist of widely distributed convenience goods which consumers purchase at frequent intervals (e.g., once a fortnight) and where, as a consequence, advertising,[1] branding and product differentiation predominate. (Included in this category is a case history of a product, typical of many others, which after being carefully researched and rigorously tested at every stage of its development, failed to get established in the market place.) Another case history describes the marketing of an industrial product where advertising has a subsidiary role in promotional policy compared with the sales force, direct mail and exhibitions; although advertising is utilized as an effective and economical method of contacting the firm's customers who are spread throughout a wide variety of trades and industries. In the quite different product area of higher education publishing the case history of an academic textbook illustrates the relative importance of word-of-mouth recommendation, sampling, the sales force, and exhibitions, compared with expenditure on advertising. Finally, in the field of arranged holidays by rail, the case history reveals the reliance placed by potential holidaymakers on the recommendation of satisfied customers and the advice of travel agents compared with advertising.

Furthermore, despite their limited number the case histories provide examples of the major factors and conditions in the market which affect competition, the type of advertising and other promotional expenditure employed by firms, and the different forms of competition other than price which help firms to compete.

That it is the characteristics of a product, for instance, which determine the proportions in which different sales promotions are combined is demonstrated in several case histories—short shelf life (Mr. Kipling Cakes); joint demand (Persil Automatic); spare capacity (Golden Rail); low cost limited service (Argos Catalogue Discount Showrooms); long-life, multidecision purchasing (Lansing material handling equipment); course recommendation (accountancy textbook).

Some of the case histories show the major influence of the structure of retailing (intense competitive pressures from large-scale retailers as buyers and as suppliers of distributors' own brands) on pricing and product policies, types of promotion, and that it may be a significant factor which has to be taken into account when a firm is considering entry into a new product market. There are also case histories which demonstrate that it may be a firm's distribution organization which is at least as important as—if not more important than—sales promotion expenditure in determining its competitive position in the market.

Other case histories (Persil Automatic, Batchelors Quick Custard) illustrate the varying demand for products according to the changing habits, tastes and life-styles of consumers. Another case history indicates how the changing role in management of a profession may alter the academic requirements of students. These changes in the competitive environment then provide the opportunity for the entry of new products and/or firms into established markets.

That the pricing and promotion policies of firms can be profoundly influenced by

---

[1] Packaged food, drink, household goods, toiletries and cosmetics comprised approximately half of manufacturers' consumer advertising in the 1970s.

changing market conditions such as the shift in the balance of power between manufacturers and retailers is evident in some case histories. It is also apparent in some that it is the threat of potential entry by other firms which may be the deciding factor in determining the timing of the launch of a new product, even where uncertainty surrounds its potential size and future rate of development.

There are examples among the case histories of the specific functions performed by various types of non-price competition (free offers, competitions, samples) which may be employed to enable firms to compete more effectively (Macleans Toothpaste, Persil Automatic), and to get a product established more quickly than would otherwise be possible (*Accounting and Finance* by Alan Pizzey).

Several case histories reveal the difficulty of attempting to delineate a market precisely (Mr. Kipling Cakes, Batchelors Instant Custard) which effectively widens the area of competition and thereby the number of competing firms.

Finally, the significance of rival innovations—which stem from a combination of technical developments and the changed social and economic requirements of consumers—as a means of stimulating competition between firms is also demonstrated in several case histories.

8 The effect of advertising in practice

BARRIERS TO ENTRY AND PRICES

Conventional economic theory maintains that advertising is at least as important as technology as a barrier to market entry. Advertising is then considered as an additional and unnecessary factor in deterring entry, reinforcing concentration, and enabling firms to set high prices and reap high rewards without fear of the competitive effects. (Part 1, Bain, Cave.) Advertising may therefore curtail competition by putting up the cost of entry, and limit price competition by making demand curves more inelastic and lowering cross-elasticities of demand as a result.

Macleans Toothpaste (CH 1) is a leading brand in a typical oligopolistic industry. Four manufacturers in 1978 were responsible for 88 per cent of turnover. Whereas in 1941 three manufacturers were responsible for 43 per cent of the market, by 1973 their share had risen to 88 per cent. For more than 30 years no new firm entered this market on a large scale. Advertising expenditure is high: 12 per cent of sales, although this proportion has declined from 18 per cent over five years, from 1973 to 1977.

As toothpaste is technically easy to manufacture, complex technology is unimportant as a barrier to entry. How far has advertising been effective in deterring newcomers, and in contributing towards increased concentration? Several characteristics of the toothpaste market impinge on this question.

Although the market may give the outward appearance of having remained stable and static over several decades, many changes have occurred within it. In particular, the share of the market held by each of the three major firms has altered radically and many new brands have been introduced, some of which have been short-lived (CH 1, Table 6–1). High and consistent advertising expenditure has apparently been ineffective in securing either stable brand or market shares, and in persuading British consumers until comparatively recently to brush their teeth with toothpaste to the same extent as consumers in other countries. Furthermore, although only one major competitor, Procter & Gamble, has entered the mass toothpaste market, firms (large and small) have experienced little difficulty in entering the specialized sectors of this market, and existing successfully and profitably alongside the three or four giants.

An important characteristic of this market has been the active and continuous commitment to research and development shown by the major firms. This has resulted in the incorporation of small improvements to existing products, and/or marketing of new brands. As a consequence of the high expenditure on research and development (R & D), and intensive advertising to publicize product improvements, little scope has existed for a potential competitor to find a niche in this market.

The determined search by existing toothpaste firms for continual improvements and variants to their brands, however minor, has been one factor in deterring newcomers. Another factor has been the knowledge that unless a would-be entrant could introduce a major innovation that could not be easily copied, it would be difficult to get a new brand established before it was quickly imitated by competitors. This was the experience of Procter & Gamble. When this firm introduced Crest fluoride toothpaste in 1975 it had two advantages over its rivals. First, the introduction of the brand coincided with a general awareness by the public of the beneficial effects of fluoride in preventing tooth decay, whereas in the 1960s when established firms introduced a similar toothpaste demand was so small that the brands were subsequently withdrawn. Second, the brand had received the endorsement of the dental profession, and this proved an important factor in commending it to consumers.

However, both these advantages eroded rapidly as competitors responded to the new competition with the introduction of their own brands of fluoride toothpaste which were also endorsed by the dental profession. This retaliation was accompanied by heavy advertising, price cutting and trade deals. This competitive reaction was particularly strong because the brand leader feared a repetition of American experience where Procter & Gamble had overtaken it as brand leader. Although, therefore, the share of the market held by Crest had reached 9 to 10 per cent by 1979, this had been achieved only at a high cost because of the immediate response of its competitors.

Three major reasons would seem to account for the high level of concentration in the toothpaste market. First, the R & D programmes of the established manufacturers have enabled them to introduce new brands, as well as continual improvements and variants to established brands, and this has forestalled the entry of competitors. Second, to date there has been the absence of a major innovation which could not be imitated easily. Third, in a market which is now fairly static, potential newcomers are aware that they will need to attract a share of trade away from established firms, and that market share will not be relinquished readily.

Similarly, the level of advertising expenditure on toothpaste is attributable to several factors. First, there has been the need to make product improvements and variations known to consumers as they were introduced. Second, because consumers have some 25 opportunities annually to choose toothpaste, and the unit price is low, they have frequent opportunities to switch brands, and therefore frequent reminders of the reputation of the brand are necessary. Third, toothpaste is a low-interest product; this characteristic means that a minimum threshold of advertising expenditure on television is necessary to maintain the position of a mass market brand (see for example the experience of Aquafresh where newspaper advertising proved ineffective). Moreover, advertising has been deployed to maximize sales in order to sustain economies of scale. Finally, the market is dominated by oligopolistic competition between a small number of firms, none of which has been prepared to risk losing sales of one of its major products that might be recovered only by a larger promotional expenditure.

Although no one toothpaste firm has been prepared alone to reduce advertising expenditure as a percentage of turnover, such a reduction has occurred through changing market conditions, that is, sales through supermarkets have replaced, to a large extent, sales through the traditional channel of distribution, the chemist. This change in the pattern of distribution, the growing concentration of food retailing among a few large-scale firms, and the intense competition between food retailers has led them to exert pressure for improved terms and trade discounts which has resulted in lower prices. Toothpaste manufacturers have also competed for special retail displays and participation in retailer promotions by the widespread use of temporary price reductions and price marked packs which again has led to lower prices. As a result, reduced expenditure on advertising has been transferred increasingly to expenditure on temporary price reductions, trade discounts, and other promotions in the total promotional budget.

In 1978 the Price Commission (PC) Report on Toothpaste (HC 125) was prepared, albeit reluctantly, to accept the high level of toothpaste advertising for several reasons: it had not deterred the entry of Procter & Gamble in 1975; the dental profession had commended the 'therapeutic' copy which had become widespread in toothpaste advertising as being more likely to persuade consumers to brush their teeth than informative booklets on dental care issued by the dental profession or health councils; as a consequence of the changing structure of retailing, advertising expenditure as a percentage of turnover had steadily declined during the 1970s and had been supplanted at least by intermittent price competition; toothpaste prices had risen less quickly than the general rate of inflation between 1974 and 1978.

If, however, the PC had been considering the toothpaste market before the advent of these changed market conditions it may perhaps have condemned advertising as a barrier to entry and the cause of high prices in the toothpaste market, as it had in its Reports on sanitary protection products. In HC 436 (1978) the Commission concluded:

'Consumers in the sanitary protection market are particularly vulnerable to a lack of real competition. They have no choice but to buy the products. They purchase mainly for reasons other than price and the prices paid reflect high costs of advertising and promotions . . . the main effects (of advertising) in this type of market are to apportion the static overall market between existing manufacturers and to limit competition by establishing very high levels of expenditure as necessary to effect entry.' [para 5.10]

However, the Commission seemed to have overlooked certain market factors and characteristics of the product which had affected competition in this market. The description of the market as 'static overall', for instance, did not accurately describe the fact that retail sales had increased by 18 per cent between 1970 and 1978 due, among other factors, to population increases in the relevant age group, and higher standards of hygiene. Furthermore, and resembling the situation in the toothpaste market, high levels of advertising had not been able to inhibit active competition between the established firms which had led to changes in market shares and the introduction of new products. More than one-third of the product by type had changed between 1970 and 1978, and half the products had not existed a few years earlier.

Notwithstanding the high level of advertising expenditure the Commission had itself acknowledged that a new competitor

'. . . has entered the market in recent years, another manufacturer has made an unsuccessful attempt to re-enter. A further manufacturer is currently test marketing.' [para 2.11]

This was followed a few months later by the entry of a newcomer into the market with a new product which had not been test marketed but which was being advertised extensively.

In its earlier Report (No. 9, 1975, and Supplementary Report, No. 26, 1977), the PC had attributed the manufacturers' practice of recommending retail prices (RRPs) as the cause of 'higher prices being charged . . . in some shops than is necessary or desirable', and thereby inhibiting price competition among retailers. The Commission recommended that RRPs should either be abandoned on these products or alternatively reduced by 10 per cent. There was little analysis or data in the Report to suggest how the Commission had reached this conclusion, apart from their agreement with the view of one manufacturer who had abandoned RRPs: '. . . the practice of recommending retail prices tends to put up shelf prices'. The Commission added: 'We share this view'. (34. 14).

Evidence in the Report revealed that price competition was relatively new on sanitary protection products: the gross margins of multiple firms had declined between 1972 and 1975. At the time of the Report the reason for the widespread adherence of most retailers to RRPs was that these products were still being sold predominantly through their traditional distribution outlet, the chemist. Supermarkets, who were primarily responsible for the limited price competition, stocked only a narrow range of fast-selling lines, and price reductions were confined to these lines.

Although the Commission concluded that its original recommendations regarding RRPs had contributed to this more competitive situation, it recognized that other market forces had been operating at the same time. As long as sanitary protection products were packed in brown paper and supplied from under the counter on request, supermarkets and other open display retailers had shown little interest in stocking them. With the change in social attitudes which occurred during the 1970s it had become possible for the first time for such products to be promoted aggressively on open display in brightly-coloured packs, and this factor had led to the increasing willingness of supermarkets to stock sanitary protection products. This transfer in the pattern of distribution towards retail outlets engaged in intense price competition had been the major contribution to the lowering of retail prices. Unfortunately, at the time when 'double pricing' (where the actual retail price is shown next to a higher reference price usually suggested or recommended by the manufacturer) would have been a valuable means of alerting consumers to the introduction of price competition in this product field, as has been the experience with other types of merchandise (see CH 7), the Commission had recommended the abolition or reduction in value of RRPs.

Furthermore, the Commission's stricture, that '. . . prices paid reflect high costs of advertising and promotions' (HC 436, para 5.10), seems to have failed to take into account that lack of retailer competition (a consequence of the characteristics of this product until comparatively recently) had been a major factor affecting the level of prices.

In several case histories, advertising expenditure by firms well-established in a market has been insignificant compared with other market factors in inhibiting entry, for example, (a) the cost and organization required to achieve economic and widespread distribution (Mr. Kipling Cakes); (b) the difficulty of predicting the speed with which rivals would introduce a similar product, and DOBs would appear before the firm could achieve an adequate return on investment (Batchelors Quick Custard).

Mr. Kipling Cakes. When Manor Bakeries contemplated the introduction of a brand of packaged cakes in the 1960s the cake market was very fragmented and with relatively little expenditure on advertising. The two best-known firms were a manufacturer, J. Lyons, which advertised, and a DOB (Marks & Spencer) with no advertising expenditure; the remaining market share was divided among a number of DOBs, regional brands, and cakes sold by bakers' shops.

The most formidable hurdles to entry were a series of distribution barriers: the high cost of setting up a distribution system for a short-shelf-life product, and operating it economically; the need to market a wide range of lines from the outset as a condition of being accepted by retailers; the knowledge that profits in this market would inevitably be squeezed by the lower prices of DOBs and the buying power of multiple food firms.

The chief product characteristic of packaged cakes—their short shelf life—means that distribution necessitates a carefully controlled and expensive van selling system combined with an efficient stock rotation system. In order to achieve an economic drop it was desirable to sell to multiple retailers who owned the larger stores. The merchandise policy of such retailers was to stock a few brands of cakes only, but to offer a wide range of a particular brand. This requirement prevented the firm from building up a range over a period of time; it was compelled to begin with a minimum of 20 lines. In addition, the limited shelf space allocated to cakes by supermarkets suggested that an early entry into this market was advisable before other competitors became well established. Finally, research had revealed that consumers appeared to show little brand loyalty towards particular brands of cakes.

This indicated that widespread distribution would be essential because availability would determine to a large extent the level of sales.

Batchelors Quick Custard. When Batchelors decided to enter the custard market it was in long-term decline because of changing economic and social conditions, for example, a growing percentage of working housewives, wider choice of sweets, change in taste towards lighter sweets.

The introduction of canned custard (by Heinz, Ambrosia, and later Bird's) in the 1960s helped to expand the total market, and indicated that a demand existed for a more convenient form of custard. Quick Custard was more convenient still because it did not require a saucepan, its thickness could be varied, and it was lighter to carry home from the shop. Batchelors possessed two important attributes to enter the market: (1) an efficient handling and distribution organization geared to the grocery trade; (2) in the short run it had a technical advantage in the formulation of Quick Custard, and the company believed that if it could get established first in this market competitors would find it less easy to achieve distribution.

Advertising as a barrier to entry was relatively unimportant because despite the advertising of canned custard, advertising expenditure on custard powder which comprised the major share of the market had virtually ceased as the market for it continued to decline. The two major barriers were the intense competition in food manufacturing and retailing, plus the search for distinctive products by retailers, namely the intense competition in food manufacturing caused by excess capacity and a consequent tendency for marginal costing leads (when products are technically simple to copy) to their speedy introduction by competitors followed by severe price discounting. On the other hand, the increasing homogeneity of supermarkets and the competitive pressures on distributive margins stimulated grocery multiples to seek out DOBs to sell at a lower price than the manufacturer's brand, but at a higher retail margin.

The examples from the case histories reveal that various factors influence a firm's decision to enter a market. These include its financial resources, how far the product is likely to prove profitable, whether the product possesses a distinguishing feature or cost advantage which will appeal to consumers compared with established products, the extent to which the market is expanding, the degree to which the company possesses or can acquire easily the skills and expertise to operate in a market different from its own (Argos Distributors established a new method of retailing by utilizing its existing strengths—expertise in producing catalogues, in acquiring retail property, in buying, and in operating retail establishments which stemmed from its position as the then associated company of the Green Shield Trading Stamp Company).

Finally, an increasingly important factor in influencing the decision to enter a market in recent years has been the ability to gain acceptance by retailers. This is the reason why in several case histories (Batchelors Quick Custard, Mr. Kipling Cakes) firms considered early entry into the market essential before retailers became reluctant to stock additional brands on their limited shelf-space. It also explains why some firms were prepared to curtail test marketing and thereby risk launching their product nationally before sufficient experience had been gained of its performance in a small sector of the market. The wide variety of factors which firms find it necessary to take into account when deciding whether to enter a market would appear to weaken the significance often attributed to advertising expenditure as a barrier to entry in public policy pronouncements, namely:

'. . . a high level of advertising by existing sellers will often create a significant barrier against the entry of newcomers into the market. Consequently, it is possible that high advertising may not only raise unit costs but also contribute to excessive prices and profits.' [Monopolies and Mergers Commission (July 1973) Cmnd 5330, p. 26][1]

'. . . various forms of entry barrier have been uncovered by the Monopolies and Mergers Commission which found that they were against the public interest . . . A high level of expenditure on advertising or other sales promotion will also act to discourage new entrants.' [*Review of Monopolies and Mergers Policy*. (May 1978) Cmnd 7198, 3.44][2]

The high level of expenditure on advertising and promotion 'not only results in wasteful expenditure but also deters potential competitors who might otherwise provide a safeguard against excessive profits'. [Monopolies and Mergers Commission (1966) HC 105, p. 39][3]

Advertising and promotion 'help to create and maintain the kind of market in which it is possible . . . to have substantial freedom to determine . . . prices'. [Monopolies and Mergers Commission (1973) HC 2, p. 88]

In such pronouncements there would appear to be a tendency to overlook other important factors which reduce the extent to which firms can raise prices, for example:

1. In an increasing number of markets firms face competition from the private brands of multiple retailers (e.g., in the case histories, Mr. Kipling Cakes, Persil Automatic, Macleans Toothpaste) which act as a restraining influence on price.
2. In many markets competition is far wider than that emanating from immediate rivals, because of the existence of substitutes or near substitutes. As part of the dessert and sweet market Batchelors Instant Custard (CH 5) is in competition with ice-cream, yoghurts, cheese and biscuits, and fresh fruit, to name only a few items, besides competition from other manufacturers of instant custard, canned custard and custard powder. Similarly, the sales of manufacturers of packaged branded cakes, such as Mr. Kipling, are influenced not only by the competition from one another and other types of cakes (e.g., fresh cream cakes, frozen cakes, bakers' cakes) but by a wide variety of products which can substitute for cakes.
3. In most markets the existing firms are aware that they face potential competi-

---

[1] All subsequent references will be to Cmnd 5330.
[2] All subsequent references will be to Cmnd 7198.
[3] All subsequent references will be to HC 105.

tion from other large firms who possess the capital and management expertise, besides the financial resources for investment and advertising should profits and/or prices become unduly high. There are other potential competitors who possess not only the above requirements to enter a market but also possess the distribution expertise. Thus Procter & Gamble entered the toothpaste market when it felt the market situation was propitious. Batchelors, Brown & Polson and DOBs (i.e., firms with distribution 'know how' and financial resources for capital investment) entered the custard market when new technical developments presented the appropriate opportunity.

Similarly, Golden Rail entered the package holiday market and offered additional competition to the existing rail package holiday operators, and to packaged holidays by coach in this country.

ADVERTISING AS A SOURCE OF PRODUCT DIFFERENTIATION AND BRAND LOYALTY

For many years the view that advertising enables firms to differentiate products and to create brand loyalty, thereby accentuating market imperfections, has been an integral part of the literature on advertising and competition (Part 1—Marshall, Pigou, Chase, Braithwaite, Chamberlin, Robinson, Lewis, Meade, Harbury, and Comanor and Wilson).

A further distinction is made in the literature between informative and persuasive advertising. It is the latter type of advertising, in particular, which is claimed to create product differentiation, build up brand loyalty and reputations, and manipulate demand against the interests of consumers. It is the ability of advertising to differentiate a product and sustain brand loyalty which is then claimed to result in higher prices, monopoly profits and excess capacity.

Despite the constant reiteration of these viewpoints the concepts of product differentiation and brand loyalty remain vague (Part 1—Robinson, p. 13 Comanor and Wilson, p. 13). It is not apparent, for instance, from conventional theory why product differentiation would no longer occur if it became possible in practice to isolate persuasive from informative advertising and rely solely on the latter. It is also difficult to discern whether the critics of product differentiation would propose, say, that only one type of washing powder should be available to consumers, or whether there should be different types of washing powder but only one brand of each. There is the implication, however, that the differences between brands are superfluous, trivial or negligible, and therefore unnecessary.

The identification of product differentiation as a source of market imperfection appears to stem from the model of perfect competition which postulates many sellers of the identical product or service, in identical circumstances, so that every buyer is indifferent between all the sellers and has no reason (other than price advantage) to choose one rather than another. On the other hand, in the marketplace sellers are not identical for reasons of geography, personality, and, above all, the different and varying needs of different buyers. Product differentiation is, therefore, an inherent factor in the market which occurs because consumers are not homogeneous and have varying preferences, requirements and incomes which change over time. As a result it is worthwhile for manufacturers to offer variations in price, size, quality, packaging, convenience, flavours, durability, service, design and comfort to meet the requirements of different groups of consumers. Retailers also cater for the varying needs and preferences of shoppers by competing not only on price, but also on the quality of their merchandise, the width and depth of their ranges, the degree of credit available, the extent of their delivery service, the amount of personal service they provide, their car parking facilities, the thickness of their carpet, and the provision of fitting rooms.

Product differentiation may emanate from changes in technology and/or changes in demand, as examples from the case histories illustrate. Argos Distributors (CH 7) were encouraged to introduce a new form of retailing, for instance, as the result of a technical development (computers), changes in legislation (Resale Prices Act 1964), and the increasing price awareness of consumers. Persil Automatic (CH 4) was developed to meet the needs of consumers who had acquired a new type of washing machine which required a detergent with a formulation different from those currently on the market. Holt-Saunders (CH 9) published an accountancy textbook in order to meet the changed syllabus of accountancy courses brought about by the changing role of accountants in business. Quick Custard (CH 5) was marketed in response to changing styles of living and tastes which had created a demand for more convenient sweets and desserts. Golden Rail (CH 2) was a response by British Rail to the growth in car travel at the expense of the train, and the expansion of the packaged holiday trade, particularly abroad, during the 1950s and 1960s.

To some extent, therefore, product differentiation acts as a competitive device in that established firms develop new products, or variations on existing products, in order to meet changing demand, and to forestall the entry of potential competitors. Conversely, firms outside an industry are constantly looking for the opportunity to occupy segments of a market which have been created by changes in technology or tastes, but which established firms may have overlooked. Product differentiation may thus provide a means of entry into a market which at the same time intensifies competitive pressures on existing firms by providing consumers with additional choice.

Product differentiation also performs other functions. To many consumers an established brand with which they have become familiar offers security, and saves time in selecting and decision-making because its quality and performance are known. (As Robertson, 1958, explained: 'There is real spiritual comfort in buying a pack of cocoa rather than ⌐ shovelful of brown powder of uncertain origin.') The time and cost of retailing and wholesaling may also be reduced by a brand of a known standard and performance and the rate of stockturn increased; when Persil Automatic (CH 4) was originally test marketed under the name Skip, retailers proved reluctant to stock a little-known brand which justified a low expenditure on advertising only on account of its small initial market. With limited distribution consumers experienced some difficulty in obtaining the product, and were some-what unwilling to try it. However, when the product was subsequently test marketed under the name Persil Automatic, still with little expenditure on advertising, retailers were far more willing to stock a brand associated with a long-established brand name with a high reputation, and consumers were also more prepared to try a product with a brand name similar to one with which they were familiar. Furthermore, as CH 7 illustrates, one criterion determining the inclusion of a line in the catalogue of Argos Distributors is that it should preferably be a well-known manufacturer brand, because shoppers then find it easier to identify a price reduction, and such lines have a faster stock-turn which leads to economies of operating costs.

Moreover, since branding facilitates identification, consumers are able to avoid purchasing a product once it has been found unsatisfactory or unsuitable. The ease of identification provided by branding also acts as an incentive for manufacturers to provide products of consistent quality since their long-term success is dependent upon satisfied customers making repeat purchases.

Finally, an important function of branding, which has been accentuated by present-day methods of organization in manufacturing and retailing, is to assist a firm to build up a reputation for the value and performance of its product and/or name and thus secure a degree of consumer 'loyalty' which will enable the advantages of economies of scale and lower unit costs to be achieved.

Consumer 'loyalty' comprises several elements besides satisfaction, including habit, inertia, and irrationality, which may persist after the original reasons for them have passed. 'Loyalty' is also a measure of the rate of turnover of customers. The lower costs which may be achieved by increased customer loyalty stem from (1) the economies of quantity buying, and (2) the economies of regularity (Lewis, 1949). The importance of the economies of 'loyalty' have intensified through the need of many manufacturers and/or retailers to secure the potential economies of large-scale operation and lower unit costs. Firms cannot get an economic return from high capital investment unless sufficient customers purchase their products or visit their shops regularly. This means that shoppers must be able to identify a firm's products, and be encouraged to make repeat purchases if they have been satisfied.

There would appear, however, to be little awareness in public policy pronouncements that branding and product differentiation can perform specific functions in the market which may be beneficial to manufacturers and consumers. The Monopolies and Mergers Commission (Cmnd 5330, 1973) has taken the view that in oligopoly

'Costs may be higher, firstly, because the factors that inhibit sellers from engaging in active price competition may encourage them to compete in other ways, for example in advertising or in minor product styling changes.' [p. 26]

In the *Review of Monopolies and Mergers Policy* (Cmnd 7198, 1978) a distinction is made between product differentiation which is worth while and that which is undesirable:

'. . . while the new and better products which are one of the objectives of innovation are usually desirable from the customers' point of view this will

not always be the case: planned obsolescence and minor styling improvements can be wasteful and may even operate to discourage competition.'
[para. 3.15]

In its discussion document (*Real Money, Real Choice*, September, 1978) the
criticism is made by the National Consumer Council that

'. . . forms of useless product differentiation make it very hard for consumers
to identify the best value for money among alternative brands, because of the
additional information they have to assimilate.' [p. 51]

Thus, combined with the view of conventional theory that product differentiation
consists primarily of competing brands with negligible differences is the planned
obsolescence theory that suggests that existing products are deliberately made out
of date by the introduction of new models with minor or superfluous differences
which add little or nothing to their intrinsic merits, and which have the effect of
complicating consumer decision-making.

In practice, it is more difficult to make arbitrary distinctions and value-
judgements between different types of product differentiation because although
changes in a product may be slight they may be valued by some consumers. Some
improvements in products become possible through the development of new
materials and new technology. On other occasions modifications and variations in
products are made to meet changes in the living standards and habits and tastes of
consumers. It would be difficult to predict in advance with certainty which products
with minor differences will appeal to consumers.

The desire by economic theory and by public policy statements to curtail product
differentiation would seem to be an attempt to oblige sellers to conform more
closely to the theoretical model of perfect competition. To the extent that such a
situation would fail to cater for the unstandardized needs and requirements and
preferences of consumers, it would be a less efficient state of affairs than a less
'perfect' market.

In conventional theory advertising acts as the concomitant of branding and
product differentiation to persuade consumers to purchase a product automatically
and permanently. This power of advertising to create and sustain durable brand
loyalty is also put forward in the 'management of demand' thesis of Galbraith
(Part 1, p. 29). Unlike the proponents of the traditional theory of the firm,
however, Galbraith accepts that oligopoly in the modern economy has become
inevitable, but maintains at the same time that it is the dominance of the large
corporation which has eroded the sovereignty of the consumer. According to this
proposition, advertising is employed to shift the decision to purchase from the
consumer to the firm because the market has become incompatible with the
operation of the large corporation and the high financial risks associated with
modern production techniques which have lengthened the period from the
initiation of the product to its purchase by consumers. As a result, large
corporations manipulate markets, and hence consumers, through the employment
of a wide variety of sales promotion techniques, which ensure the disposal of
whatever products they have decided to make.

The power of advertising would seem to be in practice more limited than these deterministic theories suggest. The high incidence of product failures demonstrates that although advertising may successfully stimulate the initial purchase of a product it is less capable (CH 3) of encouraging the consumer to make a repeat purchase (Part 2, p. 48). The reasons for the decline and withdrawal of many products are varied and include technical obsolescence, inadequate distribution, unexpected changes in demand, and incorrect pricing. Furthermore, for many reasons firms may misjudge the timing of their entry into a market, and advertising does not seem to be able to overcome this error. In CH 1, for instance, the introduction of fluoride toothpaste in the 1960s by three well-known firms was unsuccessful because at that time there was insufficient interest among consumers in the dental preservation properties of fluoride.

The limitations of advertising are also evident from the findings of empirical research (Part 2, p. 45) and the market place (CH 1) which show that, despite high and continuous advertising expenditure in many product fields, consumers switch and experiment with different brands which result in changes in market shares over short periods of time.

Public policy statements, however, often appear to overlook these many other factors which counteract the ability of the large firms in the long run to control demand and prices. Mrs Shirley Williams (then Secretary of State for Prices and Consumer Protection), for instance, supported the Galbraith thesis of consumer behaviour, that consumer wants can be artificially fabricated by advertising and other sales techniques, when addressing the Annual Conference of the Advertising Association, May 1974:

'You create demands, in many cases artificially, by conjuring up worlds of fantasy',

and the EEC seemed to accept the Galbraith view as the basis of consumer behaviour:

'. . . but can anyone refute Galbraith's assertion that in the relationship between producers and consumers the balance of power is often held by the producer, in that the consumer's needs are, in fact, "suggested" to him?' [1976, p. 2]

Such statements depend upon two implicit assumptions about consumer behaviour which do not seem to be in accordance with their shopping behaviour: first, that consumers are prepared to rush out and buy every new product that advertising commends to them. In practice, inertia, habit and tradition inhibit the acceptance of new products, and although advertising is one of the methods used to inform and persuade consumers to try them it does not follow that even when this is successful that they will continue to buy them (Part 2, p. 48). Second, this theory of consumer behaviour assumes that the consumer relies on advertising as the sole source of shopping information whereas it is only one source of communication among many others, and is recognized as being biased and exaggerated compared with the advice of relations, neighbours, and friends and articles in newspapers and magazines.

The weakness of the 'management of demand' theory stems from exaggerating the degree to which the technical requirements and planning implicit in large-scale production have been accompanied by an increase in the ability of producers to gain effective control over demand. In particular, many of the generalizations made about the relation of the modern industrial concern to the market are so extreme and sweeping as to render them invalid, and these generalizations are also too often based on a static economy. In this hypothetical situation manufacturers are able conveniently, if unrealistically, to ignore the marketing policies of their rivals and competition from substitute products, retailer brands and overseas firms, although these are decisive factors in reducing the extent to which the large corporation can 'manage wants'. There is increasing evidence from painstaking and detailed studies of economists[4] that the experience of industry both in the United Kingdom and the United States of America has been inconsistent with the Galbraithian assertions about the economy, and the theory is also contradicted by research findings on consumer behaviour and advertising, particularly the high rate of product failures and the ease with which consumers switch brands.

RETAILERS' BRANDS AND COMPETITION

As a means of reducing advertising and other selling costs Kaldor (p. 15), like Lewis (p. 15), maintained that the distributive system should be dominated by the retailer, and by retailer brands rather than those of manufacturers. The manufacturers would supply large retailers (chain stores, Co-operative Societies) who would tell them what consumers wanted, and thus drastically reduce or eliminate the expense of manufacturer advertising because, combined with only a modest advertising expenditure, the retailer achieves comparable publicity by using his shop windows and display shelves as his principal form of sales promotion. Furthermore, both Lewis and Kaldor envisaged that the pressure of retailer-domination would lead to a reduction in the variety of products; and they distinguished retailer advertising as 'desirable' because it was 'informative' compared with manufacturer advertising which was 'undesirable' because it was combative or persuasive. These conclusions were based on an analysis of the success of certain large-scale retailers in promoting their own brands (notably Marks & Spencer) at a time when distributive trends appeared propitious for their widespread introduction.

Over the past quarter-century the 'countervailing power' of the retailer has arrived in many product fields. The distinguishing features of distribution during this period have been the increase in retailer concentration (see CHs 1, 4, 5), the development of retailer brands (CHs 3, 6), and the increasing intensity of competition between retailers. The growing concentration in retailing has made the orders of large-scale retailers, or their absence, important to many manufacturers. This

---

[4] Among others, Professor John Jewkes, Sir Frank McFadzean, Professor G. C. Allen, Professor Harold Demsetz, Professor R. M. Solow, Professor James Meade; e.g., Allen (1969), McFadzean (1968), and Sharpe (1973).

factor, combined with excess capacity (particularly in food manufacturing) has meant that few manufacturers any longer refuse to pack private brands. In this period, too, some large-scale retailers have become household names, and have built up a reputation for quality and competitive prices with the result that shoppers are prepared to try DOBs without extensive advertising. The increasing homogeneity of retail outlets, particularly supermarkets, and the competitive pressures on distributive margins have stimulated many large-scale retailers to seek out DOBs. These are then sold more cheaply than the manufacturer's brand but with a higher retail margin. At the same time DOBs help to differentiate to some degree a retailer from his rivals, and may contribute towards an increase in 'loyalty' among his customers—both factors which have become increasingly difficult to achieve in the present organization of retail distribution.

The acceptance of DOBs by the shopper has been aided by the favourable publicity they have received from consumer bodies such as the Consumers' Association,[5] and the Department of Prices and Consumer Protection,[6] although both of these bodies have also acknowledged that DOBs are not necessarily of the same quality as the leading manufacturers' brands.

Nevertheless, the development of private brands has been by no means uniform across retail distribution. Wide variations exist in the degree of their penetration in different product groups, and within a particular product category. In groceries, for instance, DOBs vary from 50 per cent in cooking oil (CH 3), 28 per cent in washing-up liquids and 5 per cent in breakfast cereals. Retailers selling the same merchandise also differ in their policy towards the adoption of DOBs: of the four leading grocery multiples, Sainsbury and Tesco sell a higher proportion of DOBs compared with ASDA and Kwik-Save who rely predominantly on stocking manufacturer brands.

Several factors, including length of time and penetration of retailer in the market-place, characteristics of the product, size of product market, and degree of price differential compared with manufacturer brands determine the extent to which retailers are likely to introduce DOBs. Newcomers into retailing, for instance, often prefer to rely on the reputation and goodwill of established manufacturer brands in order to build up sales quickly. Similarly, well-known manufacturer brands can be a valuable sales aid to the catalogue discount retailer (CH 7) because they enable consumers to identify price reductions easily. DOBs have made relatively little penetration into such product areas as domestic electrical appliance because retailers have been reluctant, for the most part, to introduce their own brands into high-price merchandise which is purchased infrequently, and for which consumers seem to prefer the security of a well-known name. Furthermore, DOBs have been introduced only on a small scale in product

---

[5] 'Last year, we found that by buying own-brands . . . you could save yourself 12p in the £ on groceries. This year, the overall saving fell to 8½p in the £. But, with some items, the saving was much more than this . . . Our tests have shown that the quality of own-brands is often as good as branded versions (not always though . . .)'. 'Grocery prices', *Which?* October 1976, p. 219.

[6] A pilot survey into the Department's price monitoring scheme claimed that savings of up to 20p in the £ could be achieved by choosing the cheapest shop and using own-brands where these were the cheapest in price. Circular No. 4/75, however, also recognized that retailers' 'own brands' were not necessarily of precisely the same quality as the leading manufacturers' brands.

fields where intensive distribution is required in order to maximize sales (e.g., chocolate and confectionery, and razor blades). Retailers have also shown little interest in developing DOBs in products with a relatively small turnover. Similarly, if the price of the manufacturer's brand is very low (CH 5), this factor may inhibit the retailer from introducing DOBs because a worthwhile price differential is usually necessary to attain a high level of sales. On the other hand, retailers find it worth their while to stock DOBs in product areas such as fashion where branding cannot be a guarantee of a uniform product. In this type of merchandise styling, colour, price, etc., are generally more important than a manufacturer's brand name.

With certain notable exceptions (e.g., CH 6), the outstanding characteristic of DOBs is that they are normally introduced once manufacturer brands have become well established in a particular product. For the most part, retailers seem to prefer to avoid the risk, financial resources, product and market research, and extensive sales promotion necessary for successful product innovation and to concentrate instead on retail innovation by exploiting their skills and expertise in locating sites, merchandising, buying and pricing. Moreover, the large-scale retailer may well gain more benefit from using his increased bargaining power to acquire better terms, advertising allowances, and promotions from manufacturers rather than by introducing competing products. Although, therefore, when the opportunity occurs many retailers introduce own brands they do so selectively, and continue to depend predominantly on the sale of the leading manufacturer brands which have a high degree of customer acceptance, and active promotional support.

There is also some evidence that although the degree of concentration in food retailing accelerated during the 1970s, there has been a slight decline in the share of DOBs in this market. This seems to be attributable to the intensification of price competition from 1977 onwards with the introduction of price-cutting schemes by two leading multiples (i.e., Sainsbury and Tesco). As a result of these schemes both retailers increased their share of the packaged grocery market,[7] and in each instance their share has expanded to a greater extent through the sales of manufacturer brands rather than sales of DOBs. The price promotional schemes of such retailers tend to be associated to a large degree with manufacturer brands because it is easier for consumers to identify and compare price reduction on them.

As envisaged in conventional theory, when DOBs become prominent in a particular product category a decline in the variety of brands stocked usually takes place. Whereas retailers may formerly have stocked four or five brands of a product, once a DOB is introduced the two brand leaders are normally retained, and the remaining minor brands replaced by the DOB. This policy has several consequences: first, that minor manufacturers find it increasingly difficult to gain acceptance by retailers; second, that this policy has accentuated the trend for manufacturers to try to introduce a new product ahead of their competitors in order to ensure wide distribution; finally, it has become increasingly difficult for a new brand to achieve distribution in an established product field.

The evidence of the past three decades suggest that when DOBs are introduced

---

[7] Television Consumer Audit, Audits of Great Britain Ltd, 1979.

selectively they are profitable to retailers, good value to the shopper, and act as a warning to manufacturers that their marketing policies must heed potential and actual competition from the brands of large-scale retailers. Although DOBs have become an additional competitor in many products there has been little sign to date that the success of limited categories of DOBs can be extended ipso facto to the whole field of retailing, or even uniformly across one product category such as food. As a consequence, the prediction that

'by the end of the century manufacturers' brands could be a rarity'[8]

seems unlikely to be realized, because it is based on the assumption of conventional theory that consumers know what they want, and already know the facts about products.

RETAILER ADVERTISING

The view that advertising and selling costs would be reduced if retailers dominated the distributive system, because, combined with a modest advertising expenditure, they could utilize shop windows and display shelves as their principal form of sales promotion, has not been borne out in practice.

Since 1970 retail advertising has been the most rapidly growing sector of United Kingdom advertising expenditure; it has expanded fourfold compared with little more than a doubling of manufacturer consumers advertising;[9] and in 1979 retail firms comprised nine of the ten largest spenders on advertising.[10] Within retail advertising, expenditure by non-food retailers has expanded at a more rapid rate than that of food retailers.

The expansion of retail advertising from a very low level is related to the fundamental changes which have taken place in the organization and structure of retail distribution. These have included increased consumer mobility and leisure which have widened the geographical area of competition; the abolition of resale price maintenance, which has accentuated the trend towards the stocking of specialist merchandise by non-specialist retailers and stimulated the emergence of new types of retail firms who offer varying combinations of service and price; the homogeneity of products and shops which in certain types of products has reduced the scope for some retailers to compete on quality or individuality, and this has led competition to become more concentrated on range, convenience and price. The trend towards fewer but larger outlets has widened the range of products stocked by retailers, and similarly increased the competition between them. Not least, the relative growth in overhead costs has changed the cost structure of retailing and emphasized the importance of operating at full capacity as a means of giving better value or improving profits, and has stimulated consumer promotions and advertising

---

[8] Caspar Brook (then Director, Consumers' Association) in 'Fresh deal for shoppers', *Observer*, 11 February 1962.
[9] Advertising Association and Management Horizons.
[10] MEAL Digest of Advertising Statistics.

including advertising retailers' own brands to encourage more shoppers to enter the shop and/or increase the value of their individual purchases. The bargaining power of large-scale retailers vis-à-vis manufacturers has resulted to some extent in a transfer of advertising expenditure from manufacturers to retailers through advertising allowances and additional discounts in return for special displays of a manufacturer's brand.

Many of the new types of retail outlets such as hypermarkets and discount stores (e.g., furniture and electrical appliances) advertise widely to make consumers aware of their ranges, low prices, and convenient parking facilities, especially when these are located away from traditional shopping centres. Whereas previously furniture advertising was confined largely to local advertising by retailers and national advertising by the branded manufacturers, in 1976 manufacturers' advertising amounted to M£5.2 while that of the three major retailers (Williams, MFI and Queensway) amounted in the same year to M£5.6, thus illustrating the change in emphasis from manufacturer to retailer advertising (Fulop and March, 1979).

Finally, in response to the varied changes which have occurred in distribution, many established retailers have found it necessary to alter their operating methods (e.g., the establishment of voluntary groups in food retailing and to a lesser extent in other merchandise fields, and/or extend their product ranges). Such retail firms undertake more advertising than formerly to alert shoppers to their adapted policies, to create a corporate image, to promote their own brands, and to illustrate their price competitiveness.

In view of the many factors which have influenced the expansion of retailer advertising, the supposition that a retailer-dominated distribution system should lead to lower advertising and selling costs would seem to stem from a static concept of competition which cannot take into account the changes in demand and supply over time which influence how firms compete in the market.

ADVERTISING AS A MEANS OF CONVEYING INFORMATION

It has been generally conceded in conventional theory that although under perfect competition where buyers and sellers have perfect knowledge there is no place for advertising, nevertheless in the real world some selling techniques are necessary either because information is not perfect and/or indivisibilities in production techniques require the expansion of markets.

As a means of conveying information, however, advertising has been criticized on two counts: first, that the information provided by advertisements is designed by the sellers of goods and is consequently biased; second, that in many advertisements the building up of brand image is given priority at the expense of the provision of information. These criticisms have led to proposals (Part 1, pp. 14–15) that independent information services could be an effective substitute for advertising expenditure because their costs are lower (whereas advertising in 1938 cost M£68 the information supplied by advertising could be provided more cheaply, according to Kaldor, by an independent information service, i.e., around M£14), and that such bodies would widely disseminate

'. . . information about the real qualities of different products [which] would increase the forces of the market mechanism to which the producers would have to submit'. [Meade, 1975, pp. 49–50]

This proposition appears to take a narrow view of the functions and purpose of advertising, since it implies that its raison d'être is to convey information to the consumer about products already on the market in the same way that the primary function of a consumer association is to offer comparative information on products and services. This viewpoint seems to be derived from conventional demand theory where consumer preferences are given and changes in them largely ignored. Consequently, conventional demand theory does not inquire into how consumers' preferences are formed in the first place nor, because it is a static theory, does it take into account the effects of the changes in the composition of consumers in a market (e.g., the half-a-million newly-marrieds who set up house annually, and who are choosing many products for the first time).

Examples from the case histories illustrate the wide variety of functions undertaken by advertising in practice, apart from conveying information about existing products.[11] In the launching of a new product advertising, in conjunction with other selling techniques, is an important aid in making consumers quickly aware of its existence and in explaining its properties and purposes if a high level of demand and the economies of large-scale production are to be achieved. Advertising is also used widely as a platform for responding to the doubts and reservations consumers may have expressed about certain aspects of the product in market research investigations. Thus the initial advertising of Mr. Kipling Cakes (CH 6) attempted to dispel the apparently widely-held belief that factory-baked cakes per se are of a lower quality than the home-made variety. Firms, too, utilize advertising in order to announce a change in policy such as the diversification by British Rail into the packaged holiday trade with the introduction of Golden Rail (CH 2) with a combination of hotel accommodation, train and taxi travel, at a large number of holiday centres.

Besides employing advertising to draw the attention of consumers to new products and services, to explain their attributes, and to deal with doubts that consumers may have expressed about their efficacy, once a product has become well-established advertising helps to maintain sales because over a period of time the needs and requirements of the purchasers of a particular product alter, their composition changes and competing brands enter the market. With a long-established brand such as Macleans Toothpaste (CH 1), for instance, the need to provide information may well diminish, but consumers still require to be reminded about the brand when they go shopping, particularly with a low-cost, low-interest line which is frequently purchased, and where consumers may be tempted to switch

---

[11] In a product group outside the remit of a consumer information service (i.e., industrial products (CH 8)), and where informative advertising might be considered pre-eminent, advertising is employed to undertake a wide range of functions including to act as a reminder for an infrequently-purchased product; to build up confidence in the firm by familiarizing potential customers with its name and thus easing the task of the sales force; and to make the company better known to the various decision-makers in a firm.

brands. In another case history (CH 7) the issue of Argos' catalogue at twice-yearly intervals is accompanied by advertising to remind and encourage potential customers to visit their nearest branch and pick up a copy.

Moreover, in order to retain existing users, and to encourage potential new consumers to purchase a brand, advertising is often deployed either to announce changes and improvements in the formulation or the extension of a range which offers a wider choice. In 1978, for instance, Golden Rail (CH 2) advertised the introduction of self-catering holidays and the addition of the Channel Islands to its list of holiday resorts. Similarly, continuous advertising of Persil Automatic (CH 4) has been necessary to ensure that consumers who enter the low-suds detergent market through their acquisition of a new type of washing machine are aware of the brand, and its relevance to their changed requirements.

Finally, many of the case histories illustrate that advertising to retailers has become as important as advertising to consumers. This situation has been brought about by the changing position of retailers vis-á-vis manufacturers and the need to stimulate retailers to stock the manufacturers' products and to encourage them to provide favourable displays. In this instance, the purpose of advertising is designed to achieve a faster stock-turn and a higher distribution penetration.

In view of the employment of advertising for a wide variety of purposes, most of which it would be unnecessary for a consumer information service to replicate, it is not perhaps surprising that a wide discrepancy should exist between the estimated costs of such a service and consumer advertising expenditure. This differential is also very wide because no allowance appears to be made for the promotional expenditure which consumer associations find it necessary to expend in order to attract new members to replace their high rate of turnover of subscribers.

Furthermore, these figures do not take into account the fact that the relative expenditure on advertising varies over time. The case histories show that advertising is only one among several selling techniques (temporary price reductions, samples, trade bonuses, special offers) which are designed to stimulate consumers to try and re-try a product, and that are combined by firms in varying proportions which reflect the characteristics of a product and its changing competitive position. The efficiency and importance of these selling techniques, including advertising, increase and diminish according to how strongly manufacturers think they will appeal to consumers and retailers as a sales stimulant. Over the past decade, the relative importance of these components in the 'promotion mix' has been changing with the result that advertising tends to represent a smaller proportion of total sales promotion expenditure than formerly in many products.

The proposition that much advertising expenditure could be replaced by consumer information services also appears to overestimate the extent to which the consumer relies on advertising as the sole source of shopping information. In practice, shoppers have many avenues of information open to them, including that of retailers, advice of neighbours and friends, articles in newspapers and magazines and previous experience. To a large extent, it would appear to be continuous shop talk among housewives which helps to establish the reputation of a product, and to decide how far repeat sales will be made (see also p. 49).

Finally, the view that a consumer information service could be an effective and economical substitute for advertising also overlooks the idea that although such a service can be a valuable supplementary source of information which complements that available from a variety of other sources it nevertheless also suffers from certain drawbacks and weaknesses (see Fulop, 1978).

Since 1957 the Consumers' Association (CA), an independent consumer testing body which publishes comparative test reports on a wide range of products and services in its monthly journal *Which?*, has become well established in this country. During that time the membership has reached around 700 000 (readership, however, is much higher; in the region of three to four million). Subscribers to CA tend to be confined to a narrow range of occupations and incomes and both the old and the young are under-represented among its members. Over the years the CA has experienced some difficulty in enlarging and broadening the representativeness of its membership. This situation would seem to indicate that many people find the assimilation and collection of detailed information too time-consuming, and sometimes more technical than they understand or require.

Furthermore, there are limitations in the testing procedures of CA which were pointed out by the Molony Committee (Cmnd 1781, 1962). Over the years, CA has made strenuous efforts to overcome the earlier criticisms of its test reports. In order to minimize the problem that sampling may not be representative, for instance, increasing emphasis is placed by CA on user panels which simulate ordinary use as closely as possible, and utilizes the experience of its members which are collated by means of questionnaires. However, there remain certain inherent weaknesses in comparative test reports and it is not easy to remedy them (e.g., financial constraints, length of time required for testing, and volatile market conditions which make it difficult to keep up to date with changes in prices). In addition, the selection of questions for a comparative test to a large extent determines consumer testing procedures, and the conclusions drawn from testing depend on interpretation and judgement. If undue weight is given to certain attributes of a product such as price, or durability or safety, because they are quantifiable criteria and objective qualities compared with other sources of satisfaction which may be less measurable such as convenience, styling, or security, or brand name, then many shoppers may find that the results of a comparative test do not correspond with their requirements. Similarly, if certain questions are omitted, not through negligence or oversight but from a different assessment of a piece of research, a test report may not meet user needs.

Thus even seriously-intentioned consumer research with ostensibly object test procedures has limitations because such testing inevitably involves subjective interpretations and value-judgements. Such subjectivity has tended to be obscured because *Which?* no longer has a competitor with which it can be compared. Ever since *Shopper's Guide* ceased publication in 1963, *Which?* has been the sole source of comparative reports, and the consumer has had no independent alternative with which to compare it. Both *Which?* and *Shopper's Guide*, for instance, reported on electrical kettles and contradicted each other at some points. It was also possible to detect other points of disagreement running through various reports in the two journals, which is not surprising once the difficulty of devising satisfactory tests is appreciated.

The associated criticism of advertising as a source of information, that too much emphasis is placed in advertising on building up brand loyalty compared with the benefit to the consumer of informative advertising, was made by the Price Commission (PC) Report on Southalls (1978, HC 436):

> 'Advertising has been directed mainly towards establishing brand image; informative advertising which aids the consumer has played a minor role. This marketing strategy, based on strong brand loyalty, and reinforced by heavy advertising and promotional expenditure, adds to costs. We accept that in recent years advertising has included a growing element of information to consumers, but nonetheless, the overall marketing strategy continued to be designed to build up brand loyalty and thus it restricts competition.' [2.11]

Apart from the fundamental difficulty of defining 'informative' advertising in this particular product, the PC seemed to have overlooked that until very recently social attitudes towards sanitary protection products have not been conducive to informative advertising. The advertising of these products, for instance, continues to be banned on television.

The Commission itself acknowledged that

> 'Market research carried out by the industry has shown that consumers have not sought detailed information on products from advertisements, point of sale material or the outside of product packs. Accordingly detailed information is mainly conveyed in leaflets inside product packs . . . To supplement this consumers are actively encouraged through advertisements and pack leaflets to write to manufacturers for advice . . .' [2.17]

In other words, the characteristics of the product have made it more appropriate for firms to convey information discreetly through an information service which consumers can contact individually, and by the offer of trial samples, rather than by the provision of detailed information in advertisements. Furthermore, the PC appeared to exaggerate the extent to which the type of advertising used to market this product has been able to raise costs and restrict competition, because brand switching rather than brand loyalty, and innovation, have been features of this market, and prices have risen less than the rate of inflation.

9 Competition under oligopoly

OLIGOPOLY AND PRICES

In the theory of the firm imperfect competition is generally regarded as inferior to perfect competition, particularly the 'imperfections' brought about by oligopoly, that is, the domination of an industry by a few firms (Part 1, p. 10).

These imperfections stem from the chief characteristic of oligopoly—the diminution of price competition either tacit or overt. This diminution is the result of the mutual interdependence among oligopolists which arises from the awareness by each firm that its pricing policies will affect demand and the policies of its competitors.

Unlike the situation in perfect competition firms operating in such a market structure will not respond to impersonal market forces but personally and directly to the policies of their rivals. The inevitable outcome of oligopoly is, therefore, the emergence of price leadership, with a leading firm setting prices and others following (i.e., parallel pricing). The second inherent feature of oligopoly which follows from interdependence is that firms will prefer not to compete by price but by less direct forms of competition such as advertising, sales promotion, and product innovation. The conclusion is then drawn that since an oligopolistic market structure may encourage both high advertising expenditure and parallel pricing behaviour the forces of competition will be effectively blunted and prices and/or profits will be higher than the competitive level.

Although it is generally agreed by economists, as outlined above, that independent price changes under oligopoly are unlikely (particularly if demand is relatively inelastic) unless changes in costs and demand occur, there is less agreement whether an oligopolistic industry per se will have higher prices, higher profits and weak competition. Hence the distinction made between disciplined price leadership where the assumption is made that interdependence leads automatically to rigid and sluggish prices, and barometric price leadership where it is maintained that although prices may be more or less parallel they are more likely to resemble those which would emerge where there are many sellers because in practice there are frequent changes in demand and costs and market conditions which make it difficult for firms to sustain highly coordinated pricing. This latter situation would seem to be prevalent in several of the case histories where the firms operate in oligopolistic markets (e.g., Macleans Toothpaste and Batchelor's Quick Custard).

The toothpaste market, for instance, is characterized by oligopoly. Four firms were responsible for 85 per cent of turnover in 1977; sales promotion expenditure comprised 20 per cent of sales (of which advertising accounts for 12 per cent, and promotions for 7 per cent). Nevertheless, the industry is highly competitive, as is evidenced by the achievement of an 8 to 10 per cent share by Procter & Gamble following its entry into the market in 1975, and significant changes in the market share of the other companies and brands (see Table 6–1). Brands have been introduced and then withdrawn after four or five years. Macleans Toothpaste, at one time the brand leader, has become the second brand. Boots and Co-operative Societies have successful own brands, and one company, Stafford-Miller, has achieved significant growth in the sales of its specialized product Sensodyne. There is indirect price competition between manufacturers, largely in the form of temporary price reductions, intensified by vigorous retail competition as a result of which the 'real' price of toothpaste fell between 1973 and 1977 by 7 per cent at manufacturers' selling price and by rather more than this at retail prices (PC Report, HC 125, 1978).

High advertising expenditure did not deter the entry of a new firm when circumstances seemed propitious; and there are other major pharmaceutical companies with the financial resources and distribution expertise either to enter this market or expand their existing lines should the opportunity occur to introduce a product innovation. Three further factors have helped to keep prices and margins down. First, there has been a major change in the type of retail outlet through which toothpaste is sold; whereas toothpaste was formerly sold predominantly through chemist shops, it is now distributed largely through multiple retailers, and 13 multiple organizations are responsible for 50 per cent of sales. As a result Macleans has been compelled to compete with its rivals to get special displays and participation in retailer promotions. Second, the intensity of competition among retailers themselves has accentuated price competition. Both these factors have led to price cutting at the retail level. Finally, there has been the influence on price of a well-known DOB of a multiple chemist.

Toothpaste is a product category with no substitutes or near substitutes. Nevertheless, in this oligopolistic industry with high advertising expenditure, market conditions have reduced prices in real terms. (In another product category with no near substitutes, sanitary protection products (PC Report, HC 436, 1978), the manufacturers were reprimanded for their high advertising and sales promotion expenditure. However, in this market too there has been severe competition leading to the introduction of new products, new firms, variations in brand shares, and price rises less than the overall rate of inflation.)

Another factor which constrains prices in an oligopolistic market is the existence of substitutes or near substitutes. Batchelors Quick Custard (CH 5), for instance, faces competition not only from its immediate competitors within the instant custard powder market but also from the wide variety of products suitable for sweets and desserts. Moreover, the experience of this market has been that a firm is compelled to optimize product quality and technology as quickly as possible, since any degree of success will almost automatically attract competition from other well-known food manufacturers who have the R & D facilities to develop a similar technical advance, an efficient distribution network to facilitate their distribution of a competitive product, the existence of excess capacity to encourage the supply of DOBs, and a competitive retail milieu which stimulates retailers to stock DOBs. In consequence, these specific marketing conditions have led to a competitive situation in which increased expenditure has been made on trade discounts and promotional activity, and this has resulted in the lowest prices that can be economically operated by manufacturers and retailers.[1]

Another case history (CH 2) illustrates the fact that although British Rail is a statutory monopoly Golden Rail operates in a very price competitive market because of the prevalence of substitutes and near substitutes such as packaged coach tours, independent self-catering holidays, etc.

The evidence from the above examples would seem to suggest that, apart from the short term, it is unrealistic to assume that the stable market environment required to maintain disciplined price leadership will persist. Over a period of time, changes in demand are brought about by changing social and economic conditions, and in supply by technology, the entry of new firms, and the introduction of retailer brands. In several case histories, for instance, intense price cutting has developed at the retail level (including 'bargain offers' by manufacturers, as well as retailers' price competition), there is the growing bargaining power of large-scale retailers, both as buyers and, in many instances, suppliers of their own brands, and with some products there is the threat of potential entry by other international companies. Many of these market factors are sufficiently strong to outweigh some of the main characteristics associated with disciplined price leadership such as inelastic industry demand, static or only slow growing market, and similar products, with the result that the prices that emerge in many oligopolistic industries will be related to market conditions. Furthermore, disciplined price leadership would seem to imply a degree of homogeneity among the firms in an oligopolistic industry which in practice is rarely attained because firms are not equally efficient and aggressive in production, distribution and marketing; they are not equally successful at innovation; their market shares do not expand at a uniform rate. Under such an unstable state of affairs, one or other firm will be compelled or stimulated to introduce price reductions, for instance, or a product variant, or a more vigorous marketing policy which affects the relative positions and profitability of all the competing firms. Where firms are constantly vying to improve their

---

[1] The absence of an automatic correlation between oligopoly, advertising and higher prices in the food trade is illustrated in a study (King, 1978) which showed that the prices of the old-established 'heavily advertised' food brands—those on the market in 1964 and spending over £250,000 on advertising in 1977—rose by 220 per cent between 1964 and 1978, compared with 309 per cent for food prices generally.

position in a market which can be brought about by a variety of means, it will be more difficult to sustain higher prices.

Finally, as examples from the case histories illustrate, in many oligopolistic markets (e.g., Batchelors Instant Custard, Mr. Kipling Cakes) firms are in competition with firms in other markets which provide substitutes or near substitutes on which consumers can spend their money.

Public policy pronouncements, however, have tended to underestimate the effectiveness of the many factors in the market which help to constrain prices in an oligopolistic market structure, and particularly to overlook the time element which is most likely to undermine most efforts at disciplined price leadership. The MMC's Report for instance, which surveyed the effects of pricing policy under oligopoly, concluded:

'However oligopolists choose to co-ordinate their behaviour, the result is likely to be a level of prices and profits higher than would prevail with a large number of sellers . . .' [Cmnd 5330, 1973, p. 13]

and to alleviate this situation recommended that Government control of prices and costs will often be the appropriate practical remedy (p. 38).

Likewise in the *Review of Monopolies and Mergers Policy* (Cmnd 7198, 1978) it was claimed that

'. . . the market power arising from high concentration may permit excess profits to be made. Also, market power can result in a misallocation of resources in the sense that the pattern of output does not reflect consumer preferences or changes therein.' [3.20]

There is little recognition in either of these pronouncements that an oligopolist per se cannot be insulated either from competition from the other large firms in its particular industry, or the threat of entry from large firms engaged in other industries who see opportunities in markets quite different from their own, the influence of distributors' own brands, and changing consumer demand. There is, however, the implied assumption that has already been noted that brand loyalty can be enforced permanently by advertising, although there is little evidence from the case histories to support that view.

Finally, when the Price Commission was strengthened and given powers for new and more detailed investigation of individual prices, this policy was justified on the grounds that increased concentration, 'price leadership' and 'parallel pricing' with big companies taking the lead were increasing the danger of monopoly (Under-Secretary of State for Prices and Consumer Protection, *Trade and Industry*, 18 March, 1977). However, there is no general agreement among economists whether concentration has been increasing in industry (Part 1, p. 17). Furthermore, no distinction is made between disciplined and barometric price leadership, nor does there appear to be an appreciation that price leadership and parallel prices are often ways in which competition under oligopoly exerts its effect.

In a review of the work of the Price Commission Lord Cockfield, its first chairman (1973 to 1977), argued that there was a need for

'. . . a permanent facility to protect the community at large in the field of pricing . . . We suffer in this country from market domination, price leadership, parallel pricing, the lack of effective competition, unwillingness to compete on price.' [p. 23]

Although oligopoly typifies most industries, this proposal also pays insufficient attention to factors which may counteract the ability of markets dominated by a handful of firms to control prices in the long run. To give one example: a feature of present-day retail distribution is the widespread marketing of distributors' own brands by large-scale retailers. This development acts as a deterrent to excessive advertising, curtails monopoly tendencies over a growing range of merchandise, and exerts a beneficial influence on prices. The reputation of a retailer with a household name, and a prominent display in his branches, is sufficient for a shopper to try out a private brand without extensive advertising. Retailer brands, moreover, receive widespread publicity and favourable comment from public and private consumer bodies and the media.

The restricted view of competition and the assumption of a static economy implicit in the argument that firms in an oligopoly can raise prices with impunity would also appear responsible for the concept that retaliatory advertising and marketing costs can be wholly or largely added to the price the consumer is asked to pay as summed up in the MMC's Report (Cmnd 5530, 1973)

'But advertising which merely seeks to expand one seller's market share at the expense of other sellers' shares is likely to be partly self-cancelling and the overall unit cost of unchanging output is then likely to be higher than it would be with a smaller expenditure on advertising. Such an increase in unit costs would represent a waste of resources and would constitute a serious public interest issue.' [para 77]

The supposition that advertising expenditure merely persuades consumers to buy one brand rather than another and hence results in higher unit costs is based on several fallacies; for example, that the demand for particular types of merchandise is saturated and cannot be expanded; that all firms are equally efficient or inefficient; that there is no scope for introducing cost-reducing methods, and that no firms can expand their turnover more than proportionately to compensate for the cost of the advertising. In particular, it fails to acknowledge that changes in market shares are the raison d'être of competition in practice, and that advertising and other types of promotions are deployed to increase market share which, if successful, can lead to better quality merchandise, improved service or servicing, and act as a stimulus to firms with diminishing market shares.

NON-PRICE COMPETITION AND OLIGOPOLY

In the theoretical model of perfect competition there is uniformity of products and services so that competition is concentrated on price which will reduce costs and profits to the minimum. In this model, therefore, the only form of competition analysed is price competition. Since all consumers are assumed to be perfectly informed of all competing offers, advertising and other forms of competitive sales promotion have no place. It may then be argued that the presence of other forms of competition is evidence of 'imperfect competition', and thereby inferior to price competition:

> 'Under oligopoly competition no longer takes place by means of prices, but by means of packaging, samples, coupons, gifts and other attractions that might be considered secondary.' [Kaldor, Part 1, p. 24]

Although in a sense this premise is correct, nevertheless it is invalid unless either perfect competition is a practicable alternative to imperfect competition or methods of non-price competition are no more than a poor substitute for price competition.

It is now generally accepted that oligopoly is the prevalent form of industrial structure. In recent years in the areas of manufacturing and retailing where competition has been most intense there has been an increase in both price and non-price competition, which suggests that the latter may serve some specific functions in generating competitive activity.

Various types of non-price competition are employed in marketing products, as shown in many of the case histories. These include forms of indirect price competition such as temporary price reductions (TPRs) and multi-unit pricing, samples, competitions, 'free' offers, and rival innovations.

Temporary price reductions (TPRs)

TPRs are widely used by Persil Automatic, Batchelor's Quick Custard and Macleans Toothpaste. With toothpaste, for instance, TPRs are now more important than media advertising and other forms of promotion (CH 1).

Their increased use over the past decade has been due to three developments in retail distribution: (1) the enhanced bargaining power of retailers vis-à-vis manufacturers; (2) the increased price consciousness of consumers which has led the major retail firms to intensify their own promotional activities; and (3) the growth of distributors' own brands (DOBs).

1. The growth of large-scale retailing, and retailer concentration, (50 per cent of Persil Automatic is sold by four retail firms), has led many manufacturers who distribute through supermarkets to transfer some of their promotion through advertising to promotion through TPRs as a means of competing for special positions on the shelves of supermarkets, and gaining participation in retailers' promotional activity. In particular TPRs enable manufacturers to ensure that the discounts they make to retailers are actually passed through to consumers, whereas reducing manufacturers' list price would not necessarily have the same effect. With 'flash' offers the retailer can sell at no more than the recommended price less the 'money off' from the manufacturer. With price-marked

packs a significant contribution to the price reduction is required from the retailer, the manufacturers' discount from list prices being perhaps only half the discount from recommended prices imposed on the retailer by the price marking. The retailer's permitted margin is correspondingly reduced. In this case both the manufacturer's discount and the retailer's discount are passed on. Moreover, the retailer often discounts the retail price even further. As a result, the consumer has benefited from lower prices.

2. At a time of increased price consciousness of consumers, manufacturers have found that reduced price packs and 'flash' offers have proved more effective in achieving consumer trial and retrial of products and thus securing extra sales than other types of promotions such as advertising. First, they help to influence the less brand loyal consumer and perhaps persuade her to switch brands, and also to sustain the 'loyalty' of existing customers. Second, in the impersonal environment of self-service, they are a means of attracting the consumer at the point of sale in the supermarket when she is considering her purchases.

3. The intensification of retail competition has stimulated some manufacturers (e.g., Persil Automatic) to use TPRs to meet the competition of low price DOBs. TPRs can encourage shoppers to sample the manufacturers' brands at a low price while at the same time maintaining the quality image of the manufacturer brand.

For manufacturers TPRs can be a flexible sales promotion device because the amount of the price reduction and the duration of the TPR can be varied, which makes them less easy for competitors to imitate. Furthermore, an intermittent price reduction may be more noticed by consumers than an overall, and consequently much smaller, price reduction.

The extent to which a manufacturer will find it worth while to use TPRs will depend, inter alia, on its market position. Since Macleans Toothpaste has a smaller share of the market than the brand leader it has by definition a smaller number of 'loyal' customers and consequently finds it necessary to promote more frequently and intensively than the major brand (e.g., in 1979 40 per cent of all packs on promotion were TPRs).

Persil Automatic is the brand leader (CH 4) in the growing market for low-suds washing powder. In order to gain as large a market share as possible at the expense of its major competitor, 100 per cent of its packs were carrying TPRs for a short period although the amount of the price reduction and the length of the promotion varied, which made it more difficult for its rival to retaliate exactly.

Multi-unit pricing

The selling technique of 'three for the price of two' is used by Macleans Toothpaste. It is an example of a promotion which reduces the unit cost of selling by raising the value of the average transaction and transferring part of the cost of holding stock to the customer. In addition, it is an example of an effort to retain the 'loyalty' of the customer for a longer period than when single units of the brand are sold. Other promotions are also designed to encourage shoppers to purchase a product on more than one occasion by offering a price reduction off one pack which includes a coupon for another price reduction off a subsequent purchase. A variation on this type of promotion is to send the shopper a cash rebate if she submits proof of purchase of three packs of a product.

Samples

With new products (Persil Automatic), samples are regarded as an expensive but effective method of stimulating consumers' trial. By this means, it is anticipated that the brand will be accepted by consumers more quickly than would otherwise occur, and thereby expand sales and lower average costs of production. In addition, it is hoped that the issue of samples will enable a firm to gain a larger share of the market than its rivals. Persil Automatic, for instance, had been in the low-suds washing powder market for three years before the arrival of its major competitor, and samples were a means of quickly consolidating its position.

With Persil Automatic, contracts have been negotiated with domestic equipment manufacturers to include samples in their products. As a result, this ensures that consumers are enabled to try the brands exactly at the time they purchase the equipment which will be used in conjunction with them. Since many consumers may be reluctant to buy a product with which they are unfamiliar, a sample allows them to experiment with it without payment, and to make a decision on whether they wish to buy it in the future. As a result, samples would appear to be the most informative type of advertising which many manufacturers would like to issue if the size of their market justified the expense; it hardly seems appropriate, therefore, to describe samples as 'a secondary attraction'.

The aforementioned promotions are effective but costly. Manufacturers, therefore, intersperse them with lighter and less expensive promotions which may, nevertheless, be sufficient to focus trade interest on the product, achieve a display in the supermarket, and thus attract the consumer's attention. Competitions, for instance, are employed for this purpose by Persil Automatic. In addition, they have two further advantages: first, the prizes cost less than their cash equivalent. Second, the competitions may feature as prizes the products of manufacturers of washing machines (e.g., hi-fi equipment) which help to emphasize the link between the brand and front-loading washing machines. When a competition was organized by Persil Automatic with a specific supermarket chain, the effects were threefold: the retailer was prepared to give the products special displays, feature the products in advertising, and to match the manufacturers' price reduction during the period of the promotion.

Free offers

In 1979 to 1980 Lever Bros. and British Rail organized a joint promotion in which, in return for proofs of purchase from one or any combination of eight Lever Bros. brands including Persil Automatic, the consumer was entitled to a free rail ticket on the purchase of a rail ticket. For the company the promotion was designed to secure trial and a degree of 'loyalty' towards its brands, and to encourage the retailer to display the company's products in a valuable, and sought after, selling position. For British Rail, the promotion was designed to generate additional income at little extra cost.

Rival innovations

A continual flow of rival innovations reaches the market (of which only a small proportion are successful; e.g., CH 3) for one or a combination of factors: as a result of technical developments, in response to the changing requirements of consumers, to diversify out of a static or declining product area into an expanding market, to forestall the entry of a potential competitor into a product field and in order to compete more effectively against rivals.

Innovation can be an effective, if risky, competitive weapon because it may take longer to emulate than any other type of competitive activity (e.g., price reductions or promotions). This provides a firm with the opportunity to establish its product with the consumer and the trade before the arrival of second and subsequent brands. Under the existing organization and structure of retailing, the first arrival in a product field is likely to find it easier to obtain adequate distribution than later competitors, and provided that customers have found the product satisfactory it will be more difficult to tempt them to change brands unless a later entrant can offer a superior product. Both these factors can give the first entrant into a product field a significant advantage over competitors.

The changing habits and needs of consumers provide a constant challenge and opportunity for innovation. A technical advance enabled Batchelor's Quick Custard (CH 5) to meet the changed preferences of the consumer in the desserts market. Similarly, automation and legislation made it possible for Argos Distributors (CH 7) to introduce a new type of retail outlet in response to the changed attitudes of consumers towards price competition.

At the same time that firms innovate to meet the changing habits and needs of consumers, such innovations provide the means of replacing markets which have, or are about to decline, as the result of these changed consumer requirements. Thus in view of the continued slow decline in the volume of bread sales British Bakeries (CH 6) needed to generate new sources of turnover and profit, and decided to capitalize on its existing skills and advantages, particularly distribution facilities, by entering the packaged cake market. Two factors determined this decision: packaged cakes were the fastest expanding sector of the cake market, and grocers were becoming more important as distribution outlets. It was found essential to enter the market early and become established, in particular in multiple grocers, as large-scale food retailers appeared willing to stock only a handful of brands. Persil Automatic (CH 4) was introduced to meet the needs of a new type of washing machine. In this instance, however, the product replaced the firm's existing product (Persil), and was introduced before the market was economically viable as a means of pre-empting the entry of competitors. The entry of Persil Automatic into the low-suds washing powder market three years ahead of its main rival has altered the share of the heavy-duty washing powder market held in favour of Lever Bros.

The examples from the case histories illustrate that promotions perform several functions: encourage shoppers to try a product for the first time (samples); detach shoppers from their customary brand, in the hope that once they have been persuaded to try the particular brand they will wish to purchase it again (TPRs); to boost turnover at certain periods of the year (TPRs); to stimulate consumers to obtain the new season's catalogue; to achieve retail displays (multi-unit pricing, competitions); to maintain interest of retailers in the product ('free' offers); to encourage more 'loyal' customers when only marginal differences exist between products (gift or money for sending in three tops).

All forms of competition lead eventually to retaliation by competitors. The advantage of many forms of non-price competition, compared with price competition, is that they are more difficult to imitate, are more varied and unpredictable, and vary in their value to consumers and the skill and efficiency with which they are implemented by manufacturers and retailers. With non-price competition rivals cannot retaliate directly and exactly; during this intervening period the initiator gains an advantage in the market at the expense of potential imitators.

Non-price competition may also be preferred by manufacturers and retailers as a substitute for, or in addition to, price reductions because more value can be given as a 'gift' than as a price reduction; it may be more effective as a publicity weapon; a lower price may not be significant or dramatic enough to be noticed; and it may help to secure more consumer 'loyalty'. As a result, forms of non-price competition (including advertising) may be more effective in building sales than the equivalent outlay on a price reduction. In addition, it is possible that many of the effects, and possibly the benefits of the competitive process may be obtained through non-price competition.

Finally, the efficiency and importance of types of non-price competition increase and diminish according to how strongly manufacturers think they will appeal to retailers and consumers as a sales stimulant (e.g., case histories illustrate the increasing importance of sales promotions compared with advertising).

The functions performed by different types of non-price competition which can increase competitive activity under varied and changing trading circumstances tend to be disregarded in public policy pronouncements. Instead, non-price competition is considered inferior to price competition despite the fact that the latter cannot operate under oligopoly in the way that it does under perfect competition.

This view led the Prices and Incomes Board, in its Report on Detergents, to suggest that

> 'The consumer would benefit if the area of competition on price could be increased at the expense, if need be, either of outlays on advertising and promotion or of profit.' [Cmnd 2791, 1965, para 65]

The MMC's Report on Household Detergents did not seem to recognize that although one purpose of sales promotion is to secure trial of a product this does not mean that consumers will not then decide to purchase the product according to its merits.

> 'Lever Bros. and Procter & Gamble seem . . . to assume that the housewife will be moved to prefer one brand to another less by superior washing powder

than by the competing attractions of plastic daffodils as compared with whatever concomitant "gift" may be offered with another brand',

and that sales promotions

'. . . distract the customer's attention from the merits or demerits of the detergent.' [HC 105, p. 33]

The *Review of Monopolies and Mergers Policies* concluded that non-price competition could raise prices because it is an additional cost:

'The various forms of non-price competition involve, to a greater or lesser extent, resource costs and these in turn can mean higher prices to the consumer. The creation and defence of a position of market dominance can also involve resource costs which do not necessarily yield a social gain. Thus the accretion of market power through greater concentration can result in a range of practices which are unique to markets characterised by dominant firms which are potentially against the public interest'. [Cmnd. 7198, 1978, 3.40]

In this analysis of non-price competition there appears to be little awareness that manufacturers add to their costs in a variety of ways such as advertising or bargain offers because they will have found by trial and error that they will be more than compensated by the additional sales turnover that will be generated (e.g., plant may be utilized more fully, and manufacturing unit costs may be reduced).

Associated with the view of non-price competition as a market imperfection which raises prices, there is the further argument that the widespread employment of such selling techniques as temporary price reductions, free gifts and bargain offer claims confuses consumers. They are claimed to obscure the relationship between price and value unnecessarily, thereby complicating the comparison of competing offers, and this confusion prevents the most satisfactory choice of merchandise or retailer (Consumer Council, Price Commission, Office of Fair Trading, EEC). For example, the Consumer Council has stated (28 November 1963):

'. . . *any practice is undesirable* which makes it more difficult for consumers to compare values'. [my italics]

and the Price Commission Report (HC 657, 1978) commented on Lever Bros.:

'. . . we knew that consumer bodies believed that the scale and nature of the company's promotional activity tended to confuse the general consumer as to price, and to result in a higher price level than might otherwise prevail.' [1]

Furthermore, the issue of 'consumer confusion' has been included in legislation; under the Fair Trading Act 1973 (Section 17 (2)), where trade practices 'adversely affect the economic interests of consumers by misleading or confusing them' the Director General of Fair Trading can put forward proposals to prohibit or modify them.

Over the past decade two sales promotions which feature prominently in the case histories—recommended retail prices (RRPs) and the corollary 'double pricing',[2] and Temporary Price Reductions (TPRs)—have been the subject of considerable public controversy and official investigation on two main counts, namely whether they hinder competition and whether they confuse or mislead consumers.

The MMC (HC 100, 1969) investigated RRPs when they were still being generally observed in many trades. The MMC found RRPs a complex subject matter with retailers and manufacturers divided over the extent to which the practice contributed towards inhibiting or stimulating price competition. Between 1975 and 1978 the PC investigated the effect of RRPs and double pricing on several individual products including sanitary towels and tampons (No. 9, 1975) and Supplementary Report (No. 26, 1977); small electrical household appliances (No. 18, 1976); and beds (HC 650, 1978), and undertook a wider factual study (No. 25, 1977) to supplement the MMC's investigation.

The Commission's fact-finding Report appeared anxious to emphasize that RRPs do not form a homogeneous subject that permits easy conclusions, but a combination of separate, quite diverse, phenomena. In particular, it noted that, compared with the MMC's findings in 1969, the number and type of products covered by RRPs had changed, which seemed to indicate that they were not a monolithic or static practice but a part of fluid and constantly changing market conditions. However, this study did not include research into consumer attitudes or behaviour.

All the Commission's Reports on individual products commented adversely against double pricing, although often for different reasons (see for one example p. 128 on sanitary protection products). On small electrical household appliances the Commission recommended the abolition of RRPs because these products were rarely sold at the recommended price; as a result RRPs were valueless as a guide to prices, encouraged impulse buying, confused the consumer and discouraged shopping around. Unfortunately, the Commission's recommendation for prohibition was weakened by its price survey which was based on 25 brand leaders estimated to account for some 30 per cent of sales in each product group. Since brand leaders are the lines most likely to be discounted it does not follow that secondary brands have been discounted to the same degree. Furthermore, consumer confusion was simply inferred in the Report; no attempt was made to ascertain whether consumer behaviour in the market-place would support the view that double pricing effectively halts the shoppers from shopping around.

Similarly, in the Commission's Report on Beds[3] it was recommended that

---

[2] This is the practice where the actual retail price is shown next to a higher reference price usually suggested or recommended by the manufacturers. When RRPs are used in double pricing they are claimed to confuse consumers in one of three ways: (1) where RRPs have been deliberately inflated by manufacturers to enable all retailers to 'cut' prices to some degree; (2) where the traditional mark-up used to calculate RRPs has become obsolete through changes in the structure of distribution; and (3) where variable RRPs have been introduced and calculated for a particular product at the request of the individual.

[3] Examined under the Price Commission Act 1977 which enabled double pricing to be investigated and, if necessary, prohibited on a sectoral basis.

'. . . double pricing at the point of sale and in media advertising should be prohibited except for prescribed "sales" periods of limited duration . . . and . . . RRPs for beds should be prohibited.' [para 13]

Despite this recommendation, the Report also revealed that consumers generally bought at the 'market price', which seemed to indicate that double pricing did not adversely affect consumers' behaviour. The Report also found that bed manufacturers were not earning excessive profits.

The distinguishing feature of this Report was a survey into consumer attitudes and buying behaviour which conflicted with that depicted in earlier Reports. This showed, not unexpectedly, that purchasers of beds relied on several sources of information to help them choose what to buy, and where to buy it: window shopping and looking around were the two most important sources, followed by press and television advertising. Two out of three purchasers looked at beds in three or more shops. Although price was important in determining the shopper's selection of a retail outlet, the survey showed it was by no means the only factor. Discounts, 'sales' and credit facilities, and knowing or trusting a particular shop were all important factors for patronizing a particular outlet. Similarly, while price was important in the choice of a particular bed or mattress, aspects of quality and design were also significant elements in choice.

In 1975 the Office of Fair Trading (OFT) had widened the debate on RRPs into a discussion on the whole area of bargain offer claims, including TPRs, and contrary to the PC's recommendation for the prohibition of RRPs suggested proposals to strengthen 'double pricing'. At the same time it made detailed proposals to reduce the apparent confusion caused by one type of TPR, 'flash offers'. It had not investigated whether such offers mislead consumers but placed reliance on the investigation carried out by the National Federation of Consumer Groups in 1974. On the other hand, it had not accepted the Federation's conclusion that 'flash offers' should be abolished. When, however, the OFT's proposals to reduce confusion were examined their weaknesses became apparent, and they were shelved.

In 1978 the OFT issued two recommendations for action on bargain offer claims to the Secretary of State for Prices and Consumer Protection. Whereas its original proposals on RRPs had been designed to strengthen double pricing as a competitive device by removing ambiguities and vagueness, the OFT now concluded that most RRPs were 'notional' and recommended that they should be prohibited when used to indicate that the seller's price is less than a recommended price. This proposal to ban double pricing had the effect of effectively prohibiting TPRs and flash offers since manufacturers could no longer relate them to RRPs! This contradicted its Consultative Document which had considered flash offers as a suitable form of short-term price cutting, and had suggested how they could be made less confusing.

The OFT's recommendation to abolish double pricing seemed to be based on the assumption that 'their intention is to dissuade the consumer from further shopping around' (para 11), although no evidence was offered for this conclusion. Neither the OFT nor the PC seemed to take into account that double pricing or comparison pricing has been the marketing technique which has contributed towards the intensification of competition by acting as a 'bench mark' by providing retailers with an effective and shorthand way of publicizing their price reductions; that they help to reveal the lack of competitiveness of other retailers; that they are useful for the little-known firm entering a noisy and crowded market-place; that they are particularly effective when price competition is being introduced into a product field; and that for some new types of retail outlets, such as catalogue discount selling (CH 7) they provide a more economical method than advertising for communicating price reductions to consumers.

Furthermore, the OFT 1978 recommendations failed to make clear whether the effective prohibition of TPRs and flash offers had been the unintended side-effect of proposing the abolition of RRPs, or whether the proposal arose from the difficulty previously experienced of making such offers less confusing. In either event, the OFT had failed to take into account that these offers provide price reductions over and above those given by retailers (CHs 1 and 4), which is beneficial to consumers, and that since they are associated with low value items bought at frequent intervals the element of confusion which they generate is likely to be small.

In 1978 the PC commissioned for its investigation into the price of soaps and detergents (HC 1) a consumer survey into the effect of TPRs and flash offers. The results indicated that consumers are mainly product and brand conscious, and seem to be satisfied that they have no difficulty in assessing value for money. Nor did the survey confirm a picture of widespread consumer confusion which the Commission attributed to 'the frequency with which this type of product is purchased' (para 3.53). The PC Report on toothpaste (HC1 125, 1978) also confirmed that TPRs are unlikely to cause widespread consumer confusion, and that its price survey indicated that TPRs result in lower prices.

Despite these consumer and price surveys which were at variance with the earlier conclusions on RRPs and flash offers, a draft Order to implement the OFT's recommendations to prohibit, inter alia, price comparisons with RRPs and flash offers was published by the Department of Prices and Consumer Protection at the end of 1978. However, the eventual Price Marking (Bargain Offers) Order 1979 permitted double pricing on all products, apart from four (with the proviso that other products could be investigated on a sectoral basis), and permitted TPRs.[4]

The conclusion of the early Reports of the PC and the proposals and recommendations of the OFT that consumers were confused by double pricing seemed to be based on two assumptions: that price is almost the sole factor taken into account by shoppers when making purchasing decisions; that double-pricing inhibits shopping around because the shopper believes she is getting a bargain.

These assumptions were not, however, confirmed by the consumer surveys commissioned later by the PC on detergents and beds respectively which showed that, for instance, with detergents the reasons for choosing a particular brand were more often to do with the quality of the powder than the price. Moreover, and not

---

[4] In 1979 a voluntary agreement for a year was signed by many trade associations on behalf of their membership that no more than 50 per cent of their members' packs would carry TPRs.

unexpectedly, of those buying for reasons of price, 20 per cent chose a distributor's own brand compared with only 6 per cent of all housewives who did so. With beds, the survey revealed that shoppers took a variety of factors into account, besides price, when selecting a retail outlet. In other words, with both these products double-pricing (including TPRs) was only one factor among many others which affected the buying decision of the shopper, and if considered in this context their ability to mislead consumers would appear to be somewhat diminished. From the attitude adopted by public policy towards recommended prices there appears to be a tendency to underestimate the knowledge possessed by the shopper which develops over time and which has become more perfect through such social and economic developments as ownership of cars and telephones, widespread retail advertising, compound trading (the sale of specialist merchandise by non-specialist retailers), the consumer movement. As a result shoppers have better and speedier facilities for comparing prices than in the past.

The shift in emphasis on the issue of RRPs over a short period of time (1969 to 1979) also illustrates the difficulty of legislating under changing trading conditions without adversely affecting competition. Originally, RRPs were condemned as contrary to the interests of consumers because of the widespread adherence to them by manufacturers. They were often regarded as a substitute for resale price maintenance, and as a hindrance to price competition. More recently, the abolition of RRPs has been recommended because the difference between the actual and the recommended price has become so wide that consumers are misled and confused by them! In the intervening period, as the Price Commission's fact-finding study revealed, changes have taken place in the number and type of products covered by RRPs which, apart from the incentive of the Trade Descriptions Act to introduce them, has reflected the impact of new forms of retailing, and the varying rate at which price competition has emerged in different product fields.

10 Conclusions

The discrepancies which have emerged in Part 3 between the theory and practice of advertising and competition stem from several omissions and fallacies in the theory of the firm. The basic omission is the element of time, the importance of which economists like Marshall were well aware, and which in practice limits the ability of advertising to determine demand, and the ability of firms to raise prices and costs.

Furthermore, (1) premises such as advertising as a barrier to entry and as a creator of durable brand loyalty appear to have limited validity in the market-place. (2) The neglect of the influence of the organization and structure of retail distribution on advertising and competition has also resulted in a failure to recognize the increasing need for firms to attain the economies of 'loyalty' and widespread distribution in order to maximize sales and achieve economies of scale.

Finally, (3) the assumption that oligopolists should compete in the same manner as firms operating under the abstract model of perfect competition has led to the conclusion that any other form of competition apart from price is an imperfection and thereby detrimental to consumer welfare, whereas practice shows that under conditions of oligopoly non-price competition can be an effective means of competition.

1. The conclusion, for instance, of conventional theory that advertising enables prices and/or profits to be higher than the competitive level is based on three main premises: that advertising acts as a barrier to entry; that advertising can create automatic and durable brand loyalty; and that firms operate in a static market.

In the market-place the concept of 'barriers to entry' appears as a more complex and varied phenomenon than in economic theory because advertising may be only one, and even an insignificant, variable compared with all the other factors which influence a firm's decision to enter a market, such as financial resources, the complexity of technology, the ease or difficulty of achieving distribution, the potential size of the market, whether existing firms have already reached economies of scale, whether the market is expanding or contracting. All these factors are as 'barriers to entry' to some degree; they are utilized by firms as a means of protecting themselves as long as possible from their competitors while they build up their reputation and goodwill with a product which is well distributed, well advertised, and sold at the 'right' price. Conversely, firms contemplating entering a market take it for granted that it consists of established competitors whose brands are well known and acceptable to consumers, and that this is a major obstacle that they will need to overcome. Both groups of firms would assume that this is the essence of competition!

The implicit assumption in theory that advertising can create automatic and durable brand loyalty is not borne out in practice where many products either fail to get established in the market-place, or remain in existence for only a short period. Although advertising may have been successful in stimulating the shopper to purchase a product in the first instance, unless she/he is willing to make a repeat purchase the brand will fail after a few months. With established brands, wide fluctuations occur in their market shares. This is due to the fact that only a proportion of purchasers are completely loyal to a particular brand. The remainder, which in many product groups constitutes the major part of the market share of a brand, is made up of customers who vary their purchases between two or more brands of the same product, and who, on occasion, decide to purchase from a different product group. The two major reasons why consumers behave in this way is the desire for variety, and that one brand offers an intermittent price reduction or promotional offer. The latter will occur in order to remain competitive when the brands have become interchangeable to some customers so that only the price or the promotion differentiates them.

Under these circumstances, a high proportion of advertising is devoted to encouraging those who already purchase the brand to do so more frequently, or in larger quantities. This means that advertising is often directed towards customers who are already familiar with a product, and who are able to compare the promises made in advertisements against their own experience of the product.

The tacit assumption that advertising can create durable and automatic brand loyalty also implies a static market, since over time firms are vulnerable to the impact of competition from the introduction of new brands and products, and changing consumer habits, demands and tastes. These are all factors which cause brand shares to fluctuate and brands to be withdrawn from the market, and which impose severe limitations on the power of advertising.

Associated with the assumption that advertising can assure durable brand loyalty is the implicit—and sometimes explicit—supposition that consumers are gullible and passive acceptors of advertising and sales promotions. This fallacy arises through the tendency of theory, first, to isolate sales promotion from the many other sources of information (i.e., retailers, the media, friends and relations, and consumer bodies) available to consumers and which they take into account before deciding on a purchase; and, second, to take a static view of the economy which thereby ignores the fact that consumers learn from experience and reject products in the future which have proved unsatisfactory, and underestimates the knowledge of the consumer which develops over time, and which has become more perfect because of certain economic and social developments (e.g., ownership of cars and telephones, retailer advertising, etc.).

2. Conventional theory tends to overlook the effect of the organization and structure of retail distribution on advertising and on types of sales promotions. Conventional theory considers advertising predominantly from the supplier's viewpoint, and seems to ignore advertising as a beneficial source of information to consumers. It also ignores the effect of advertising on retailers, although advertising and sales promotion are as necessary to persuade the retailer to stock a product as to stimulate the consumer to buy it. While advertising may successfully create awareness of a product, and encourage the consumer to try it, this will be of little avail unless the potential purchaser can easily find it in his/her local shop. There is evidence that on many occasions consumers are prepared to take an alternative brand or substitute product if their preferred brand is unavailable. Many of the case histories confirm that a firm's success in achieving widespread distribution of its product has been an essential factor in obtaining a major market share. It is perhaps not surprising that, in the current competitive and cost conditions in distribution, retailers prefer to stock brands with a rapid turnover. Conversely in the competition for the limited shelf space in the store the retailer is least likely to eliminate the most popular selling brands. In these circumstances, the advertising of many manufacturers is often intended to reassure retailers that a product will sell well. Likewise, the promotions of many manufacturers are often introduced to encourage the retailer to display the product prominently.

The implied insistence in conventional theory that advertising and brand loyalty are synonymous has led it to overlook the need of manufacturers and retailers for 'loyalty' which has become more necessary under present-day conditions of production and distribution, but which many market developments have made it more difficult to achieve.

In retail distribution impersonal methods of shopping, standardized merchandise, and the mobility of shoppers have diminished the ability of retailers to achieve the economies of 'loyalty'; at the same time expensive capital investment and high overheads have accentuated the need to attract maximum customer traffic. In their efforts to operate stores at full capacity, lower operating costs by handling fast-selling merchandise, and to differentiate themselves from their rivals, retailers have increased their advertising, their range of distributors' own brands, and the frequency of 'special offers' and promotions, with a further trend as competition has intensified towards exclusive promotions with a particular manufacturer.

Manufacturers have likewise been affected by recent retail developments, in particular by the increased concentration in retail distribution. On the other hand, the potential economies of large-scale production, and the cost savings which result from more intensive utilization of expensive machinery can only be achieved if manufacturers can encourage sufficient customers to make regular and repeat purchases.

The growing power of a few large-scale retailers vis-à-vis manufacturers has led to the development of consumer promotions whose primary objective is to induce retailers to give a product a prominent display, and to provide a price reduction directly from the manufacturer to the consumer over the heads of retailers. Furthermore, the impersonal service of the supermarket and the superstore has shifted competition to the point of sale, and this is where the manufacturer is faced with the task of trying to gain the attention of the shopper, without the aid of a sales assistant. This has led to the expansion of promotions to encourage trial of a new product; stimulate repeat buyings; facilitate entry into an established product field; boost turnover at certain times of the year, and encourage shoppers to try out larger sizes. Other promotions such as temporary price reductions lessen substantially the price differential between the manufacturer brand and the distributor's own brand in order to stimulate trial by the price conscious and/or indifferent customer.

To some extent the expansion of promotions has been at the expense of advertising expenditure, although advertising is widely used to bring them to the notice of consumers. Moreover, in these examples of non-price competition manufacturers support the retailer with improved terms and advertising allowances because they are keen to have their lines chosen in preference to their competitors, and the retailer usually matches the manufacturer's price reduction. Non-price competition, therefore, often takes place in conjunction with, and not in place of, price competition. Under current trading conditions manufacturers and retailers employ particular types of non-price competition because they can perform certain identifiable selling tasks more efficiently than other selling techniques including price. Sales promotions have increased over the past 20 years chiefly as a consequence of changes in the organization and structure of retail distribution.

The efficiency and importance of different forms of sales promotions increase and diminish according to how strongly manufacturers and retailers think they will appeal to consumers as a sales stimulant. Just as advertising expenditure in food retailing has risen over the past five years, trading stamps, for instance, have disappeared during the same period. Similarly, manufacturer expenditure on advertising has relatively declined in recent years and has been replaced by increasing expenditure on promotions.

3. Non-price competition is widespread under oligopoly because the interdependence of firms leads the oligopolist to consider how his rivals will react before changing its prices or output. Under these circumstances, the oligopolist usually prefers not to compete directly on price for fear of setting a downward price spiral in motion which will lead to a price war, squeeze profit margins, and be self-defeating. Instead, the oligopolist tends to compete by other means such as advertising and sales promotion to achieve increased sales turnover.

In conventional theory non-price competition is regarded as inferior to price competition because, for the purpose of simplifying the analysis, sales promotions including samples, indirect price competition, free gifts, competitions, etc., are relegated to the category of ceteris paribus and regarded as evidence of imperfect competition and therefore as detrimental to consumer welfare. This error has led to the view that if these 'imperfections' could be eradicated then direct price competition would once more prevail.

Non-price competition is, however, inherent in the nature of oligopoly which has become the prevailing form of organization in industry. Oligopolists tacitly refrain from direct price competition because of the ease and speed with which it can be followed by rivals, particularly when cost conditions in an industry are similar. (Occasional outbursts of aggressive price competition will tend to be confined to product innovations and major technical developments.) On the other hand, firms vary in the calibre of their marketing, advertising and sales promotion expertise, and particularly in their ability to innovate. Not only are these forms of competition more flexible and unpredictable, and more difficult to emulate exactly, but it is less easy for rivals to retaliate effectively against a promotion or an advertising campaign since these do not have an identical appeal for retailers or consumers, and manufacturers vary in the efficiency and aggressiveness with which they implement them. Even more important, it takes time to retaliate and during this period the initiator gains an advantage at the expense of his competitors.

The conclusion of conventional theory that non-price competition adds to costs and raises prices is a misconception based on a static view of the market. If non-price competition helps to encourage consumer 'loyalty' to the retailer and to the brand, reduces costs in the shop and the factory, and innovation has a competitive value, then it may be an effective means of competition in increasing sales turnover and in keeping prices down. The argument that the cost of sales promotions must ipso facto be transferred to consumers in the form of higher prices is based on the supposition that all manufacturers/retailers are equally efficient or inefficient, that there is no scope for introducing cost-reducing methods, and that no manufacturers/retailers can expand their turnover more than proportionately to compensate for the cost of the sales promotion.

Since there are obvious practical limits on the degree to which the abstract theoretical assumptions of 'perfect competition' can be reproduced in modern industry, non-price competition which varies according to trading developments may be more applicable than direct price competition where oligopoly prevails. Legislation, therefore, which curbs or eliminates particular types of non-price competition without understanding its function in the market-place, or that it is likely to expand and then recede, and perhaps be replaced by other sales techniques under changing market conditions is likely to be detrimental to consumer welfare.

Finally, in Part 1 it was shown that the weaknesses and fallacies in the theory of the firm which make it inappropriate as a basis for competition policy have been demonstrated by many eminent economists. Nevertheless, in my examination of public policy pronouncements in Part 3 it is evident that public policy is predominantly based on the theory of the firm and the need to curb or eliminate imperfections in the market such as oligopoly, product differentiation, advertising, and non-price competition.

Bibliography

Aaronvitch, S. & Sawyer, M. C. (1974) The concentration of British manufacturing. *Lloyds Bank Review*, Oct.

Achenbaum, A. A. (1972) Advertising doesn't manipulate consumers. *Journal of Advertising Research*, **12**(2), 3–13.

Adelman, I. G. (1958) A stochastic analysis of the size distribution of firms. *Journal of the American Statistical Association*, Dec.

Adelman, M. A. (1951) The measurement of industrial concentration. *Review of Economics and Statistics*, Nov.

Alderson, W. (1968) *Dynamic Marketing Behaviour*. Richard D. Irwin. Quoted in Doyle, P., Economic aspects of advertising: a survey. *Economic Journal*, Sept., 582.

Allen, G. C. (1969) *Economic Fact and Fantasy*. 2nd Edition OP 14, Institute of Economic Affairs.

Allen, G. C. (1970) *The Structure of Industry in Britain*. 3rd Edition. Allen & Unwin.

Bain, J. S. (1956) *Barriers to New Competition*. Harvard University Press.

Bain, J. S. (1968) *Industrial Organization*. John Wiley.

Bannock, G. (1971) The *Juggernauts*. Weidenfeld & Nicholson.

Baumol, W. J. (1959) *Business Behaviour, Value and Growth*. Macmillan.

Berle, A. A. & Means, G. C. (1932) *The Modern Corporation and Private Property*. Macmillan.

Boulding, K. (1955) *Economic Analysis*. 3rd Edition. Hamish Hamilton.

Braithwaite, D. (1928) The economic effects of advertising. *Economic Journal*, **38**, 16–37.

Brozen, Y. (1970) The anti-trust force deconcentration recommendation. *Journal of Law and Economics*, **13**, 279–292.

Brozen, Y. (1971) Bain's concentration and rates of return revisited. *Journal of Law and Economics*, **14**, 351–369.

Burns, A. R. (1936) *The Decline of Competition*. New York: McGraw Hill.

Cave, R. E. (1968) *Britain's Economic Prospects*. Brookings Institute, Allen & Unwin.

Chamberlin, E. H. (1956) *The Theory of Monopolistic Competition*. 7th Edition. Harvard University Press.

Chamberlin, E. H. (1957) *Towards a More General Theory of Value*. Oxford University Press.

Chase, S. (1925) *The Tragedy of Waste*. Macmillan.

Chatfield, C., Ehrenberg, A. S. C. & Goodhardt, G. S. (1966) Progress on a simplified model of stationary purchasing behaviour. *Journal of the Royal Statistical Society*, Series A, **60**. (See also under Ehrenberg.)

Clark, J. B. (1901) *The Control of Trusts*. New York.

Clarke, K. & Rowe, M. (1977) The marketing mix test—relating expectations and performance. *Market Research Society Conference Proceedings*.

Clarkson, G. P. E. (1968) Interactions of economic theory and operations research. In *Models of Markets* (Ed.) Oxenfeldt, A. R. (1963), pp. 339–361. Columbia University Press. Reprinted in *Managerial Economics* (Ed.) Clarkson, G. P. E. Penguin.

Cockfield, A. (1978) The Price Commission and price control. *Three Banks Review*, March, **117,** 23.

Comanor, W. S., & Wilson, T. A. (1967) Advertising market structure and performance. *Review of Economics and Statistics* Nov., **49,** 423–440.

Comanor, W. S. & Wilson, T. A. (1974) *Advertising and Market Power.* Harvard University Press.

Comanor, W. S. & Wilson, T. A. (1967) Advertising market structure and performance. *Review of Economics and Statistics*, Nov., **49,** 423–440.

Cyert, R. M. & March, J. G. (1963) *A Behavioural Theory of the Firm.* Prentice-Hall.

Davidson, J. H. (1976) Why most new consumer brands fail. *Harvard Business Review*, March/April, 117–122.

Davis, E. J. (1964) Test marketing: an examination of sales patterns found during 44 recent tests. *Market Research Society Conference Proceedings.*

Demsetz, H. (1973) Industry structure, market rivalry and public policy. *Journal of Law and Economics*, **16,** 1–9.

Dobb, M. (1973) *Theories of Value and Distribution Since Adam Smith.* Chapter 7. Cambridge University Press.

Downie, J. (1958) *The Competitive Process.* London: Duckworth.

Doyle, P. (1968) Advertising expenditure and consumer demand. *Oxford Economic Papers*, **20,** Nov., 394–416.

Doyle, P. (1968) Economic aspects of advertising: a survey. *Economic Journal,* Sept., 570–602.

Economists Advisory Group (1967) *The Economics of Advertising.* Advertising Association.

Ehrenberg, A. S. C. et al (1966) Progress on a simplified model of stationary purchasing behaviour. *Journal of the Royal Statistical Society*, Series A.

Ehrenberg, A. S. C. et al (1969) Towards an integrated theory of consumer behaviour. *Journal of the Market Research Society*, **11,** 305–337.

Ehrenberg, A. S. C. et al (1972) *Repeat Buying and Applications.* North Holland.

Ekelund, R. B. Jr & Gramm, W. P. (1970) Advertising and concentration: some new evidence. *Anti-Trust Bulletin*, **15,** Summer, 293–249.

Ekelund, R. B. Jr & Gramm, W. P. (1971) More on tests of the Kaldor hypothesis. *Anti-Trust Bulletin*, **16,** Spring, 105–109.

Ekelund, R. B. Jr & Maurice, C. (1969) An empirical investigation of advertising and concentration: comment, *Journal of Industrial Economics*, **18,** Nov., 76–80.

Engel, J. F., Kollat, D. T. & Blackwell, R. D. (1968) *Consumer Behaviour.* Holt, Rinehart & Winston.

Engel, J. F., Blackwell, R. D. & Kollat, D. T. (1978) *Consumer Behaviour,* 3rd Edition. Dryden Press.

EEC (1976) *European Consumers: their interests, aspirations and knowledge on Consumer Affairs*, Doc. 309/76–E.

Farley, J. V. & Ring, L. W. (1970) An empirical test of the Howard–Sheth model of buyer behaviour. *Journal of Marketing Research*, 427–438.

Ferguson, J. M. (1974) *Advertising and Competition: Theory, Measurement, Fact.* Ballinger.

Festinger, L. (1957) *A Theory of Cognitive Dissonance.* Stanford University Press.

Foxall, G. R. (1976) Advertising and the critics: who is misleading whom? *Advertising Quarterly*, **48,** 5–7.

Fulop, C. (1971) *Markets for Employment.* Research Monograph 26, Institute of Economic Affairs.

Fulop, C. (1978) 20 Years of Which? European Journal of Marketing, **12**(4), 283–298.

Fulop, C. & March, T. (1979) The effects of the abolition of resale price maintenance in two trades. *European Journal of Marketing*, **13,** 7.

Galbraith, J. K. (1948) In *A Survey of Contemporary Economics* (Ed.) Ellis, H. S. Philadelphia: Blakestow.

Galbraith, J. K. (1958) *The Affluent Society.* Hamish Hamilton.

Galbraith, J. K. (1963) *American Capitalism.* Penguin.

Galbraith, J. K. (1969) *The New Industrial State.* Pelican.

Galbraith, J. K. (1977) *The Age of Uncertainty.* André Deutsch.

Gibrat, R. (1931) *Les Inégalités Économique.* Paris: Siret.

Guth, L. A. (1971) Advertising and market structure revisited. *Journal of Industrial Economics*, **19,** 179–198.

Hallett, G. (1967) The role of economists as government advisers. *Westminster Bank Review*, May.

Harbury, C. D. (1958) Efficiency and the consumer. *Fabian Research Series*, No. 199.

Harris, R. & Seldon, A. (1962) *Advertising and the Public.* André Deutsch.

Hart, P. E. (1965) *Studies in Profit, Business Savings and Investment in the United Kingdom.* Allen & Unwin.

Hicks, J. R. (1962) Economic theory and the evaluation of consumers' wants. *Journal of Business*, **35,** 257.

Howard, J. A. & Sheth, J. N. (1969) *The Theory of Buyer Behaviour.* Wiley.

Jevons, W. S. (1927) *The Theory of Political Economy*. Macmillan.

Jewkes, J. (1977) *Delusions of Dominance*. HP 76, Institute of Economic Affairs.

Johnson, H. G. (1967) The economics of advertising. *Advertising Quarterly*, **13**, 9–14.

Johnson, P. S. (1970) *Industrial Structure*. Key Discussion Books, No. 9. Longman Group in association with the Institute of Economic Affairs.

Joyce, T. (1975) What do we know about how advertising works? (read at Esomar Seminar 1967). In *The Three Faces of Advertising* (Ed.) Barnes, M. Advertising Association.

Kaldor, N. (1950) The economic aspects of advertising. *Review of Economic Studies*, **18**, 1–27.

King, S. (1980) *Advertising as a Barrier to Market Entry*. Advertising Association.

Kirzner, I. M. (1973) *Competition and Entrepreneurship*. University of Chicago Press.

Kotler, P. (1970) Mathematical models of individual buyer behaviour. *Behavioural Science* (1968), **13**, 274–287. In *Market Research* (Ed.) Seibert, J. & Wills, G. Penguin.

Kraushar, Andrews and Eassie Ltd (1976) *New Products in the Grocery Trade*. Based on Shaw's Price List.

Lambin, J. J. (1975) What is the real impact of advertising? *Harvard Business Review*, May–June, 139–147.

Lancaster, K. J. (1971) Excerpts from a new approach to consumer theory. *Journal of Political Economy* (1966), **174**, 132–157. In *Consumer Behaviour* (Ed.) Ehrenberg, A. S. C. & Pyatt, F. G Penguin.

Lewis, W. A. (1945) Competition in retail trade. *Economica*, **X11**(48), 202–234.

Lewis, W. A. (1949) *Overhead Costs*. Allen & Unwin.

Lind, H. (1975) The economic aspects of advertising—a reply to Nicholas Kaldor. In *The Three Faces of Advertising* (Ed.) Barnes, M., pp. 183–194. Advertising Association.

Lowe Watson, D. (1971) Advertising and the buyer–seller relationship. *Journal of the Market Research Society* (1969), **11**(2), 125–146. In *Modern Marketing Management* (Ed.) Lawrence, R. J. & Thomas, M. J. Penguin.

Lunn, J. A. (1974) A review of consumer decision process models (read at Esomar Congress, 1971). In *Analytical Marketing Management* (Ed.) Doyle, P. et al. Harper & Row.

Mann, H. M. (1966) Seller concentration, barriers to entry and rates of return in thirty industries, 1950–60. *Review of Economics and Statistics*, August, 296–307.

Mann, H. M. & Meehan, J. H. Jr (1971) Advertising and concentration: new data and an old problem. *Anti-trust Bulletin*, **16**, Spring, 101–104.

Mann, H. M. et al (1967) Advertising and concentration: an empirical investigation. *Journal of Industrial Economics*, **16**, Nov.

Mann, H. M. et al (1969) Testing hypotheses in industrial economics: a reply. *Journal of Industrial Economics*, **18**, Nov., 81–84.

Marcus, M. (1969) Advertising and changes in concentration. *Southern Economic Journal*, **36**, 117–121.

Markham, J. W. (1951) The nature and significance of price leadership. *American Economic Review*, **XLI**, Dec.

Marris, R. (1964) *The Economic Theory of 'Managerial' Capitalism*. Cambridge University Press.

Marris, R. (1972) Why economics needs a theory of the firm. *Economic Journal*, March, **82**, 321–352.

Marshall, A. (1919) *Industry and Trade*. Macmillan.

Marshall, A. (1920) *Principles of Economics*. 8th Edition. Macmillan.

Martin, S. (1978) *Theoretical Issues in the Specification of Models of Industrial Organisation*. Unpublished Paper presented at 1978 Meeting of the Econometric Society, Chicago, Michigan State University, Jan.

Mason, E. S. (1957) *Economic Concentration and the Monopoly Problem*. Oxford University Press.

McDonald, C. (1970) What is the short-term effect of advertising? *Esomar Congress Proceedings*, and *Admap*, Nov.

McFadzean, F. S. (1968) *Galbraith and the Planners*. University of Strathclyde.

Meade, J. E. (1964) *Efficiency, Equality and the Ownership of Property*. Allen & Unwin.

Meade, J. E. (1975) *The Intelligent Radical's Guide to Economic Policy*. Allen & Unwin.

Menger, K. (1950) *Principles of Economics*, 1871. Free Press of Glencoe.

Molony Committee (1962) *Final Report of the Committee on Consumer Protection*. Cmnd 1781. HMSO.

Monopolies and Mergers Commission (1966) *Household Detergents*. HC 105. HMSO.

Monopolies and Mergers Commission (1969) *Recommended Resale Prices*. HC 100. HMSO.

Monopolies and Mergers Commission (1973) *Parallel Pricing*. Cmnd 5330. HMSO.

Monopolies and Mergers Commission (1973) *Report on Breakfast Cereals*. HC 2. HMSO.

National Board for Prices & Incomes (1965) *Prices of Household and Toilet Soaps. Soap Powders and Soap Flakes, and Soapless Detergents*. Cmnd 2791. HMSO.

National Consumer Council, *Real Money, Real Choice*. Sept. 1978.

Needham, D. (Ed.) (1971) *Readings in the Economics of Industrial Organisation*. Holt, Rinehart and Winston.

Nicosia, F. M. (1966) *Consumer Decision Processes*. Prentice-Hall.

Nielsen Researcher (1970) The realities of new product marketing. No. 1. A. C. Nielsen Co Ltd.

Nielsen Researcher (1973) Building a million pound product. No. 5. A. C. Nielsen Co Ltd.

Office of Fair Trading (1975) *Bargain Offer Claims*. A Consultative Document. HMSO.

Office of Fair Trading (1978) *Bargain Offer Claims Excluding Claimed Reductions from Recommended and Similar Prices*. A recommendation by the Director General of Fair Trading for Government Action. Feb.

Office of Fair Trading (1978) *Bargain Offer Claims: Claimed Reductions from Recommended and Similar Prices*. A recommendation by the Director General of Fair Trading for Government Action. March.

Ozga, S. A. (1960) Imperfect markets through lack of knowledge. *Quarterly Journal of Economics*, **74,** Feb., 29–52.

Parfitt, J. H. & Collins, B. J. K. (1974) The use of consumer panels in brand share prediction. *Journal of Marketing Research*, **68**. In *Analytical Marketing Management* (Ed.) Doyle, P. et al. Harper & Row.

Parkin, M. (1972) *The Growth of the Firm*. Audio Learning, London.

Penrose, E. T. (1959) *The Theory of the Growth of the Firm*. Basil Blackwell. A new edition, with an Introduction by M. Slater, was published in 1980 by Basil Blackwell.

Pigou, A. C. (1932) *The Economics of Welfare*. 4th Edition. Macmillan.

Porter, M. E. (1974) Consumer behaviour, retailer power and market performance in consumer goods industries. *Review of Economics and Statistics*, Nov., **56**(4), 419–436.

Prais, S. J. (1976) *The Evolution of Giant Firms in Britain*. Cambridge University Press.

Price Commission (1975) *Prices of Sanitary Towels and Tampons*. No. 9. HMSO.

Price Commission (1977) *Prices of Sanitary Towels and Tampons: Supplementary Report*. No. 26. HMSO.

Price Commission (1976) *Small Electrical Household Appliances and Recommended Prices*. No. 18. HMSO.

Price Commission (1977) *Recommended Retail Prices*. No. 25. HMSO.

Price Commission (1978) *The Pricing of Beds*. HC 650. HMSO.

Price Commission (1978) *Lever Bros—Soaps, Detergents & Related Products*. HC 1. HMSO.

Price Commission (1978) *Procter & Gamble—Soaps and Detergents*. HC 1. HMSO.

Price Commission (1978) *Prices, Costs & Margins in the Production and Distribution of Toothpaste*. HC 1 125. HMSO.

Price Commission (1978) *Southalls (Birmingham) Ltd, Sanitary Protection and Other Hygiene Products*. HC 436. HMSO.

Reekie, W. D. (1977) The market in advertising. In *The Consumer Society* (Ed.) Hirst, I. R. C. & Reekie, W. D. Tavistock Publications.

Review of Monopolies and Mergers Policy: a Consultative Document (1978) Cmnd 7198. HMSO.

Riesman, D., Glazer, N. & Denney, R. (1956) *The Lonely Crowd*. Doubleday.

Ricardo, (1817) *The Principles of Political Economy and Taxation*. 3rd Edition, 1821.

Robertson, D. (1958) *Lectures in Economic Principles*. Staples.

Robinson, J. (1964) *Economic Philosophy*. Pelican.

Robinson, J. (1969) *The Economics of Imperfect Competition*. 2nd Edition. Macmillan.

Rogers, C. (1951) *Client-Centered Therapy*. Houghton Mifflin.

Schmalensee, R. (1972) *The Economics of Advertising*. North-Holland.

Schnabel, M. (1970) A note on advertising and industrial concentration. *Journal of Political Economy*, **78,** 1191–1194.

Schumpeter, J. A. (1976) *Capitalism, Socialism and Democracy*. 5th Edition. Allen & Unwin.

Sharpe, M. E. (1973) *Galbraith and the Lower Economics*. Macmillan.

Sheth, J. N. (1967) A review of buyer behaviour. *Management Science*, **12,** 13.

Sheth, J. N. (1974) *Models of Buyer Behaviour*. Harper & Row.

Simon, J. L. (1975) Advertising and Market Power (Chapter from his *Issues in the Economics of Advertising*, University of Illinois Press, 1970). In *Three Faces of Advertising* (Ed.) Barnes, M. Advertising Association.

Simons, H. C. (1948) *Economic Policy for a Free Society*. University of Chicago Press.

Slater, M. (1980) see Penrose.

Smith, A. (1904) *An Inquiry into the Nature and Causes of the Wealth of Nations*, 1776. The World's Classics, Grant Richards.

Steiner, P. O. (1966) The economics of broadcasting and advertising—discussion. *American Economic Review*, **56,** May, 472–475.

Stigler, G. J. (1947) The kinky oligopoly demand curve and rigid prices. *Journal of Political Economy*, **LV**, Oct.

Stigler, G. J. (1961) The economics of information. *Journal of Political Economy*, **69**, June, 213–225.

Stigler, G. J. (1968) *The Organization of Industry*. Richard D. Irwin.

Strickland, A. D. & Weiss, L. W. (1976) Advertising, concentration and price–cost margins. *Journal of Political Economy*, Oct., **84**(5), 1109–1121.

Telser, L. G. (1964) Advertising and competition. *Journal of Political Economy*, **72**, Dec., 537–562.

Telser, L. G. (1966) Supply and demand for advertising messages. *American Economic Review*, **56**, May, 457–466.

Telser, L. G. (1968) Some aspects of the economics of advertising. *Journal of Business*, **41**, April, 166–173.

Telser, L. G. (1969) Another look at advertising and concentration. *Journal of Industrial Economics*, **18**, Nov., 85–94.

Treasure, J. (1975) How advertising works (Paper given at University of Chicago, 1973). In *The Three Faces of Advertising* (Ed.) Barnes, M. pp. 261–277. Advertising Association.

Walras, L. (1954) *Elements of Pure Competition*, 1874. Richard D. Irwin.

Williamson, J. H. (1966) Profits, growth and sales maximisation. *Economica*, **33**.

Wilson, T. (1962) Restrictive practices. In *Competition, Controls and Their Regulations* (Ed.) Miller, J. P. North-Holland.

Yamey, B. S. (Ed.) (1973) *Economics of Industrial Structure*. Penguin.

Yarrow, G. K. (1973) Managerial utility maximisation under uncertainty. *Economica*, NS, May, **40**, 155–173.

Yarrow, G. K. (1976) On the predictions of managerial theories of the firm. *Journal of Industrial Economics*, June, **24**, 267–279.

Index